"*Brexit Unfolded* is a must-read for anyone who ... happened following the momentous decision Britain took in the 2016 referendum. Grey is not a neutral observer, but his analysis is scholarly and balanced. He writes with engaging clarity as he navigates through toxic headlines and political slogans. It will be a long time before this illuminating account is rivalled."

JONATHAN DIMBLEBY, BROADCASTER AND AUTHOR

"A fascinating, thoughtful, clear and authoritative analysis of Brexit and its ongoing aftermath."

PROFESSOR BRIAN COX, PHYSICIST AND BROADCASTER

"Chris Grey has blown away the fog and obfuscation surrounding Brexit and revealed it in all its stark wretchedness. His writing is thrilling; his conclusions, tragic."

SARAH CAREY, COLUMNIST, *IRISH INDEPENDENT*

"It is hard to imagine a clearer, more detailed, more dispassionate analysis of the journey and execution of the UK's departure from the European Union than this brilliant and readable book by Chris Grey. Everyone who cares about the issue, for and against, needs this level of expertise and knowledge at their fingertips. Masterly."

HOWARD GOODALL, COMPOSER AND BROADCASTER

"An absolutely compelling account of how Brexit first muddied and then poisoned the well of political debate in Britain and left us with a reputation for political untrustworthiness which still haunts our relations with the EU. Above all, it's a searing account of the deep failure of political leadership in our country at a moment when it was so desperately needed."

CAROLINE LUCAS MP

# BREXIT

## UNFOLDED

### HOW NO ONE GOT WHAT THEY WANTED (AND WHY THEY WERE NEVER GOING TO)

## CHRIS GREY

Biteback Publishing

First published in Great Britain in 2021 by
Biteback Publishing Ltd, London
Copyright © Chris Grey 2021

ISBN 978-1-78590-692-3

10 9 8 7 6 5 4 3 2 1

A CIP catalogue record for this book is available from the British Library.

Set in Adobe Caslon Pro

Printed and bound in Great Britain by
CPI Group (UK) Ltd, Croydon CR0 4YY

*Every organization of men, be it social or political, ultimately relies on man's capacity for making promises and keeping them.*
HANNAH ARENDT, *CRISES OF THE REPUBLIC*

# CONTENTS

# ACKNOWLEDGEMENTS

As I explain in the Introduction, this book grows out of the weekly blog I have written since 2016, so I am hugely grateful to all those who have read and publicised it, or in other ways helped to get an audience for my work on Brexit, and particularly to Sarah Murphy for her unflagging private and public support and encouragement, especially in the early days of building a readership for the blog.

Dr Jennifer Zerk, of Jennifer Zerk Consulting and an associate fellow of Chatham House, an expert on international trade and human rights, has week-in and week-out for five years supplied me with media reports to use for the blog, which she constantly encouraged me to write. She then read and provided detailed and hugely helpful comments on the entire first draft of this book, for which I am profoundly grateful. I have never before received feedback on anything I have written which has been so astute and smart, and yet so supportive. She provided exactly the mixture of engagement and detachment needed to help me develop the text, a skill that is very rare indeed. Needless to say, she bears no responsibility for the content of the book, including any factual errors.

Peter Ungphakorn, former Senior Information Officer at the World Trade Organization, very kindly read and commented on the sections in Chapter One of this book about different trade models for Brexit. Again, he bears no responsibility for the content, including any factual errors, of those sections or any other part of the book.

Professor Katy Hayward of Queen's University Belfast, an expert on the Ireland/Northern Ireland border, was equally kind in commenting on the section in Chapter Two setting out the overall issues Brexit posed for that border. Once again, she bears no responsibility for the content, including any factual errors, of that section or any other part of the book.

I am grateful to Alex Dean, senior editor at *Prospect* magazine, for allowing me to include in Chapter Two edited parts of my article originally published as 'The ultimate Brexit counterfactual' in *Prospect* on 1 August 2018.

I am grateful to Martin Stanley for providing me with an introduction to James Stephens, publisher at Biteback Publishing, who commissioned this book. Also at Biteback, I would like to thank Olivia Beattie for encouraging the development of the book and giving some useful feedback on draft chapters, Vicky Jessop for her assiduous work dealing with digital marketing issues (and no doubt much else), James Lilford for his consummate professionalism in completing the editorial process and, especially, Molly Arnold, my original editor, for her extraordinary and exemplary efficiency, skill, knowledge and professionalism.

Finally, and most importantly, I am far more than grateful to my wife, Dr Nathalie Mitev-Grey, whose Franco-Polish-Bulgarian heritage and British/French citizenship tell a story of twentieth-century Europe, and to whom I am for ever indebted for emotional and intellectual support too extensive to describe, which encompasses her encouragement of my work on Brexit and much else besides.

# ACRONYMS

BRINO: Brexit in name only
CBI: Confederation of British Industry
CETA: Comprehensive Economic and Trade Agreement
CPTPP: Comprehensive and Progressive Agreement for Trans-Pacific Partnership
CTA: Common Travel Area
DExEU: Department for Exiting the European Union
DUP: Democratic Unionist Party
EBA: European Banking Authority
ECHR: European Convention on Human Rights
ECJ: European Court of Justice
EEA: European Economic Area
EFTA: European Free Trade Association
EMA: European Medicines Agency
ERG: European Research Group
FTA: Free trade agreement
GATT: General Agreement on Tariffs and Trade
GFA: Good Friday Agreement
IMB: Internal Market Bill
Lib Dem: Liberal Democrat (party)
LPF: Level Playing Field
MFN: Most favoured nation
NAFTA: North American Free Trade Agreement
NI: Northern Ireland

NIP:    Northern Ireland Protocol
NTB:    Non-tariff barrier
SNP:    Scottish National Party
TCA:    Trade and Cooperation Agreement
TUC:    Trades Union Congress
UKIP:    United Kingdom Independence Party
WAB:    Withdrawal Agreement Bill
WTO:    World Trade Organization

# INTRODUCTION: UNFOLDING BREXIT

On 23 June 2016 a referendum was held in which the majority of the people of the United Kingdom voted to leave the European Union.

Just that short, apparently factual, statement contains within it implications which are still heavily contested.

It was a majority of the 'people', but only of the 72 per cent who voted amongst those eligible to do so. Those ineligible included sixteen- and seventeen-year-olds, EU nationals living in the UK* and UK nationals who had lived abroad for over fifteen years. The people of England and Wales voted by a majority to leave, but those of Scotland or Northern Ireland did not. Legally, the vote was an 'advisory referendum', which did not automatically entail leaving the EU but simply gave advice to Parliament which it could, in principle, refuse to take. That it was advisory was the reason given in Parliament as to why only a simple majority of anything over 50 per cent, rather than a super majority of some higher percentage, was required for a vote to leave. So how could a very small simple majority – 52 per cent to 48 per cent – now mandate leaving? Above all:

---

\* I use United Kingdom (UK) and Britain interchangeably, and Great Britain to refer to England, Wales and Scotland.

I

what did it mean to 'leave the EU'? Clearly it meant not being a member of the EU, but which of the many different ways of 'not being a member' was to be followed?

Yet this account of the issues raised by the referendum result would be regarded by many Brexiters and leave voters[*] as absurd, if not downright dishonest. More specifically, it would be seen as a 'remainer' account, and perhaps as an illustration of remainers' refusal to accept the referendum result. They would see it as an irrelevant truism that only those eligible to vote and choosing to do so were the ones who got to decide. The distribution of votes between the constituent parts of the UK is also irrelevant since it was a national vote. The advisory nature of the referendum is irrelevant because the then Prime Minister, David Cameron, had written to every household saying that its outcome would be implemented by the government. A narrow majority is a majority, and that is all that matters. As for what leaving the EU means, things get much murkier, as is discussed at length in this book, but many Brexiters would say that it meant leaving all the institutions of the EU without exception.

## THE SIGNIFICANCE OF COMPETING ACCOUNTS OF BREXIT

Without evaluating these competing accounts of the referendum result, what is important is simply that they exist. That matters in two ways. Firstly, it matters because it illustrates

---

[*] I use 'Brexiter' to mean a high-profile public advocate of Brexit, including politicians, journalists and other leaders or opinion-formers. I use 'leaver' or 'leave voter' to mean a member of the general public who supports or voted for Brexit. I use 'Brexit Ultra' to mean someone highly committed to a hard or very hard form of Brexit (in senses I will subsequently define). I do not draw the same distinction amongst 'remainers' because remaining in the EU only took a single form in the Brexit process, i.e. to stay in the EU. I use 'remainer' to mean a voter for or advocate of staying in the EU, and I use 'leading remainer' to refer to a high-profile advocate of remaining in the EU in the same sense as for such advocates of Brexit.

that anything that anyone writes about Brexit will almost certainly be hotly disputed by someone, and is likely to be seen as reflecting the biases of the person writing it. I will say more about my position shortly, but for now will just note that such disputes are part of the wider sense in which Brexit has created a kind of culture war.

This is partly to do with the demographics of the referendum vote itself. Polls conducted afterwards showed that leave voters were likely to be older, less educated and less economically active than remain voters (these things were partially linked, because older people are less likely to have been able to go to university and more likely to be retired), more likely to be in lower socio-economic groups than remain voters, and more likely to hold socially illiberal views.[1]

This suggests that the way people voted in the referendum coded a set of social and cultural divisions that went deeper than the ostensible question of EU membership and, therefore, that the Brexit process was going to be about more than Brexit itself. One consequence was that, almost from the beginning, there emerged fundamental differences in how the two groups saw Brexit, to the extent of there being almost 'remainer truth' and 'leaver truth'.

From this flows the second significance of the competing accounts. It is that whatever position anyone takes on Brexit, they cannot deny that these accounts do, as a matter of fact, exist. Whatever motivations or inadequacies each side attributes to the other in a sense don't matter. The very fact of their existence structures what has happened since the referendum and to some extent explains it: had there been more consensus then Brexit would not be the deeply contested issue that it is. Even now, there is very little sign that members of either side have been persuaded by each other. If anything, each is more deeply entrenched than before. That can't be wished away, but has to be accepted and understood in order to make sense of what has happened since the referendum.

## MY POSITION

This book is, precisely, an attempt to make sense of what has happened and, given that it is such contested terrain, it is necessary that I say something about my own position, and in the process something about the basis on which this book is written.

I regard Brexit as a very serious national mistake, which has already done and will continue to do untold economic, geopolitical and cultural damage to the United Kingdom. However, from the day of the referendum result, I did not expect the decision to be reversed. In that sense I 'accepted' the result, not because of any particular 'respect' for it but because it seemed to me politically impossible to change it. Except for a brief period during 2019, that view did not change. In the immediate aftermath of the referendum, I believed that a 'soft Brexit', in the sense discussed below, would be viable in fully meeting the requirements of the vote whilst minimising the damage. That did not happen, but I continue to believe that in 2016 there could have been a national consensus for such an approach which would largely have avoided the bitter and toxic divisions we have experienced.

It's also worth saying that prior to the run-up to the referendum I was neither especially interested in the EU nor a passionate advocate of Britain's membership of it. Like a lot of people, including many who became deeply partisan on both sides, it simply didn't feature in my mind as much of an issue. To that limited extent, I approached things with an open mind – and certainly had no life-long involvement in debates about the EU. In view of some of the accusations that fly about in discussions of Brexit, it's also necessary to say that I have never received any money, for example research grants or other funding, from the EU.

My interest only really started in the year or so before the referendum, when it was in prospect but no date had been set, as I began to notice a huge amount of confusion and downright falsehood about what EU membership meant, and especially how it functioned as a trade and regulatory institution. This touched on my own academic expertise because I work in the field of organisation studies – a rather strange, hybrid discipline at the interface of psychology, sociology, economics, business and politics which is concerned with how organisations of all sorts operate. As such, I had worked in business schools for over twenty-five years. My own research had never been concerned with the EU, especially, but as part of the general background knowledge of my subject I had a working knowledge of how it operated. Moreover, ever since writing a PhD on the regulation of financial services my academic research and teaching has been on the intersection between politics and business.

In the run-up to the referendum, I wrote some short articles trying to clarify the trade and regulatory issues, which led to invitations to give various public talks. In the course of these, I deepened my own knowledge but also observed that many people valued these explanations and felt they were more useful than the material they were getting during what, by then, was the official campaign. It was not simply that I was providing them with 'the facts' but also with an analysis which grew out of my work as an academic even though it had not in the past been applied to Britain's membership of the EU.

That analytical mindset is the basis of this book. For whilst it may be that there is in some sense 'remainer truth' and 'leaver truth', I continue to believe that it is possible to use the tools of rational argument and evidence in order to make sense of events, including Brexit. Of course there are endless questions of judgement, values and interpretation, as in all political questions (were that not so, they would not be political questions). But that does not mean that there is no basis on which to evaluate evidence and nothing to differentiate good arguments from bad ones. Moreover, whilst some things about Brexit are legitimately and probably endlessly debatable, there are some things which are straightforwardly true or false.

What matters is to avoid starting from the position that Brexit is 'good' or 'bad' despite facts, evidence or argument to the contrary and to avoid twisting those facts to support that position. Having not started with a particular position but having acquired one as a result of evidence and argument I have tried, within human limits, to continue in that analytical vein. I am not 'neutral', therefore, and do not pretend to be, but I am not tribalist either.

Concretely, shortly after the referendum result, I decided to start a weekly blog to catalogue and analyse Brexit events as they transpired. Inevitably, at first very few people read it but even within the extremely crowded market for Brexit analysis it gradually acquired a wide and enthusiastic readership. In time, it came to be highly praised by leading journalists and commentators, and read by politicians and others on both sides of the Brexit debate, and in many countries. It was also frequently quoted in the media and led to me making several media appearances to comment on events.

This book grows out of that blog, but it is certainly not a print edition of it, not least as that would run to ten or more volumes. Rather, it draws out what emerged over time as the recurring analytical themes in the blog and attempts to use these to explain how Brexit has unfolded since the referendum.

## THE UNFOLDING OF BREXIT

To speak of the unfolding of Brexit is, in itself, to make an important point. Brexit is not, and was never going to be, a single event. It was and is an ongoing process. That explains why – to the consternation of some, especially those Brexiters for whom securing it had been their life's ambition – the vote to leave the EU was not the end of anything but, rather, the beginning of something very different and much more complex. For that matter, the day that Britain left the EU, 31 January 2020, was only a staging post, albeit a very important one, in the Brexit process. It was followed by a transition period during which a future terms agreement, the Trade and Cooperation Agreement (TCA), was negotiated. This book ends at that point but, as will become clear, that in itself was only the beginning of a new phase of Brexit.

As the process has unfolded, it has become possible to see recurring themes within it, some more important than others. One of them is simply that lack of agreement about basic facts – or, perhaps, it might be truer to say that all of them are variations on that theme.

### Lack of definition of the outcome of Brexit

A particular, and crucial, case of lack of agreed facts was the absence of an agreed definition before the Brexit vote as to what that vote would mean. In outline, from the outset at least three fundamentally different versions of Brexit were in play, which will be discussed in detail in Chapter One. One version, known as 'soft Brexit' or the 'Norway option', meant remaining as a member of the single market and possibly even (unlike Norway) in some form of customs union. Another, which was usually called 'hard Brexit' or the 'Canada option', meant leaving the single market but seeking a free trade agreement (FTA) with the EU. A third, 'no-deal Brexit' or 'the WTO option', meant leaving without a trade deal and trading on World Trade Organization terms.

These very different versions of Brexit were the subject of the first thing I published on Brexit, on a website devoted to making academic research publicly accessible, in October 2015.[2] This was after it was known that there would be a referendum, but before the campaign had started. In the piece, I outlined these main models of Brexit and argued that the debate at that time suffered from conflating or confusing them. If this persisted, and the vote were to leave when the referendum was held, then I warned it would be too late and the country would have voted for something without knowing what it was.

This turned out to be prescient. Not only were all the models touted at different times by different advocates of Brexit during the referendum, but their differences were concealed, especially by persistent references to 'single market access' which could have meant any of them. The Vote Leave campaign did not specify which version of Brexit it advocated, and explicitly said that it would be for the government, not it, to do so if the vote were to leave. It was only after the referendum that Brexiters claimed the vote had been for any particular form of Brexit. But that was not true, as was shown by the fact that for many months after the referendum all the versions were being debated as possible outcomes. Clearly that debate would not have happened had Brexit been pre-defined.

### Ever-hardening definitions

The existence of this debate is a prelude to the next recurring theme. At every stage of the process, some Brexiters, whom I refer to as 'Brexit Ultras', argued that 'true Brexit' was a harder form of Brexit than whatever was currently envisaged. So whereas in the years before the referendum Nigel Farage and UKIP (as well as some of those on what was then called the Eurosceptic wing of the Tory Party) were extolling the soft Brexit Norway model, by the time of the referendum only hard or FTA Brexit would do. Some who campaigned during the referendum for soft Brexit afterwards championed an FTA hard Brexit. Still others who had argued for soft or hard Brexit came to say that 'no deal' was the only true Brexit. Within this, there have been many twists and turns but the direction of travel was always the same – as soon as anything was conceded to the Brexit Ultras, they always demanded something more extreme.

As a consequence, the terminology shifted confusingly as Brexit unfolded. Soft Brexit came to be called, by Brexit Ultras, 'Brexit in name only' (BRINO), or simply not Brexit at all. The hard Brexit of leaving the single market and customs union came sometimes to be described as soft Brexit, with hard Brexit sometimes referring to the more extreme position of WTO Brexit, or no-deal Brexit.

### Lack of definition of the process of Brexit

However, no-deal Brexit itself came to have two meanings which, initially, were not clear, because as well as the outcome of Brexit being undefined, so too was its process. In fact, all of the different models for Brexit were actually models of what the outcome might be, and not of the process by which it might be reached.

The legal process for leaving the EU was defined in Article 50 of the Lisbon Treaty. This specified that an agreement for withdrawal would be negotiated 'taking account of the framework for [the departing member's] future relationship with the Union'.[3] That future relationship would be agreed subsequent to the Withdrawal Agreement, and by a different process.

What it meant was that Brexit would consist of two separate agreements. One would be a Withdrawal Agreement, setting out the terms of exit. The other would be a future terms agreement, setting out the conditions of trade and other forms of cooperation, which eventually was called the Trade and Cooperation Agreement. Sitting between these two deals would, or might, be a Political Declaration accompanying the Withdrawal Agreement in which both parties agreed a non-binding general framework for the future terms agreement.

Over and over again as Brexit unfolded it became clear that many Brexiters either did not accept this process or did not understand it, and that lack of understanding was shared by many in the media and elsewhere. During the referendum, the Vote Leave campaign actually promised that the future terms would be agreed before the Article 50 process to leave even began. This was simply impossible given the terms of Article 50. After the referendum, many Brexiters claimed that both the exit agreement and the future terms agreement could be done as part of a single process.[4]

This was also untrue but it permeated almost the entirety of the Brexit process in one way or another. It led to a row over the structure of the Article 50 talks (see Chapter Three) which never really went away. It led to the idea that what was agreed in the exit terms – especially as regards a financial settlement for the past – was, or should be, conditional on the future terms agreement. It led at least some Brexiter MPs to think that the final terms agreement would override the exit terms agreement. And it led to some very complex misunderstandings about what was being voted for in the fraught parliamentary debates that occurred. To give one example, during debates about the original Withdrawal Agreement negotiated by Theresa May (see Chapter Four), many MPs objected to it saying that, instead, they wanted a 'Canada-style' deal. But such a deal, if reached, would be the future terms agreement and so could not be a substitute for the exit terms agreement.

All of this will be explained in more detail in the coming chapters, but for now it is important to say that one consequence was that the term 'no-deal Brexit' changed in meaning as the Brexit process unfolded. Until the end of 2019 it meant no Withdrawal Agreement (i.e. no agreement on exit terms). From early 2020 it meant no Trade and Cooperation Agreement (i.e. no agreement on future terms).

## Nativism and globalism

In addition to recurrent confusions about the outcome and process of Brexit, there were others about its meaning. On the one hand, it was sold to many, if not most, leave voters on an anti-immigration and economically protectionist or 'nativist' prospectus. On the other, especially since the referendum, it has been proclaimed as a licence for a free-trading 'Global Britain' open to the 'brightest and the best'. Whilst being contradictory, combining these two strands arguably helped to build the coalition to win the referendum because it enabled the combination of two quite different critiques of the EU. The EU was depicted as a neo-liberal agent of globalisation which cared nothing for the nation state but was solely concerned with satisfying the interests of the business elite, including for the supposedly cheap labour that freedom of movement of people supplied. However, the EU was also derided as a 'protectionist racket', inhibiting free trade and preventing Britain from being globally competitive.

This has inflected the Brexit process in several ways. As regards immigration, it partly explains the shift away from soft Brexit, since this would have entailed freedom of movement of people within the single market, including the UK, and hence would not fulfil the 'nativist' strand. At the same time, it has led to a far greater emphasis on the globalist agenda of independent trade deals (which entail not being in a customs union with the EU) than was the case during the referendum. But the two remain in tension. It is highly likely that post-Brexit Britain will have higher levels of immigration than before, though probably not from the EU, in order to meet skills needs, and also because immigration liberalisation is likely to be a precondition of some trade deals. Meanwhile, erecting new barriers to free trade with the UK's biggest trading partner is hardly a sign of pursuing a global free trade agenda.

## Economics and sovereignty

Nested inside all that is yet another theme, which is the tension between Brexit as an economic project and as one purely concerned with political sovereignty and national independence. Again, there are many complexities and sub-plots. In brief, whilst one of the main referendum slogans – 'taking back control' – articulated Brexit in terms of sovereignty, the other main slogan – '£350 million a week for the NHS' – was plainly an economic argument for Brexit. Indeed, the Vote Leave campaign made numerous claims of economic benefits in terms of higher wages and better access to housing and public services, often linked to reducing immigration. It was only later, when even the most disingenuous could no longer say that the economic effects were going to be anything other than negative, that it began to be widely claimed that it was 'never about the money'.

That this claim is false is shown by the fact that any suggestions of economic damage (or any other kind of damage, for that matter) were dismissed as 'Project Fear'. The reason for that was because Brexiters knew that if voters were persuaded that leaving would cause economic damage they would not vote for it, or not in sufficient numbers to win, in the name of sovereignty. The central achievement of their campaign was to persuade voters that 'taking back control' was cost-free, but this also turned out to be its central flaw. For it was the fundamental reason why, as the subtitle of this book suggests, Brexit in reality could never deliver the Brexit promised. One of the commonly used terms during the Brexit process was 'cakeism', deriving from Boris Johnson having said that he favoured Britain 'having its cake and eating it'. This meant, generally, having the benefits of EU membership without belonging to it but, more specifically, having the independence of sovereignty without economic cost and, indeed, with economic benefits. In fact, there was a tension, and a trade-off, between the two.

### Betrayal and victimhood

All of these issues are discussed in detail later, but with them comes another recurring theme, which is quite psychologically complex. Whilst Brexit stayed undefined, it could mean whatever people wanted it to mean. But as soon as any actual form of Brexit was articulated or defined, some group of Brexiters would consider it to be 'a betrayal of true Brexit'.

As mentioned earlier, this generally meant pushing for a harder and harder version, but its real significance went much deeper: it became ever clearer that betrayal was not just something that many Brexiters feared, but something that some of them actually wanted or even needed. There was a particular strand within support for Brexit which positioned 'ordinary people' as the downtrodden victims of the elite, meaning not so much the rich and privileged but the politically correct 'metropolitan liberals' who wouldn't let ordinary people 'say what they thought', about immigration especially. For those of this mindset, winning the referendum was, paradoxically, a disaster because by making their protest agenda central to government policy they were denied that victimhood. Thus 'betrayal' was actually quite attractive because it enabled them to stay in a mode of perpetual victimhood, perpetually railing against the elite who were thwarting them.

This contained within it the seeds of an inevitable tragedy, which was that once Brexit was done, and however it was done, not only would it be against the wishes of, by definition, remainers, but also there would be at least a hard core of Brexiters for whom it would be seen as a betrayal.

## Punishment and sabotage

From this derives the final and most culturally destructive theme, which is the search for blame. If 'true Brexit' could never be delivered in the eyes of those who most wanted it, and yet never disowned as a mistake, and if victimhood was to be maintained through a narrative of betrayal, then someone had to be to blame. Thus, almost from the beginning, various groups and people were identified. Some were external – the EU 'punishment brigade', Jean-Claude Juncker, Donald Tusk, Michel Barnier, the Irish, especially Leo Varadkar, and the global elite. Others were internal – saboteurs and enemies of the people, such as Gina Miller, judges, civil servants, the Establishment, the liberal elite, and in due course Theresa 'the Remainer'. In the end, even Boris Johnson was attacked by the most extreme Brexiters for what he delivered.

It is this theme, more than any other, that has made the politics of the Brexit process so toxic. It meant that Brexit could not be undertaken within the 'normal' parameters of policy delivery – even contentious policy delivery. The immensely complex business of enacting Brexit was constantly being scrutinised and judged through the prism of the culture war. In fact, even to describe it as 'complex' is, in the eyes of some Brexiters, a part of this culture war because, they still insist, it should have been quick and easy and was only made complex by EU punishment and remainer sabotage. But on any rational appraisal the process was bound to be complex, and Brexiters above all should have realised this, since their repeated complaint was that the UK had been sucked into a European 'super-state'. At all events, Brexit could not be made simple just by saying that it should be.

## MAKING SENSE OF BREXIT

In the years since the 2016 referendum there has been a swirl of events, often confusing, sometimes dramatic. Millions became watchers of the parliamentary TV channel as knife-edge votes were held under sometimes arcane procedures in the House of Commons. People also began to become aware of and interested in things which, in many cases – including in some respects my own – they had hardly registered before. These included the intricacies of international trade and its laws and regulations; the nature of the Good Friday Agreement; how fishing quotas work; what a customs union is; how international supply chains operate – and much else besides.

This has led to two problems, both of which are highly relevant to this book.

## The problem of expertise and Brexit

One is about expertise. Most, if not all, of those areas have (mainly) small groups of seriously knowledgeable experts, whether they be academics, journalists, business people or think-tankers. As public interest grew, they became more visible but, at the same time, they were joined by (and were sometimes irritated by) hordes of 'instant experts' who, very often, partially or totally misunderstood what are very complex subjects. This was true on both the leave and remain sides.

But the genuine experts also had their limitations, which were precisely those of expertise. Brexit is such a hydra-headed phenomenon that no one could claim to grasp it in its entirety. And that isn't just about the multiplicity of relevant 'topics', it's about the way that Brexit interweaves the domains of domestic and international politics, economics, business, culture, law, history, psychology and much else besides.

This is a problem for me, too, but also one in which it may be helpful to work in the cross-disciplinary field that I do. I'm fairly used to hopping across some of these different domains. But I am also conscious of the limitations of this. I am neither a trade expert nor a politics expert, to take what are probably the most central bodies of expertise relevant to this book. My attempt is to use the knowledge and skills that I have to dip into different areas of expertise, but I recognise that this 'jack of all trades' approach will be offensive and unsatisfactory to those who are 'masters' of any one of them. It may also lead me to make errors, for which I apologise in advance.

Equally, there is no need to be too apologetic. Academics and other experts have arguably become too narrowly focused and, in the process, lost a sense of the big picture which Brexit presents. This book is an attempt to present that big picture, which means using some broad brush strokes.

## The problem of how to make sense of Brexit

That links directly to the second problem. The Brexit process has been confusing precisely because of the scope and scale of events. That is particularly true for people who may have dropped in and out of giving attention to them, but it's also true for those who have become immersed in the thickets of those events. Making sense of Brexit requires both continuous engagement with what has happened (unlike the first group) and standing back from what has happened (unlike the second group). In this book, I aim to draw upon my efforts to do the first in order to do the second.

It is here that the recurring themes sketched above become crucial in understanding how Brexit has unfolded. What they enable is a way of making sense of the complexity and confusion of what has happened. For whilst the story of Brexit has unfolded chronologically, it has, throughout the years since 2016, shown the patterns and repetitions of these recurring themes. So I will tell that story so that it does not just chronicle what happened, but explains how and why it happened.

In doing so, I am telling it in terms of what happened in Britain and I, myself, am British. There are clearly other accounts to be given from the perspective of the EU or of individual EU members, and indeed one of the problems throughout the Brexit process was that so much of the British debate was domestically focused. However, I do seek to include in my account explanations of EU interests and motivations, and particularly those of Ireland, the country other than the UK most affected, so I hope it is not a wholly parochial one.

Underlying the idea that Brexit is a process that has unfolded via a series of recurring themes is the proposition that
what has happened was never predetermined, in part because
of the contradictions within – and in some cases between – the
themes I've outlined. Throughout the process there have always
been voices, usually those of remainers, claiming – either pre-
dictively or retrospectively – that such and such 'was always
bound to happen' or even 'was the plan all along'. Others have,
with equal certainty, claimed the same for completely different outcomes. This has applied in particular to whether or not
there would be a Withdrawal Agreement and, later, to whether
or not there would be a trade deal.

For the most part, these voices have been mistaken – not
necessarily in their predictions since, by definition, some of
those predicting contradictory things were going to be right,
but in the assumptions of inevitability. In reality, the way that
events have unfolded was contingent rather than necessary:
that is, with different decisions or different actions different
outcomes were possible. I will return to this in the concluding
chapter but, for now, will just say that no one writing in 2016
could conceivably have predicted even the broad outlines of
what actually happened over the following years.

Although I am an academic, this is not an academic book;
it does not for the most part use academic sources, and it is
not written for an academic audience. In the ways I've already
suggested, my academic background has some relevance, and
is probably what enabled me to write both this book and my
other works on Brexit. But, more, it is an example of what in
my opinion is the too-rare genre of academics writing for the
general public in a way that is hopefully intelligent and accessible without being convoluted or condescending.

In this, there is a tricky balance between what novelists call 'telling' and 'showing'. As I tell the story of Brexit, there will be constant episodes which show one or more of the themes I've outlined in this chapter. In most academic writing, the convention is to 'tell, show and re-tell', which in this context would mean drawing the reader's attention to each example of one of the themes being in play. I think that would be an unbearably didactic approach and so, instead, I rely on readers' good sense and intelligence to see when my telling of events shows the themes I have identified. However, in the conclusion, I will spell some of these out explicitly.

## BREXIT, UNFOLDED

This book does not attempt to explain what led to the referendum being held, nor to explain its result. Such explanations already exist[5] and no doubt there will be many more in the future. Instead, it starts from the point at which that result was announced and discusses the events since then, culminating in the Trade and Cooperation Agreement and the end of the transition period on 31 December 2020.

The chapters are arranged chronologically, and structured around the main political phases, to show the unfolding process but sometimes, in the interests of clarity, there are slight overlaps in that arrangement and I also refer forwards and backwards as the story proceeds so as to show links or to provide reminders. In giving an account of these Brexit years, part of my purpose is to correct some of the more flagrant rewritings of history that have already occurred. In this respect, the blog mentioned earlier has acted as a valuable 'archive' in that it contains a contemporaneous record of events and helps to avoid errors arising from hindsight, although, used properly, hindsight can also be useful to make sense of what was not necessarily obvious at the time.

However, this book is very far from being a complete history of what has happened. It is probably too early to write anything which could properly be called a history, partly because the events are too recent for the application of a historical gaze and partly, as I will make clear, because although the end of the transition period marks a certain moment in the Brexit process, it is very far from an end. It is a semi-colon, rather than a full stop.

In any case, this cannot be a 'complete' account of all the twists and turns of the almost five-year period it covers. That would require many large volumes rather than a single book. It would also need insider access to the political actors and papers to provide such a completeness, whereas this book is based on (a wide range of) publicly available sources.

From those sources, and my own interpretation and analysis of them, what this book provides is a chronologically structured account of how the major events of these years unfolded. It is an attempt to make sense of what we, as a nation, have just lived through in this period which has changed so much in our lives, as well as to explain to those abroad who have looked on, often with bemusement. I hope, along the way, to convey the drama of these events for, whatever else may be said of the Brexit process, it has at times been highly engaging in ways that contrast with the perhaps rather drab and technocratic nature of 'normal' British politics.

Be that as it may, this book is also, as its subtitle implies, a critique of what has happened. Because of the polarised landscape which Brexit has created, some will reject that critique out of hand. In particular, although there are places at which I criticise remainers, or say things which some of them will find deeply unpalatable, I am well aware that some readers will dismiss my entire account as 'remainer truth' (or even as 'remainer lies'). To them I would say a few things. First, that I have attempted to show at several points how and why a Brexiter account would differ from mine. Second, that reading the book will, if nothing else, give an insight into how some of their compatriots see Brexit. And, third, if they at least agree with my argument that the Brexit process has not given them what they wanted then it may be that they will come to agree with my explanation of how and why that came about. If so, it may also be that they will come to think, as I do, that what I provide in this book is an accurate and damning chronicle which might serve as a warning for the future.

## CHAPTER ONE

# BREXIT MEANS BREXIT

*From the 2016 referendum to the Lancaster House speech*

It is hard now to recreate the shock of the hours and days following the announcement of the 2016 referendum result. As the headlines went around the world, Boris Johnson and Michael Gove, the leading figures in the Vote Leave campaign, appeared on television seeming bemused and, to many eyes, frightened by their victory. David Cameron, the Prime Minister, stood outside 10 Downing Street to announce his resignation, surely guessing, even then, that his permanent historical legacy was going to be one of having made a colossal political blunder in calling and losing the vote.

The pound immediately plummeted in value by as much as 13 per cent against the dollar within the first few hours, hitting its lowest level for thirty years. Both the FTSE-100 and FTSE-250 fell dramatically, the latter, which includes many of the smaller and more domestic companies, especially so. About the only adult in the room during this political vacuum and economic firestorm seemed to be Mark Carney, the Governor of the Bank of England. He swiftly announced the Bank's willingness to take extraordinary measures to guarantee financial stability, including provision of an immediate £250 billion to lend to banks if needed.

One thing did not happen. Whereas Cameron had said

during the campaign that if he lost then he would immediately trigger Article 50 of the Lisbon Treaty – that is, begin the formal process to leave the EU – he did not do so. That inaction, along with Carney's actions, had an important consequence. In the economic modelling of what would happen after a vote to leave, amongst many other things it had been assumed that Article 50 would be invoked immediately, but not that the Bank of England would take any action.

Like all such forecasts, they were not predictions in the sense that most people would expect them to be, but models of what would happen under certain conditions. That these and other conditions were not met inevitably made the models flawed, and this allowed Brexiters to claim that they had been discredited as 'Project Fear', for whilst the pound never fully recovered from the immediate shock,[6] the stock markets did, and Carney's bank stabilisation measures were largely unneeded – it had been enough that he had announced their existence. Equally, it's not unreasonable to think that had an immediate triggering of Article 50 happened, on top of the general chaos of those post-referendum days, the economic effects would have been more dire. Even as it was, by June 2019 an authoritative study estimated that the UK economy was 2.9 per cent smaller than it would have been had the referendum result been to remain.[7] This and the fall in the value of sterling would, in any other context, have been seen as a major failure of policy rather than a vindication of it.

## Project Fear

My point is not to defend the pre-referendum economic forecasts, but that what happened, and what did not happen, in the immediate aftermath of the vote enabled a pivot from using the Project Fear accusation as a campaign tool to incorporating it into the post-referendum discussion of delivering Brexit. During the referendum campaign, Vote Leave had persistently and successfully attacked as Project Fear any warning of economic damage (or indeed any other kind of damage). In particular, Gove had famously – or infamously – declared in an interview that 'the public had had enough of experts', referring primarily to various domestic and international economic and business bodies who had issued warnings about the impact of Brexit.

Once the immediate shockwaves of the vote had passed, Brexiters were able to claim that the economic predictions had been confounded, and from then onwards every single announcement or warning of damage was dismissed by reference to that. The success of the Project Fear line was one reason why rational debate about how to 'do' Brexit became all but impossible. In ways quite unlike normal political decisions, or for that matter decisions that people take in everyday life, no balancing of pros and cons, or costs and benefits, was deemed allowable. All the cons and all the costs were written off as fearmongering and 'remainer lies'.

As time went on, it inevitably became more difficult to disentangle the economic effects of Brexit from those due to other causes. At the level of company closures or relocations, some other explanation could often be given – sometimes truthfully, sometimes half-truthfully in ignoring that such decisions are usually multi-factorial, and sometimes dishonestly. This was compounded by the fact that companies making such decisions would often have good reasons not to irritate the government or a potentially large chunk of their customer base by publicly blaming Brexit. At the level of the economy, other factors – and especially, from 2020, the impact of the Covid-19 pandemic – came to overlay the consequences of Brexit, making it all the easier to dismiss the latter.

The existence of the Project Fear rebuttal, and its aggressive promulgation both before and ever since the referendum, is significant because it gives the lie to what came to be a repeated claim that leave voters had chosen Brexit for non-economic reasons. That claim took two (related) forms. On the one hand, that the motivation had been purely one of reclaiming political sovereignty, irrespective of economics and regardless of cost. Yet had that been so, then why was so much effort put into the Project Fear rebuttal? The reality, of course, is that the leave campaigners knew that, had voters believed it would be so costly, insufficient numbers of them would have voted for Brexit.

On the other hand, the very existence of the warnings was later used to supposedly demonstrate that voters had chosen to leave with full knowledge of the economic costs. Yet, clearly, the whole point of the rebuttal line was that these costs were exaggerated, or did not exist at all. In a similar way, the idea that the remain case was based on (economic) rationality and the leave case on (nationalist) emotion does not really stack up. Both, albeit more or less successfully, made appeals to economic rationality, and both to nationalist emotion (on the remain side with, for example, the 'stronger together' slogan).

In any case, the persistence of the Project Fear rebuttal long after the referendum is also an indicator of the way that the Brexit process has remained in a kind of campaign mode ever since 2016. I will return to that theme, but it had one particularly malign, and perverse, consequence: as the reality of leaving the EU got closer, the preparations for it – the construction of new customs facilities, for example – were significantly hampered since making such preparations entailed admitting that the costs of Brexit were real.

## May's emergence

In June 2016 all that was for the future, but some o
were sown in those early hours, when the combination of
Cameron's resignation and Carney's reassurance derailed the
economic forecasts of what a vote to leave would mean. Cameron's resignation had two other effects. One, obviously, was to
create political uncertainty, if not crisis. The other was, at least
potentially, to buy the country some breathing space. The original timescale to elect his successor was meant to culminate
in September and with no immediate invocation of Article
50 that would allow time for the 'dust to settle' and, perhaps,
some collective reflection on how to proceed. At the very least,
it left the responsibility to define what Brexit meant and how
it should be undertaken to his successor.

In fact, events moved much more quickly. The story of the
truncated leadership contest has been told many times,[8] and
the outcome was to install Theresa May as Prime Minister on
13 July 2016. May was and remains an enigmatic figure,[9] but
understanding her character and conduct is crucial to understanding some aspects of how the Brexit process unfolded. Her
obvious persona – especially at that time – was of someone
serious, sensible, dutiful and competent. She manifestly lacked
the social skills that are the stock-in-trade of most successful
politicians, but she had navigated six years as Home Secretary
without the public disasters that often befall holders of that
office. She had a slightly old-fashioned air about her, whilst
also being known for having challenged the Tory Party about
its 'nasty' image years before. Both remain and leave voters
might see her as someone who would 'act in the national interest' and for a while she enjoyed substantial public approval
ratings.

But behind all this lay some more complicated and problematic things. May was less confident than she seemed, and very reliant on two advisers, Fiona Hill and Nick Timothy, whom she brought with her from the Home Office to Downing Street. She had relatively little background in economics or business, but what she *had* acquired in her years as Home Secretary was a preoccupation with controlling immigration. In that role, she had also become accustomed to dealing with the EU by opting out of security initiatives and then opting back in to selected parts of them. This was to colour her approach to Brexit even though it was a wholly different process. It was an approach that was neatly skewered by a comment from Xavier Bettel, the Prime Minister of Luxembourg, when in October 2016 he remarked that 'before, [the UK] were in and they had many opt-outs; now they want to be out with many opt-ins'.[10]

Most significantly of all, May's obvious dutifulness led her to take a narrow and dogmatic view that what that duty consisted of was the delivery of Brexit in a way which would allow no compromise and little consultation. Yet, ironically, having embraced that duty to mean – as we will see – both an uncompromising form of Brexit and, certainly, no turning back on the referendum decision, she had always to prove to Brexiters that her commitment was genuine.

That need arose because she had campaigned for remain. Yet in the very early days of that campaign there had been some question (and concern, on Cameron's part) that she might come out in support of leave. As with Johnson, the decision was for a while in the balance, and although she jumped the other way to him, her involvement in the remain campaign was limited, low-key and apparently unenthusiastic. Still, she had not been a Brexiter and, despite her embrace of their cause, in the fevered atmosphere of these years her commitment to

Brexit was always under scrutiny from the most fanatical or Ultra Brexiters – meaning, primarily, the influential members of the European Research Group (ERG) of Tory MPs who became almost a party within a party. The bigger irony was that she would never be able to satisfy them.

## May's impossible challenge

That story is a complex one which I will return to at several points in this book. In brief, as May might have learned from Cameron, or John Major before him, no concession to the extreme Eurosceptics – or Brexit Ultras, as they became – would ever be enough to satisfy them. They would always demand more. That had been clear in the way that as soon as Cameron agreed to hold a referendum, they immediately started making new demands about restricting the franchise (e.g. to exclude sixteen- and seventeen-year-olds who had voted in the 2014 Scottish independence referendum), and about the question to be asked, and the framing of the answers, on all of which they got their own way.

During May's premiership, the Ultras quickly moved to discredit soft Brexit and to demand harder and harder Brexit, as discussed later. But there was more to it than that, which is why there is far more to explaining how Brexit unfolded than analysing May's character and decisions. The key problem she or any other Brexit Prime Minister would face was an entirely insoluble one, and it persists to this day. As soon as any concrete form of Brexit was defined, it was immediately denounced by some Brexiters as a betrayal of 'true' Brexit. That might come from within the Tory Party or from outside, especially from Nigel Farage and UKIP or, subsequently, the Brexit Party, and would be amplified in the media by Brexiter journalists and commentators.

In summary, although May embraced Brexit with a ferocious and fanatical duty, that embrace always had to be 'proved' by delivering Brexit – yet since delivery of any actual Brexit was not 'true' Brexit, her attempts to prove her commitment could never succeed. Thus, in the end, despite all her efforts, she got labelled by the Ultras as 'Theresa the Remainer' and is still blamed by them for Brexit 'not having been done properly'.

And in addition to all this is the final and greatest irony of May's leadership. In a certain sense the Ultras were right, for during her premiership she seemed to realise that Brexit was a terrible mistake. She repeatedly refused to answer questions about whether, if another referendum were held, she would vote leave or remain, and the clear implication was that she would vote remain. It's difficult to think of a parallel for the leader of any country dogmatically pursuing a complete reset of its economic and geopolitical strategy whilst apparently thinking it misguided. But that is what she did. Where the Ultras were wrong was in failing to see that her lack of belief was completely overridden by her sense of duty, and that the problems of delivering Brexit lay not with her so much as with their own inconsistent and unrealistic demands.

## BREXIT MEANS BREXIT

All this was the background to perhaps the most widely quoted and widely mocked slogan in the history of Brexit, and possibly in modern British political history generally: 'Brexit means Brexit'. In the months after her installation as Prime Minister, this (or variants, such as 'Brexit means Brexit and we're going to make a success of it') was almost all that May would say of what she planned to do. It was tautologous and it was derided as meaningless. But it did have a meaning, and an important one. It was code for saying that the result of the referendum would be acted upon and that it would not be revisited, whether by another referendum or by a confirmatory parliamentary vote. In this way, it was a signal to Brexiter MPs that she had embraced Brexit and to leave voters that she saw delivering Brexit as her duty.

At this time, there was relatively little political demand for another referendum, but the question of a confirmatory parliamentary vote was, potentially, a live one. It arose because, as mentioned in the introduction to this book, legally, the referendum had been a purely advisory one – that is, its outcome would advise but not bind Parliament on the question of whether to leave or remain in the EU. Indeed, it was for this reason that there had been no requirement set for a supermajority rather than a simple 50+ per cent majority for the vote. So it would have been perfectly proper to have a parliamentary vote in the light of the 'advice' given by the public vote.

That was the legal reality, but the political reality was entirely different. That was for two reasons. First, because in general referendums are rare in the UK system and carry a sense of settling big, constitutional questions. Second, and more specifically, because during the campaign a government leaflet had been sent to every household promising to enact whatever decision was made by the public. That had no legal force, but it clearly substantially inflected the politics towards confirming that first, general, expectation. The reason for the leaflet's statement was to try to make clear to voters that they should vote on the issue seriously and not – for example – use it as an opportunity to 'send a message' of opposition to the government or of dislike of David Cameron, although no doubt some voters did just that anyway.

In the years that have followed, many remainers have attached much significance to, and expended much energy upon, the legal issue of the referendum having been advisory, but that has been misguided. In a political sense, the Brexiters are right to say that the vote was presented to the electorate as a choice that bound the government. In a similar way, the repeated complaint of some remainers that the turnout invalidates the result, since it means that less than 50 per cent of those entitled to vote endorsed leave, is fatuous. In a democracy, those who vote decide. Those who choose not to implicitly or by default endorse the decision of those who do vote.

The culprit in this part of the saga is undoubtedly Cameron, who allowed the referendum to be set up as legally advisory – presumably in the expectation that remain would win – whilst communicating it to the electorate as binding. In any case, even had there been an argument for a parliamentary vote to accept or reject the referendum result, there was no political pressure for one (I am not referring here to the different issue of a vote on triggering Article 50, which is discussed in the next chapter). Such pressure would have required, at a minimum, a demand from Labour, the official opposition party. Not only did this not come, but Jeremy Corbyn, Labour's leader, far from seeking a parliamentary vote on the referendum result, had on the day after the result called for the government to immediately issue an Article 50 notification so as to commence exit proceedings (though a few weeks later he claimed to have been misunderstood).[11]

## Labour and Brexit

The story of Brexit is to some large extent the story of the internal politics of the Tory Party, but in the post-referendum years the role of Labour under Corbyn was also important. I make no comment on his leadership of Labour in general (in fact, throughout this book, I only discuss the political parties as regards their role in Brexit), but in relation to Brexit it was consistently ambiguous and problematic.

The roots of that go deep into the history of Britain's relationship with the EU, which is not the subject of this book (although I will suggest in the concluding chapter that it has some relevance). In brief, opposition to Britain joining what was then the EEC in 1973 had come partly from the nationalist right, exemplified by Enoch Powell, but mainly from the far left, which at the time of the 1975 referendum on whether to remain in the EEC saw it as a 'capitalist club' and, subsequently, saw the EU as part of neo-liberal globalisation. In the 1970s, that position was spearheaded by Tony Benn, and withdrawal from the EEC was pledged in Labour's 1983 election manifesto. By 2016, it was the province of 'Lexiters' (left-wing Brexiters), including the leaders of some trades unions. But in the intervening period, the bulk of the Labour movement – including most MPs, most members, most voters and the TUC – had become firmly pro-EU.

Corbyn straddled those eras. An acolyte of Benn, he had been opposed to staying in the EEC in 1975, and in the early 1990s had repeatedly voted with the Tory rebels opposed to the Maastricht Treaty, many of whom became prominent Brexiters. In 2016 he campaigned, but in a fairly lacklustre way, for remain, and refused to appear on joint platforms with Cameron. Subsequently, it was never clear that he was much bothered by Brexit, and he appeared to see some advantages to it, especially as regards escaping EU rules on state aid, or subsidies, which ironically also became a central issue for the Tories (see Chapter Six).

But Brexit would have posed a problem for Labour under any leader because the vote cut across traditional party lines and, in some ways, made long-standing structural problems about its core vote more visible. In particular, its traditional working-class constituencies in the Midlands and North of England overlapped significantly with the majority votes for Brexit in most of those areas. This possibly wasn't as significant a problem as some Labour strategists thought, for two reasons. Firstly, many of the leave voters in those areas would never have voted Labour anyway, and secondly, those habitual Labour voters who voted leave didn't necessarily prioritise Brexit so highly as to determine their electoral voting choices. Even so, many Labour MPs in such seats were in an invidious position if they, themselves, were opposed to Brexit.*

The other aspect of Labour's dilemma was the extent to which the Brexit vote had been driven, including amongst the party's core voters, by anti-immigration sentiment. That cut across the internationalism of the party more generally and, in particular, brought into focus the role of previous Labour governments in failing to use the controls available on free movement of people from eastern European accession countries to the EU after 2004. This had produced the painful 'Mrs Duffy moment' for Gordon Brown in the 2010 election when a voter berated him for this policy.

Again, this reflected long-standing tensions and dilemmas within Labour's history, for which Corbyn can't be held responsible. Nevertheless, he never showed even the most basic understanding of, or much interest in, what Brexit actually meant, so that even by the time of the 2019 general election he was still talking about having 'a close relationship with' and 'access to' the single market. But, as explained below, that was a

---

* It should be noted that Brexiters made much of the supposed problem of remainer MPs who represented leave-voting constituencies, but there were several MPs who saw no problem in supporting Brexit even though they represented remain-voting seats.

meaningless formulation, and brings us back to 2016, when all we knew was that Brexit meant Brexit.

## BUT WHAT DID BREXIT MEAN?

The central triumph of the Vote Leave campaign was to deliberately avoid specifying what Brexit would mean. This enabled it to garner votes from people with widely different expectations of Brexit who were united only in what they did *not* want, namely EU membership. That was undoubtedly astute as a campaign tactic, because had any particular version of Brexit been specified it's highly unlikely there would have been a majority for it. The counterpart of this tactic was the insistence of the Vote Leave campaign that since it was not the government, it was not incumbent upon it to define a model for leaving. Rather, if the vote was to leave it would be for the government to determine how. Meanwhile, for its part, the government produced documents, such as the Treasury forecasts, which invoked all the main models of leaving (discussed below), showing that all were possible interpretations of a vote to leave.

It is crucial to recall this because, almost immediately the referendum result was in, Brexiters began claiming that it was, after all, a mandate for hard Brexit and, far from the government choosing how to implement the result, that result had provided an instruction on the form as well as the fact of leaving. This was not true, and the lack of clarity about what Brexit leavers voted for in 2016 created a situation which dogged the entire Brexit process from then right up to the present day. This lack of clarity also concealed quite fundamental and long-standing confusions within the UK about what the EU actually is.

At the heart of these issues was what the economic relationship between Brexit Britain and the EU was to be (although its implications went well beyond economics), and, centrally, whether it would mean being a member of the single market or not. That was a question because it is possible to have full or almost full access to the single market without being a member of the EU. This is the situation of Norway and Iceland, for example, or – in a different way – Switzerland. All of these countries belong to the European Free Trade Association (EFTA) and are neighbours of the EU, although Switzerland is not part of the European Economic Area (EEA) and its participation in the single market is slightly more limited than that of Norway, as well as being more complicated in that it operates through a multiplicity of bilateral agreements with the EU.*

Both 'Norway' and 'Switzerland' were touted as models for Brexit long before the referendum campaign, and often during it. But many Brexiters deemed them inadequate for two main reasons. One was that, with some minor caveats, they entailed freedom of movement of people and therefore did not meet one of the central arguments of the leave campaign: that Brexit would allow controlled (and, assumedly, reduced) immigration from the EU. The other was that these models didn't meet the hard-line version of the sovereignty argument for Brexit, because they gave limited (it can be debated how little) input into decision-making about single market rules and because (even if indirectly) they gave a role to the European Court of Justice (ECJ) in enforcing those rules.

Thus some Brexiters favoured, or came to favour, a trading relationship based not upon membership of the single market but on the more limited access afforded by a free trade agreement with the EU. This could have been associated with one

---

* Although it is not quite technically accurate, for ease of expression I will refer from now on to the full or almost full access to the single market enjoyed by Norway and Switzerland as 'single market membership'.

of the many countries that had such an FTA, but was almost invariably described as the 'Canada model' (though, as we will see in future chapters, exactly what this meant was debatable). Under such a model, both freedom of movement of people and ECJ jurisdiction would be avoided.

However, the nature of the trading relationship would be entirely different to that of single market membership. Free trade agreements are primarily concerned with the removal of all or most tariff barriers to trade – that is, the charges levied on imports and exports between countries – and they are primarily related to goods trade rather than services trade. These two things are linked, because services trade does not attract tariffs. Instead, the main barriers to services trade are the different standards and regulations that exist in different countries.

These 'non-tariff barriers' (NTBs) also exist in relation to goods trade, but do so in addition to tariffs. An example of an NTB for goods would be the different product standards – say, how much noise a lawnmower can emit – required in different countries. An example of an NTB for services might be to require professionals, say, architects, to hold a qualification gained in the country where they practise. Thus NTBs can be removed when, in these examples, countries agree to apply common standards for lawnmowers' noise emissions or to recognise each other's architectural qualifications. The result is that firms in those countries have a larger potential market and may be able to reduce their cost base as they only have to conform to one set of standards.

It's true that some modern FTAs – such as the EU–Canada agreement – cover considerably more than tariff removal and may include product customs cooperation, some standards and regulations, intellectual property (such as patents, copyrights and trademarks), investment, services, public procurement, disciplines on state aid, administrative issues such as dispute settlement, and more. Even so, such FTAs do not provide complete removal of NTBs to goods trade. Moreover, the liberalisation of services trade under FTAs tends to be weaker than for goods because services are much more complicated. Trade in services is not simply a physical object crossing a border, which is why it cannot be charged import duties or tariffs. Instead, liberalisation of services trade requires regulatory harmonisation which cuts across borders but, in so doing, entails a loss of unilateral national control of the making and enforcement of regulations.

These different models of trade vary considerably in how deeply they integrate the participants' economies. The most deeply integrated include the EU single market itself, and the agreements between the EU and the Norway–Iceland group or Switzerland. The shallowest only remove tariffs on some goods. An FTA such as that between the EU and Canada is somewhere in between.

In other words, the EU single market differs considerably from a more common FTA. The single market is the essence of EU economic integration. The idea is to create an internal market, mirroring the internal market of any single country, and indeed the EU uses the terms 'single market' and 'internal market' interchangeably. This means unfettered economic activity across the market, including freedom of movement throughout the market for goods, services, capital and people. Those freedoms apply across, say, the Italian–French border in the EU just as they do between, say, Lancashire and Yorkshire in England. This means that regulations for goods and services have to be harmonised across the member states just as they are between counties.

The EU single market is not quite complete, especially for some services. But it is the most advanced example of such a market in the world, including for services. That is especially significant for an economy like the UK's, which is 80 per cent services and consistently runs a services trade surplus with both the EU and the rest of the world. In order for the EU single market to function as such it has to have a mechanism to both set and enforce regulations across its members. In this sense, the distinction between the single market as an *economic* entity and as a *political* entity is a false one. Thus, immediately, it conflicts with the ideas of (some) Brexiters about sovereignty, which they take to mean complete national control over the creation and enforcement of regulations and laws (though, arguably, such a definition of sovereignty also conflicts with *any* form of trade agreement).

The single market's set of four freedoms of movement is not a matter of political ideology or even, as some suggest, a dogmatic 'theology', but an economic necessity for creating such a market. For, as regards the most contentious of them in the Brexit context, a fully functioning market cannot operate without freedom of movement of people. That would create segmented labour markets, so would be like trying to have a national British single market whilst enforcing restrictions on people's movement between counties like Yorkshire and Lancashire. It would also – a point not sufficiently appreciated by Lexiters in particular – mean that whereas capital could flow freely across countries, labour would be confined by national borders.

The implications of this run very deep. An insider account of David Cameron's attempt to renegotiate the terms of Britain's EU membership prior to the referendum records the frustration involved:

Nor would our counterparts in Europe acknowledge that the EU's four freedoms are very much divisible. A country can reduce tariffs and remove trade barriers and still maintain restrictions on which foreigners are allowed to enter the country. This is what the United States has done since World War II, with NAFTA being the best example.[12]

These sentences absolutely expose the core misunderstanding: NAFTA is not a single market, it is a free trade agreement between the US, Mexico and Canada. They are fundamentally different things. The four freedoms are indivisible not because the EU won't 'acknowledge' it but as a matter of definition of a single market. It is a rich irony that the development of an EU single market was championed most enthusiastically by successive British governments since the 1980s, and yet they seem not to have understood what they were championing.

From this point of view, even regarding movement of people between member states as immigration or emigration is as misguided as doing so for movement between counties or even England and Scotland. Even more misguided – indeed, totally illegitimate – is to conflate, as some leave campaigners did, such free movement with the issue of migration into the EU from outside, or with asylum seeking.

## THE CONFLATION OF THE SINGLE MARKET WITH FREE TRADE AGREEMENTS

The failure to understand the fundamental difference between a single market and a free trade agreement has bedevilled the entire Brexit debate and process. It is part of the cause, or perhaps one of the consequences, of so much of the discussion of trade being a very dated one about tariffs, rather than about non-tariff barriers to trade. It may well also be rooted in the enduring Eurosceptic myth that when Britain joined the EEC, and subsequently voted in the 1975 referendum to stay in, 'we were told we were only joining a trading bloc'. That is indeed a myth, in that the prospect of political integration was openly acknowledged and, by many advocating membership, welcomed at that time. There is more on this in the concluding chapter of this book but the present point is that it morphed into a highly misleading proposition about Brexit.

In the official Vote Leave material, repeated with minor variants in several high-profile speeches by Michael Gove and other leading campaigners, it was claimed that 'there is a free trade zone stretching from Iceland to Turkey to the Russian border' and that 'after we vote to leave we will stay in this zone'.[13] This was the core pledge of the leave campaign as regards international trade, and a major component in the rebuttal of Project Fear. But it was nonsense. There is no such 'free trade zone'. There is a single market, and that seems to be what is being referred to given the reference to Iceland which, as noted above, is a member of the single market whilst not being in the EU. Moreover, the UK would not be 'part of it' automatically and as of right, but would need to negotiate membership.

At one level, this could be interpreted as just being a sloppy use of terminology, with what was really meant being that Britain would seek to stay in the single market, presumably via EFTA. That would be a perfectly reasonable interpretation, not least as many individuals campaigning for Brexit stated explicitly that this – the Norway model – was what Brexit would mean. But ever since the referendum many Brexiters, including Gove, have insisted that it meant no such thing, and that such a model would not be Brexit at all.

So an alternative explanation is that such Brexiters

actually thought that there was some kind of trading relationship whereby Britain could not be in the single market and yet, in some unspecified way, retain all or most of the benefits of it. And, indeed, this 'cakeism' did seem to be what many Brexiters had in mind. As will be seen later, this idea persisted well into the negotiations to leave, with the claim that Britain could 'have the exact same benefits' of membership without being a member. This was in part bound up with the long-standing assertions that Britain would 'hold all the cards' in any trade negotiation because of its trade deficit with the EU.

But more often, both during the campaign and afterwards, all of these issues were simply ignored by referring only to Britain continuing to have 'access' to the single market. This was a profoundly misleading expression – or more accurately a meaningless one – because all countries have 'access' to the market, including North Korea, with its approximately €200 million a year trade with the EU. The question was access to what extent and on what terms, so using the word 'access' simply served to evade the distinction between single market membership and an FTA. It was at best unhelpful and at worst dishonest, and what it allowed was a constant slippage between, or mix-and-match of, the two. Thus, when ending freedom of movement of people was under discussion, Brexiters would point to Canada and say it was perfectly possible to have 'access' to the single market without such freedom, but when trade, and especially services trade, was under discussion they would point to Norway and say that it was perfectly possible to have 'access' to the single market without being an EU member.

## THE WTO OPTION

However, the Norway and Canada models were not the only

possibilities. Before the referendum, but much more frequently afterwards, some Brexiters proposed the idea of trading on World Trade Organization (WTO) terms or, sometimes (but misleadingly), under WTO rules. The terminology is confusing because WTO rules cover a wide range of trade situations, including those where one country gives other countries better, or more 'preferential', terms than normal, for example through a single market or a free trade agreement. In that sense, both the 'Norway option' and the 'Canada option' come under WTO rules. WTO terms, which is what the Brexiters meant, is an unofficial way of describing basic trading without any of those preferential terms, and so involves higher trade barriers than exist under preferential terms. So 'WTO terms' means the most basic, or default, terms within the overall framework of WTO rules.

Trading on WTO terms is one form of 'access' to the single market, but of the most limited sort for WTO members (non-members of the WTO, like North Korea, have even more limited access). This limitation is concealed by the counter-intuitive meaning of the often-quoted but confusing phrase 'most favoured nation' (MFN) to describe these limited terms. In ordinary speech it connotes 'the best any nation has', but actually means almost the opposite here: it means those terms which, if made available to one nation that another trades with, must be made available to all nations that it trades with. It would be better, as the US Congress does, to call these MFN terms 'normal trading relations'. In practice they mean that a country can't normally charge a 10 per cent tariff on a product imported from one country, but a 15 per cent tariff on the same product imported from another country, because to do so would break the WTO's non-discrimination rule.

One way of avoiding that rule is to sign a 'preferential'

agreement with another country, or with a set of countries, such that discrimination (i.e. preferential treatment) becomes allowable. Then, with the nation with whom you have such an agreement the tariff might be reduced from that of WTO MFN terms, or eliminated altogether, whilst the standard tariff would still apply on the same product when traded with a nation with whom you do not have such an agreement. Hence the reason why countries make FTAs involving two or more partners or, indeed, a single market and customs union (of which more below).

So to propose to trade with the EU on WTO MFN terms was to propose trading on the worst terms available from the EU for a WTO member, not the best, and in practice would mean extensive tariffs on UK goods exports to the EU. As for imports, within certain technical constraints the UK could set its own rates and, whatever these were, it would increase the cost of things it bought from the EU compared with the zero tariff of EU membership. Or, as some of the most extreme Brexiters proposed, the UK could simply set tariffs on EU imports at zero. But if so, under the WTO non-discrimination principle it would have to apply zero tariffs to all countries, and that would be hugely damaging to UK agriculture and manufacturing. It would also substantially reduce the incentive for any other country to make an FTA with the UK since the core outcome of such an agreement – reduced or zero tariffs – would already be available to them on WTO MFN, or normal trading, terms. Moreover, WTO terms offer only very limited guaranteed access to service markets, and remove relatively few NTBs.

In summary, then, in terms of market integration, if the single market represents the greatest possible degree of such integration, and an FTA somewhat less (although how much less will depend on the extensiveness of the FTA), then 'WTO terms' denotes the lowest level of all (other than not being a WTO member at all, which might be called the 'North Korea model').

## UK TRADE WITH NON-EU COUNTRIES

A further aspect of the Brexiter claim about 'WTO terms' was that this was how Britain traded with the world outside of the EU and, therefore, they would be fine for trade with the EU. But this entailed a series of falsehoods, misunderstandings and contradictions.

Firstly, it ignored the fact that the EU was (and is) by far Britain's biggest trading partner, accounting, in round figures, for about 50 per cent of its trade (in 2016, 43.6 per cent of UK exports went to the EU-27 and 53.2 per cent of imports came from the EU-27).[14] That is partly because of having been an EU member, but also because it is a general truth that countries trade most with countries geographically closest to them. This so-called 'gravity model of trade' is not a theory but is based on empirical observation, sometimes expressed in the rough-and-ready way that 'as distance doubles, trade halves'. The reasons are obvious for goods trade, mainly because of transport costs, but the relationship holds almost as well for services trade, even in the digital age.[15] So even if it were true that WTO terms would do for non-EU trade, it doesn't follow that the same would be so for trade with the EU.

But, secondly, it wasn't even true for the UK's non-EU trade, about 12 per cent of which was done through FTAs that the EU had with other countries in 2016. And even trade with those countries, such as the US and China, with which the EU does not have FTAs, was not conducted solely on WTO terms because there are numerous 'micro-agreements' – smaller than an FTA but more extensive than MFN – between the EU and those countries. This is also an explanation of why the Brexiters were mistaken in claiming that EU membership was of declining importance because the share of UK trade with the EU was declining as a percentage of its total trade. For this was in part because of these various trade agreements, as well as the more general growth of the world economy. Moreover, in many cases UK trade with non-EU countries started from a very low base and so even quite small absolute increases gave rise to misleadingly high percentage growth rates.

In any case, there were two contradictions in all this. One was that it didn't sit with the avowed primacy of national sovereignty. If setting and enforcing our own rules and laws was paramount, and following those of the EU so unacceptable, why should WTO rules and laws be so attractive? What was so appealing about 'regaining our seat at the WTO table' of 160+ countries having bemoaned how little influence we had as a member of the 28-strong EU? And where was the democratic process in the WTO?

Secondly, and perhaps more importantly, even as they claimed that WTO terms would be fine for trading with the EU, Brexiters simultaneously claimed that a great prize of Brexit was for the UK to be free to make its own trade deals (that is, to *avoid* WTO MFN terms) with other countries. Not only was this a contradiction, but it also ignored the greater leverage the EU has in making such deals, from which the UK profited. It also implied, quite incorrectly, that EU membership was holding Britain back from participation in global trade (a claim directly contradicted by the Brexiters' other argument that trade with the EU was becoming a smaller proportion of total UK trade).

However, the issue of freedom to make trade deals was not the same as the question of single market membership, nor was it a basis to differentiate between Norway and Canada models, because both those countries – the first a single market member, the second not – have independent trade policies. Rather, it was to do with the customs union.

## THE CUSTOMS UNION

The EU customs union preceded the single market, which was created around it. Customs unions exist all over the world. In essence, they are free trade agreements in goods with the additional criterion that all members charge the same tariffs on imports from other countries. By contrast, the single market relates to regulatory harmonisation for goods and services (and hence, also, moving to the elimination of non-tariff barriers to trade in both).

Thus trade amongst those countries within the customs union is duty-free, whilst a common set of tariffs applies between those countries and non-members of the customs union, although those external tariffs may be further modified by FTAs with particular non-members. A consequence of the customs union is that its members are not free to make their own FTAs for, clearly, if each member could do so, then there would no longer be a common set of tariffs established with non-members, and differentials would open up between members.

So, to give a simplified summary, members of the EU belong to both the single market and the customs union, countries like Norway are part of the single market but not the customs union, and countries like Canada belong to neither. Despite some talk about the possibility of Britain remaining in the customs union after leaving the EU, strictly speaking this would have been impossible because only EU members are customs union members. What would have been possible, though, would be for Britain to have formed a customs union with the

EU. Turkey has such an arrangement, albeit of a more limited sort than the EU customs union itself.

But whilst different in nature, both the single market and the customs union have one thing in common. Each, in its own way, entails a border. In practice, for EU countries, these appear to be one and the same thing because these countries are members of both the single market and customs union, but, conceptually, they are different borders because they do different things.

With a customs union, a border has to exist around the territory within which the common tariff policy applies. Otherwise, there is no way of separating goods on which those tariffs are due from those on which they are not. Brexiters subsequently argued that this was a connivance of the EU, but a moment's thought shows that if, as they want, Britain is free to sign its own trade agreements, then who would make such an agreement with Britain if they didn't know the territory within which it applied? And how would smuggling between territories with different tariff rates be prevented? With the single market, the border is a regulatory one. It needs to exist to ensure that goods – including things like foodstuffs and animal livestock – meet the standards of the territory within which those regulations apply. Otherwise, what is to prevent goods which don't meet, for example, the requisite safety standards from entering the market?

As a result, whilst Norway (and in a different way Switzerland) are single market members, they still have borders with the EU as regards goods traffic because they are not in the customs union. And Turkey, whilst having a customs union with the EU, still has a border with the EU, because some of its products are not included in that customs union and also because it is not in the single market. Hence all of these borders require various forms of documentation and authorisation and are subject to checks on goods traffic (which is why there are sometimes lorry queues at each of them). It became common during the Brexit process to read newspaper columnists and others declaring that as they had driven freely over, say, the French–Swiss border, this 'proved' that leaving the EU had no border implications. But, apart from the fact that Switzerland is part of the Schengen Area allowing passport-free travel, such stories failed to understand that the issue is the transport of goods across borders, not people.

The implications of all of the above for Brexit were barely discussed in the referendum campaign, but they came to be dominant issues in the following years. That was partly because of what they meant for UK–EU goods traffic generally, but far more importantly because of what they meant for the border between the Republic of Ireland and Northern Ireland. For the non-existence of such a border was central to the Northern Ireland peace process and the fraught, complex and violent politics to which that process was a response. As we will see later, this created a set of arguably insoluble conundrums which continue to the present day.

## SO – WHICH BREXIT?

Thus, as Theresa May continued to say throughout 2016 that Brexit meant Brexit, there were some enormously complicated questions about what that actually meant. Whilst primarily described in terms of different models of trade, these models also had implications for a wide range of non-trade issues. These ran from security, criminal justice and intelligence cooperation, through nuclear safety protocols, scientific and educational cooperation and aviation systems right down to pet passports, in large part because of the role of the European Court of Justice (ECJ) in these areas.

Teasing out the distinctions between different models of Brexit was only a first step because what it immediately revealed was that no model actually fitted the situation. No other country had been in the position of leaving before (Greenland being the only extremely limited and partial exception*) and, therefore, of disentangling or in some way accommodating an enormously deep set of interconnections.

On the one hand there were businesses, such as automotive and aerospace companies, with totally integrated pan-European supply chains; organisations like Euratom, which provided the entire infrastructure not just for the nuclear power industry but things like medical isotopes used in cancer treatment; and regulatory systems like REACH, which set global standards for the chemicals industry. On the other hand, there were people whose whole lives were predicated upon their freedom of movement within the EU, at the time estimated as perhaps three million EU-27 nationals in the UK and perhaps two million UK nationals in the EU-27. Families and relationships which would probably never have existed had it not been for Britain's EU membership faced uncertainty and, shamefully, many EU nationals in the UK were exposed to insults, threats and violence.

So even if Norway, Canada, or any of the other models touted – which ranged from Ukraine to Turkey to Jersey – were to be adopted as a template for the final outcome, it could hardly provide any clue as to the process by which it might be reached. Of all the many criticisms that can be levelled at

---

* Greenland had joined the EEC in 1973 because it was in effect governed by Denmark and, following increased autonomy from Denmark, left what was then the European Community in 1985. Its primary business and export sector, and reason for leaving, is fishing. With a population of about 60,000 and a GDP of less than $3 billion, its departure isn't in any meaningful way comparable to Brexit.

the Brexiters, one of the greatest is that, whilst bemoaning the extent to which the UK had been subsumed within the EU, they failed to recognise that the corollary was the complexity of leaving.

## RECURRENT MYTHS

Instead, they not only ignored warnings about that complexity, but actively denied it through an orchestrated series of myths. These included the idea that Britain would get a quick, advantageous and easy new deal with the EU because 'we are the world's fifth largest economy', 'we have a trade deficit with the EU' so 'they need us more than we need them' and, repeatedly, because 'German car makers' (or, in some variants, French cheese makers or Italian wine makers) would force the EU into granting such a deal.

None of these arguments held water. Being a large economy doesn't cut much ice in a world where there are three economic superpowers – the US, China and the EU – and, actually, came to be an impediment in that it led the EU to seek constraints on UK regulatory autonomy (of which more later). The trade deficit argument was simply a misnomer as it concealed the fact that, in percentage terms, UK trade is far more dependent on the EU than the EU is on the UK. Whereas, as noted above, about 44 per cent of UK exports went to the EU-27 in 2016, only about 8 per cent of EU-27 exports went to the UK. As regards the deficit, this was in goods trade, whereas the UK had a services trade surplus – so even if having a deficit was an advantage in terms of the former, it would be a disadvantage in terms of the latter.

In reality, EU goods exporters – including German car makers – like the EU, cared more about maintaining the rules of the single market than accommodating the UK's desire to have something like the benefits of membership without abiding by all the rules. And, beyond that, if policy was dictated by businesses then Britain would not be embarking on Brexit anyway, since most business opinion, and especially businesses that traded with the EU, was opposed to Brexit. So why would German businesses be so omnipotent? In any case, the idea that what Germany decided the EU would do was another myth, not just about Brexit but reflecting long-standing Eurosceptic propaganda about German dominance. In fact, it was predictable, and proved to be the case, that the EU would negotiate as a bloc, taking account of the diverse interests of its members. The repeated claims that Brexit would be settled between London and Berlin were false in both a procedural and a substantive sense.

None of these myths have ever totally disappeared from the Brexiter lexicon, and some version of them was espoused at one time or another by all three of the leading pro-Brexit figures whom Theresa May had appointed to her Cabinet in 2016. These were Boris Johnson as Foreign Secretary, Liam Fox as International Trade Secretary, and David Davis as Secretary of State for Exiting the European Union (DExEU) and the man who would lead the Brexit negotiations. Whilst none of them – or any other high profile Brexiter – has ever recanted on the blithe promises they made about how easy Brexit would be, by September 2016 Davis acknowledged that these negotiations might be 'the most complicated of all time'.[16] As we will see in later chapters, it was a complexity he never mastered.

### May's silence

There was little sign in the closing months of 2016 that the government was making any progress towards engaging with these complexities, or facing up to them. In September, the respected think tank the Institute for Government produced a damning report on Brexit planning, subtitled 'Silence is not a strategy'.[17] And as the year wore on, various leaks suggested the level of debate within the Cabinet was at a rudimentary level, even implying that the aspiration was still a Johnsonian 'cakeist' one[18] or, alternatively, that there was no plan at all.[19] May continued to be inscrutable, insisting she would not provide a 'running commentary' on government thinking (as, later, she said of the negotiations).

The consequence was that her every utterance was pored over by commentators trying to read coded or implicit signals. But these were contradictory and ambiguous. On the one hand, she frequently talked of maintaining Britain's services trade with the EU, which seemed to imply remaining in the single market, and in September 2016 she publicly rebuked David Davis for saying that it was very improbable that the UK would stay in the single market.[20] This was not, she said, government policy. She also eschewed talk of soft and hard Brexit (as Norway and Canada models were at that time called), seeming to imply some kind of 'cakeist' model in which, perhaps, there would be single market membership without freedom of movement of people. The government gave some assurances to car-maker Nissan – whose business depended very much on the single market and customs union – which appeared to satisfy them, perhaps implying soft Brexit, but the nature of these assurances was kept secret (later, it was revealed that Nissan had been promised millions of pounds in state aid).[21]

At the time it was obvious, and it has become even clearer since, that May was squandering the time when really imaginative leadership was urgently called for. Britain was in an unprecedented situation, deeply divided between its constituent countries and even within families, and she was at the peak of her political power. It would have been perfectly legitimate, without questioning the referendum result, to have initiated a major process of consultation and public discussion, perhaps using citizens' assemblies but at least involving other parties, the devolved administrations, businesses, trades unions and other expert bodies. Its task would have been to seek a consensus on how to proceed, both in terms of outcome and process.

It would have been an unprecedented exercise, which would have been better undertaken before the referendum rather than after, but so was the situation. It would also have been a difficult and complex exercise, but so too was any course of action in the circumstances. And, of course, it may be that such an exercise would have failed. It would certainly have encountered ferocious opposition from the ERG within May's party, and UKIP and others from outside. Yet she had a parliamentary majority, albeit a small one, and it would have been hard for her MPs to oust her within weeks of starting her premiership. At all events, she didn't even try anything like this. It was a leadership failure of historic proportions.

## TOWARDS 'HARD BREXIT'

Whilst the government's intentions remained opaque throughout the second half of 2016, the first really clear hint that Brexit was to be defined as hard Brexit came with Theresa May's party conference speech in October. In it, she gave clear priority to control of immigration and the removal of any role for the ECJ in the delivery of Brexit which, realistically, could only mean leaving the single market. Yet she did not say that in those terms, and there remained an ambiguity because of her rejection of the very terms 'soft' and 'hard' Brexit as presenting a false dichotomy, suggesting that she may still have thought that there was a way of avoiding the binary question of 'Norway' and 'Canada' models.

That there was a continuing lack of clarity is demonstrated by the fact that, as late as 19 November, dozens of Tory MPs signed a letter to May calling for a hard Brexit – leaving the single market and customs union.[22] That would have made no sense if she had already made such a commitment. The extent to which the Prime Minister's conference speech could be taken as a clear declaration of the government's plans was also tempered by the context. After all, this was a party speech which was inevitably aimed at the membership and core vote. Even so, it led May to make a commitment which came to have huge consequences, because she promised that the letter triggering Article 50 would be sent to the EU no later than March 2017. This wasn't a complete surprise, as it had been rumoured before, but it did make concrete a timescale which, like the form Brexit would take, was not entailed by the referendum result and which in turn precluded any possibility of the kind of national conversation and consensus-building that might otherwise have occurred.

In fact, in committing to that timescale, May explicitly ramped up the divisions that had already been caused, because it came against the backdrop of an impending legal challenge to the right of the government to trigger Article 50 without a parliamentary vote. I will return to that in the next chapter, but for now the point is that May explicitly positioned those who wanted such a vote as 'trying to subvert' democracy. This, along with other jibes at remainers, may again have been designed to appeal to the party faithful, but it sent a wider message that she had no genuine interest in seeking consensus, and contributed to positioning those who opposed Brexit as politically illegitimate.

This in turn fed into what was now a growing culture war in which 'leaver' and 'remainer' were becoming solidified political identities which were more deeply felt than traditional party political or left–right loyalties. That had obviously been a feature of the campaign, but it might have been expected that it would decline afterwards. The opposite was the case, partly because of the way the campaign was fought but, now, because of the way that Brexit was being pursued without any attempt at consensus-building. Unsurprisingly, that angered and further alienated remainers but, perversely, leavers seemed as enraged as ever. It was a harbinger of what was to unfold later.

## Donald Trump and the geopolitical context

To this already highly charged atmosphere was added the election of Donald Trump as President of the United States in November 2016. For Brexiters, this had huge significance for two reasons. First, it seemed to suggest that they had caught the tide of history, given the close connections between the populist politics of the two campaigns, their shared disdain for the international order and the many personal relationships between the camps. Trump had repeatedly invoked Brexit during his own campaign, even to the extent of referring to himself as 'Mr Brexit'. Second, and more concretely, it seemed to suggest that a UK–US trade deal might be imminent or at least that, contrary to Barack Obama's words during the referendum campaign, Britain would no longer be at the back of the queue for such a deal. Much of this was based on wishful thinking, as later became clear, but for some Brexiters such a trade deal would provide the ultimate vindication of Brexit.

However, Trump also presented significant problems for the British government, despite its embrace of Brexit, and they were problems, ironically, shared by the EU. Precisely because of his disdain for the global rules-based order, and in particular because of his at best ambiguous stance on Russia, his hostility towards NATO and his outright opposition to the Iran nuclear deal, he added to the geopolitical instability caused by Brexit. If Britain's acquired role during the previous four decades had been predicated on being a transatlantic bridge between the US and Europe, then both ends of that were challenged by a volatile and unpredictable US administration along with British withdrawal from the EU. And whilst Trump's election brought this into focus, it really only highlighted what had scarcely been discussed before: what exactly was Britain's post-Brexit global role to be? It could hardly, as the 'buccaneering Brexiteer' image might suggest, be that of Elizabethan global conquest, or even of Victorian imperialism, for those times had long gone. It is a conundrum that has still to be resolved, except for the placeholder of the 'Global Britain' slogan which itself sits awkwardly with the nationalist and protectionist themes of much of the Brexit campaign.

As with the question of what form the UK's relationship with the EU would take, this awkwardness arose from the way that the leave campaign mobilised quite contradictory sentiments. In relation to immigration, most explicitly, it advanced a nationalist and anti-globalisation agenda, but lurking more implicitly were ideas about how EU membership had led to de-industrialisation and that Brexit would enable the protection of British businesses.

However, many of the leading proponents of Brexit were not nationalists or protectionists but adherents of the global free trade model against which Brexit (like Trump) was ostensibly a backlash. Hence, in September 2016, Liam Fox in his Manchester speech[23] proclaimed:

> I believe the UK is in a prime position to become a world leader in free trade because of the brave and historic decision

of the British people to leave the European Union. Those
who believe that the referendum was a sign of Britain looking inwards have it completely wrong – it is the beginning
of Britain increasing its global engagement.

This vision outlived Fox's tenure as International Trade Secretary in that its emphasis on Britain's new independent trade
policy, which had been a fairly peripheral theme during the
referendum campaign, came to dominate governmental claims
for the value of Brexit. It sat uneasily not just with the protec-
tionism that had been at least implied to the voters making
their 'brave and historic decision', but also with the highly explicit 'America First' rhetoric of Brexit Britain's new best friend
in the White House.

### The failure to grasp regionalisation

The contradiction of nationalism and globalism did not just
make Brexit incoherent in its own right; it also masked the
underlying failure of both strands to appreciate that the real
transformation of the previous decades had been neither national nor global but *regional*. The development of regional
trade blocs of various sorts, including the EU, was in part a
response to the way that the WTO has made relatively little
progress towards providing a comprehensive architecture for
global trade in, especially, services and agriculture. On the
other hand, the development of regional economic structures
meant that the pure 'sovereignty' of national self-determina-
tion no longer made sense. The world of 1973, when Britain
had joined the EEC, no longer existed.

The same was true beyond trade and economics in the domains of geopolitics and international relations. In the aftermath of the collapse of the Soviet Union there had been a brief

period when the idea of the 'end of history' gained ground. Western capitalism and liberal democracy had 'won' and were now the only game in town. That analysis was bound up with the idea of economic globalisation, but it also implied a unipolar geopolitics and a trend to ideological homogeneity.

Thirty years on from the fall of the Berlin Wall, that analysis has turned out to be naïve in almost every respect. The world is not unipolar (nor is it any longer bipolar in the way it arguably was during the Cold War) but multipolar. One aspect of that, in part because of the impact of 'end of history' type thinking on reshaping the post-Soviet space, is that Russian nationalism is resurgent and notably hostile to both the UK and the EU. The rise of Chinese global capitalism – China joined the WTO in 2001 – has not been accompanied by liberal democracy and in many respects, most obviously state involvement in private enterprises, is completely different to the neo-liberal model of capitalism that had supposedly triumphed.

At all events, there are three military superpowers (the US, China and Russia), three economic superpowers (the US, China and the EU), and two and a half regulatory superpowers (the US, the EU and, the half power, China). And, of course, there is also a string of regional power-brokers – India and Iran being examples, albeit of very different sorts. The implication of this isn't so much that the UK needs to accept that it is a regional rather than a global power but, rather, that Brexiters are wrong to posit a necessary contradiction between the two. Both economically and geopolitically, regional participation is a necessary platform for having a global presence.

Even without Brexit, this would always have been a complex and unstable world within which Britain had to operate, made far more so by a US administration so radically different to those it had been used to. As it was, Brexit dropped into the middle of that complex world, with its politics of nationalism and globalism which was both contradictory in its own terms and out of kilter with the realities of the regionalised and multipolar world.

## The Lancaster House speech

This incongruence was clearly exposed when, finally, in her Lancaster House speech of January 2017,[24] Theresa May spelt out explicitly what she intended Brexit to mean. It contained no recognition at all of the wider strategic context and instead – apart from a strong repudiation of freedom of movement of people – focused relentlessly and repeatedly on the aim of being 'a truly Global Britain' as expressing the meaning and the consequence of the referendum vote. There was no discussion of, or any sign of thought about, what this could possibly mean in the economic and geopolitical context of the early twenty-first century.

What *was* made plain, for the first time, in precise and unambiguous terms was that Britain would leave the single market. In doing so, May embraced and repeated what had become two central untruths amongst Brexit Ultras. One was that retaining such membership 'would to all intents and purposes mean not leaving the EU at all'. The other, relatedly, was that 'both sides in the referendum campaign made it clear that a vote to leave the EU would be a vote to leave the single market'.

With these words she flatly contradicted all the times that Norway and Switzerland had been invoked as models for Brexit, and denied all the ambiguities of the Vote Leave campaign. It was patently untrue – as is demonstrated, if by nothing else, by the fact that it was the very first time in the six months since the referendum that she had unequivocally said it. If leaving the single market was so definitively entailed by the vote to leave, why had she refused to confirm or deny it in all that time? And why had she rebuked Davis for saying the UK would leave the single market?

In addition to ruling out single market membership, May's Lancaster House speech also, but in more hedged terms, ruled out a customs union. This arose because she emphatically rejected any outcome which would have precluded Britain from making its own trade deals. She did, however, want 'to have a customs agreement with the EU' without clarifying what form this would take, or how it would be compatible with an independent trade policy. Moreover, not only was there to be no single market or customs union membership, but the speech also made clear that there would be no role for the ECJ, with the consequence that Brexit would also mean leaving any agency, scheme or other body within which the ECJ figured.

Given the extent to which May came to be reviled by Brexiters later, it is worth recalling that at this moment she gave them exactly the hard Brexit they had been lobbying for since the vote, and that at this time they cheered her to the rooftops for doing so. Of note, too, given what was to happen, is that they did not at that point question her commitment to a customs agreement.

On the other hand, and also of relevance to what was to come, the process by which she came to her Lancaster House position is noteworthy, if not downright extraordinary. Not only had it not been preceded by any kind of national consultation exercise of the sort discussed earlier, but 'the foundational decisions of Britain's withdrawal strategy … were taken, in essence, by two people [May and her adviser Nick Timothy]. The cabinet certainly had no chance to debate them.'[25] That, at least, is the claim made by Tim Shipman, political editor of the

*Sunday Times*, and it has never been denied. It is also obliquely confirmed by an interview with the then Chancellor, Philip Hammond, who explicitly says that there was no Cabinet discussion of what was in May's 2016 party conference speech and implies the same was so for the Lancaster House speech.[26]

Apart from anything else, in this and her subsequent conduct May took ownership of hard Brexit and thereby exposed herself to attacks which would have been more difficult to make had she bound others into her decisions. She even seemed to envisage that the government could undertake Brexit without much in the way of further public discussion of what was being negotiated, which proved very wide of the mark but was consistent with the secretive modus operandi that was already her hallmark.

A further hostage to fortune in the Lancaster House speech was a phrase which came to dog May and the entire Brexit process. It was that 'no deal is better than a bad deal', and it seemed to arise from the already widely voiced paranoia of the Brexiters that the EU would seek to 'punish' Britain in the negotiations. Later they used it to punish May, for it turned out that the real problem was not negotiating with the EU but with the Brexiters in her own party.

If, for now, they were cock-a-hoop at the announcement of hard Brexit, things looked very different to that half of the country that had voted remain and, for that matter, to those leavers who had envisaged, and in some cases campaigned for, soft Brexit. For whilst May's speech spoke of the country 'coming together' after the 'division and discord' of the referendum, and whilst she cautioned that 'the victors have the responsibility to act magnanimously', its effect was the opposite. As presaged in her conference speech, she had now decreed that, despite those deep divisions, there was to be no compromise and no magnanimity.

Later, a narrative developed that May had sought concili-
ation and compromise in her approach to Brexit. That is emphatically not true. The Lancaster House speech set the stage
for years of polarised, bitter politics from which Britain has
still not escaped. It is a polarisation encapsulated in a headline
which had appeared above an article in the *Daily Mail* a couple
of months before: 'Enemies of the people'.[27] May never publicly repudiated that headline and, less than a month after her
Lancaster House speech, appointed the author of the article as
her official spokesperson.

## CHAPTER TWO

# ENEMIES OF THE PEOPLE

*From the Lancaster House speech
to the 2017 general election*

The 'enemies of the people' headline of December 2016 had arisen in the course of a legal challenge mounted by the businesswoman Gina Miller and others which asserted that the UK government could not initiate the Article 50 process to leave the EU using its executive powers, but that a parliamentary vote was required. However, it had a wider significance in both crystallising and intensifying the bitter culture war that the referendum had unleashed.

The headline was an attack on the three High Court judges who had ruled in favour of Miller. Its viciousness was especially shocking because it invoked a slogan habitually used in totalitarian regimes, and the more so because it was being used to publicly discredit the legal system. Whilst it was widely condemned, it spoke for and to a constituency of Brexit supporters who depicted the case as being about whether or not Britain should leave the EU – it wasn't, it was about the constitutional issue of how it could be done – and as an attempt to subvert, in a phrase that became ubiquitous, the 'will of the people'.

There was some irony in that, since a core Brexiter claim was that restoring parliamentary sovereignty was the purpose of leaving the EU, yet a legal action based on just that premise was deemed undemocratic. There was additional irony in the fact that the Vote Leave campaign had made the (impossible) promise that no legal process to leave the EU would begin until a new deal had been negotiated.

Those ironies reflected the wider problem of the role of referendums in a parliamentary democracy, and the attack on the judiciary and disdain for Parliament were an early suggestion of how far Brexit Ultras were willing to throw aside all sorts of constitutional conventions in pursuit of their cause. On the other hand, it would be naïve to suppose that remainers did not hope that, were there to be a parliamentary vote, it might have the effect of stymieing Brexit because the majority of MPs had campaigned against it. But that scarcely justified the bullying of judges legitimately called on to make a decision, still less the vile threats made against Gina Miller and others for posing a legitimate constitutional question.

It seems surprising that the government devoted such effort to contesting the case, appealing to the Supreme Court to overturn the High Court ruling, and one explanation may have been Theresa May's determination to demonstrate her commitment to Brexit. Yet by the time of the appeal, she had made her Lancaster House speech, so that commitment was entirely clear. Rather, her motivation seemed to be – as with her entire approach – to conduct Brexit with as much secrecy and as little consultation or scrutiny as possible. Certainly, she appeared to see no virtue in securing consent and support for it. In the event, in January 2017 the Supreme Court upheld the earlier judgment and a vote was forced upon her. But, even then, the government allowed only a brief debate and the whole episode was a foretaste of the way that both she and, later (and even more so), Boris Johnson were to treat Parliament with contempt.

In yet another irony, when the vote was actually held at the start of February MPs voted overwhelmingly in favour of triggering Article 50, and thus the thing May and the Brexiters had fought so hard to avoid, with such dire consequences for the toxicity of public discourse, actually strengthened her hand and their position. Only 114 MPs voted against, including forty-seven Labour MPs – and just one Tory, Kenneth Clarke – who did so in defiance of their party whip. That this happened was a truly shameful dereliction of duty on the part of those many MPs who believed that Brexit would be deeply damaging to Britain but still voted to enact it. It arose at least in part because of the hysterical mood that the *Mail*'s headline had both expressed and exacerbated. The size of the majority also reflected Jeremy Corbyn's decision to impose a three-line whip on Labour MPs to support the government.

One important consequence of this vote was that just as it strengthened May's hand, conversely, it meant that all those MPs who voted for it, and the Labour leadership, were complicit in the consequences. Indeed, as events progressed they were frequently taunted, by the very Brexiters who had been so adamantly opposed to a vote, for having agreed to Brexit and, supposedly, for having endorsed whatever outcome the Article 50 process might have, including that of there being no agreement on withdrawal terms (i.e. 'no-deal Brexit'). MPs even failed to carry any of the amendments that might have given Parliament, and also the devolved assemblies, some control of that process. The one which came closest would have given a 'meaningful vote' to Parliament on the final Brexit deal, perhaps the first time that the phrase was heard in the context of Brexit. Support for that was bought off with the unenforceable promise of what might be called a 'meaningless vote' whereby MPs would be given a vote on any final deal but with 'no deal' as the only alternative to accepting it. MPs, having been given the chance to assert their power over the executive by campaigners who suffered hugely for having done so, simply wrote the government a blank cheque.

## Brexit McCarthyism

Throughout these debates, Brexiters in Parliament and in the media, along with May, repeatedly framed the issue in terms of upholding rather than subverting democracy and of the 'will of the people' as expressed in the referendum. During the House of Lords stage of the Article 50 Bill, May even took the unusual step of attending the debate, glaring balefully at peers, as if to remind them of their unelected status. It was part of a wider process, illustrated by, but not confined to, the treatment of the judiciary. In particular, the civil service had from the outset been targeted by Brexiters for its supposedly obstructive pro-remain attitudes. May had voiced such criticism as early as August 2016 and the Ultras were even more vociferous.

Just before the Lancaster House speech, they claimed a high-profile scalp in the resignation of Sir Ivan Rogers, the UK's ambassador to the EU, following his vilification by some Brexiter politicians and journalists. They immediately called for his replacement to be a pro-Brexit figure,[28] and this pointed to a wider sense, that was to grow in the following years, that some of them wanted a wholesale purge of the civil service in favour of political appointments – something wholly alien to British political tradition.[29]

The underlying issue was a more complex one, and reflected an intrinsic contradiction within the Brexit process. Rogers, notably, had profound knowledge and expertise about how the EU worked and of the UK–EU relationship. Many others in the civil service had similar knowledge, and the only way to enact Brexit would be to make use of it. It is probably true that, as Brexiters said, many such senior civil servants did not personally support Brexit – that is guessable simply from the overall demographics of the vote, as well as from the statements of some ex-civil servants – but that in itself would not preclude them from delivering it since it is a deeply ingrained civil service tradition to deliver policy regardless of personal views. The real problem was that what Brexiters wanted them to do was to accept as true things which were not true, and to ignore all of the complexities which Brexiters were either ignorant of or denied. Traditionally, the civil service role would be to 'speak truth to power', but that could not work if what was said was ignored because it was 'remainer truth'.

To take perhaps the most generic example, Brexiters had repeatedly claimed that doing a deal with the EU would be the easiest in history, could be done within a day, and many similar things about the simplicity of Brexit. That may have been reassuring to the electorate, but it manifestly wasn't true and civil servants couldn't make it so, whatever beliefs they may or may not have had. More specifically, Brexiters now wanted civil servants to deliver the 'frictionless trade', or something very close to it, of the single market and customs union without being in the single market or customs union. Or, to take another example that became important, Brexiters wanted technologies as yet uninvented to do away with checks on the Irish border.

Rather than accept that such demands were impossible, they accused civil servants of refusing to deliver them because of opposition to Brexit. From there, it was a short step to saying that they were subverting the 'will of the people' and that they, like the judges, were the 'enemies of the people'.

That didn't just apply to civil servants and judges. Mark

Carney, the Governor of the Bank of England, was a particular target of Brexiter ire and so too were those many business leaders and representative groups, such as the CBI, who raised concerns about the costs and practicalities of Brexit. For to a mindset in which it was cost-free and easy, even to raise these issues was to be disloyal to the cause and to set oneself against 'the people'. As a result, what might almost be called 'Brexit McCarthyism' took hold.

As far back as 2014, leading Tory Eurosceptic John Redwood had threatened 'punishment' for firms that spoke out in favour of EU membership,[30] whilst in March 2017 it was revealed that contractors bidding for work with the government were being asked to affirm that they backed Brexit.[31] Later that same year, Chris Heaton-Harris, a committed Brexiter and at the time a government whip, wrote to every university in the country asking for the names and syllabuses of anyone teaching about European affairs and especially Brexit,[32] and the BBC was perpetually under attack for its supposed remainer bias.

Anna Soubry, former business minister and then still a Conservative MP, but opposed to Brexit, wrote:[33]

I have never known a political atmosphere like the current one in Westminster. There is a danger that the insidious methods used to silence all criticism of Brexit, no matter how reasoned and measured, will have disastrous consequences for our country ... Yet that is exactly what is happening now as a 'hard Brexit monoculture' takes hold. Some are determined to stifle all dissent in their zeal to make everyone 'conform' to their views. I and others who have done no more than dissent from supporting aspects of the Government's policy on Brexit have received vile abuse. I received an email from a Conservative-supporting clergy-man who told me to 'burn in hell, evil bitch'.

Nor was it just MPs. In the media and on social media it had become routine to see 'remoaners' accused of treason and threatened with hanging or worse.

It was in this context that the former Conservative Prime Minister, Sir John Major, in his first major speech since the referendum, argued:[34]

[The] 48 per cent care no less for our country than the 52 per cent who voted to leave. They are every bit as patriot-ic. But they take a different view of Britain's future role in the world, and are deeply worried for themselves, for their families, and for our country. They do not deserve to be told that, since the decision has been taken, they must keep quiet and toe the line. A popular triumph at the polls – even in a referendum – does not take away the right to disagree – nor the right to express that dissent. Freedom of speech is ab-solute in our country. It's not 'arrogant' or 'brazen' or 'elitist', or remotely 'delusional' to express concern about our future after Brexit. Nor, by doing so, is this group undermining the will of the people: they are the people. Shouting down their legitimate comment is against all our traditions of tolerance. It does nothing to inform and everything to demean – and it is time it stopped.

His reward for this plea for tolerance? To be denounced as a traitor and subjected to vitriolic personal abuse, with one of the milder assaults coming from Jacob Rees-Mogg – at this time a backbencher who, despite having had little profile during the referendum, was emerging as one of the most divisive Brexit ideologues in his spiteful attacks on those he deemed lacking in commitment, aided by his almost ubiquitous presence in TV studios – who called it the 'craven and defeated speech of a bitter man'.[35]

## THE POLITICAL PSYCHOLOGY OF THE BREXIT CULTURE WAR

What lay behind this vicious culture war? At first sight it is puzzling that, having won the referendum and with a Prime Minister who had endorsed hard Brexit, the Brexiters were still so angry, and acting as if they had lost. The explanation is a complex one but at its heart was the fact that a significant strand of the Brexit movement was based on a supposed victimhood at the hands of the Establishment (as briefly discussed in the introduction and as I will return to in the concluding chapter), but in winning they *became* the Establishment. A small but telling indication of the inability to accept that this was so is that the magazine *Private Eye*, which is entirely devoted to satirising the Establishment, has ever since received letters from outraged Brexiters bemoaning its repeated lampooning of Brexit. Within such a political psychology, winning was actually the worst thing that could have happened, for it removed any rational basis for self-pity and took them from the comfort zone of victimhood.[36]

From this perspective it made complete sense for Brexiters to speak of a 'remainer Establishment' and a 'liberal metropolitan elite', even when they had won and remainers and liberal metropolitans were in despair. This was not just because that restored them to the purity of victimhood but because it provided an alibi for the fact that they had no idea about how to actually deliver Brexit now they had won. That could now be blamed upon the treacherous machinations of remainers rather than their own lack of realism about the detailed, practical complexities of Brexit.

If Brexiters had had any serious, coherent ideas about what Brexit meant then, having won the referendum, they would have confidently pushed forward with these. Instead, they continued to rely on a series of half-baked slogans ('taking back control') and economically illiterate claims ('BMW exports lots of cars to Britain') girded by meaningless ideas about 'Global Britain'. None of these survived contact with reality and at least some of those making them must have at least half-known it. Hence the recourse to a facile but vicious rhetoric of loyalty and betrayal.

Clearly, the Brexiter view of this would be different, and would instead stress that remainers had failed to accept the result of the referendum, still less to 'get behind' Brexit. Yet there were several obvious reasons why that hadn't happened. The first and perhaps least important was that it was a hypocritical argument. Eurosceptics had never accepted the 1975 referendum result – even though it was much more decisive than the 2016 vote – and agitated successfully to overturn it. As regards the 2016 referendum, Nigel Farage, no less, had said before the result that if it were 52–48 to remain 'this would be unfinished business by a long way'.[37] And whilst it was true that there had been a petition to the government to hold another referendum if the vote on either side were 'less than 60 per cent on a 75 per cent turnout', which after the referendum was signed by millions of remainers, it had actually been started by a leave voter in anticipation that leave would lose.[38]

The more important reason was that the referendum result was not a moment or event from which anyone could 'move on'. It was only the beginning of a process which was always going to last for years and which would shape British politics and economics for decades. Had the remain campaign won, it would simply have meant continuing with the status quo – which would have evolved over time, of course, but would not have entailed 'doing' or 'enacting' anything in the way that the vote to leave did. So 'accepting the result' meant very different things depending what the result was.

As for getting behind Brexit, this was an unreasonable demand precisely because what it meant had not been specified but had to be defined, and when it came to be defined the preferences of remainers were not given a second thought. There could be no 'buy in' since there had been no process to construct it. Instead, on the basis of a thin victory, Brexit had been interpreted as hard Brexit – almost as if, had remain won, it had been taken as a mandate to join the Euro and the Schengen Agreement. In any case, it is notable that as that process unfolded, Brexiters themselves felt no obligation whatsoever to 'get behind' it whenever it seemed to be taking a form which they did not like. Moreover, as their subsequent treatment of Theresa May showed, no matter how much ex-remainers recanted they were never accepted as 'true believers'.

The motif of true belief is an important one, because as time went on, Brexit became ever more cult-like, on the assertion it could be made to work successfully with sufficient faith, and that the problems it encountered were due to a lack of such faith (as well as deliberate obstruction and betrayal) amongst remainers. Thus, eventually, calls for remainers to be charged with treason moved from the wilder fringes of social media to the point where a Conservative MEP proposed just such action against those with 'extreme EU loyalty' (whatever that might mean).[39]

## THE ENEMY WITHOUT

The counterpart of this 'enemy within' type narrative was, inevitably, to configure the EU as an external threat, set on punishing the UK for leaving. This had been present since the referendum and, as noted in the previous chapter, had been referenced in the Lancaster House speech. It burst out explosively at the end of March 2017 when the EU Council published its draft negotiating guidelines, a couple of days after the UK had formally triggered Article 50 on 29 March 2017. In particular this provoked a furore over a paragraph about Gibraltar to the effect that no UK–EU Brexit agreement would apply there without the agreement of Spain. This was controversial because ownership of Gibraltar is disputed between the UK and Spain (it had also voted overwhelmingly to stay in the EU as, in a previous referendum, it had voted to stay in the UK). The British media and polity erupted, with some senior political figures even discussing the prospects of war with Spain.

That this should have caused such a row provided instructive lessons about the entire Brexit process in at least three ways. First, although it had certainly not been a major issue during the referendum, the dangers of Brexit for Gibraltar's future were pointed out by the remain campaign. The reaction to this from Brexiters had been furious. Liam Fox was enraged that the possibility should even have been mentioned, saying 'I think there are limits to what you can and cannot say in any campaign that goes way beyond acceptable limits' [sic].[40] All this was inevitably reported in the media as Project Fear but, like so many other things dismissed in this way, it turned out to have genuine cause.

Anyway, and this was the second instructive point, whilst Brexiters may have shouted it down during the campaign they could not convincingly do so now. As with all slogans and false claims, when they meet reality, reality wins out. The EU had, as a matter of fact, decided to take this line and now it had to be dealt with (in the event, it proved far less contentious than it seemed it would be at the time). No amount of bluster or outrage could change that. Screaming headlines in the British press might have been effective for *domestic* purposes but were irrelevant to the EU, unless serving to make it wary of the growing extremism of Brexiters. In microcosm, this was indicative of the entire shift that occurred as a result of the triggering of Article 50. It was no longer a matter of Brexiters producing domestic slogans, but of having to take responsibility for the actual delivery of Brexit through negotiations with the EU.

The third lesson from the Gibraltar row was therefore one of realpolitik. Of course both the EU and individual member states such as Spain were going to seek to pursue their own interests. On the Gibraltar issue, the UK had done exactly the same thing at the time of Spain's accession to the EU in 1986 (by insisting on an open border). Brexiters could and did denounce the EU for 'bullying' and even, in their hermetically sealed logic, of it 'proving' that it was right to leave. But that didn't change anything in the real world of international relations.

In fact, although attracting fewer headlines, the EU Council's statement underscored in several other ways the reality of the power plays which were now going to unfold. In particular, as I will discuss in more detail shortly, the UK's desire, expressed in the Article 50 letter, for parallel talks on exit and on future trade was rebuffed. Additionally, the idea of sector-by-sector access to the single market, at this point one of the Brexiter fantasies, was emphatically squashed, as was the possibility of bilateral negotiations about Brexit between the UK and individual EU-27 states.

Whatever Brexiters may have thought, none of this made the EU's stance 'punitive'. It just meant that the UK could not dictate terms in a vacuum in the way they imagined and had proposed to the British electorate in saying that the UK would 'hold all the cards'. It also laid bare some of their other fantasies about the EU, including the idea, mentioned in the previous chapter, that dealing with it meant, primarily, dealing with Germany and, to a lesser extent, France. For although these countries are indeed significant, the EU is an association of member states and is not ruled from Berlin or Paris. The failure of Brexiters to understand this grew out of their narrative of how the UK lost sovereignty from EU membership whereas, in fact, the EU was an arena in which the UK (in particular, one might argue) could exercise and magnify its sovereignty. At all events, the row over Gibraltar indicated that other countries, such as Spain, would be influential and it was already clear (though still not fully appreciated by Brexiters or the government) that Ireland would play a key role.

So all of the compromises and trade-offs that Brexiters had bemoaned about EU membership were not going to cease, but now the UK would face them alone across the negotiating table rather than as a powerful member, with powerful allies, within the EU. In a similar way, having for years mocked the European Parliament as a 'rubber stamp', Brexiters now faced the prospect that any exit deal would be subject to the approval of that body which at this point was drafting its own red lines about what would be acceptable.

Yet alongside the narrative of EU punishment ran a quite contradictory one. At the same time as being seen as an all-powerful bully, the EU was constantly depicted as being weak, sclerotic and on the point of collapse. Indeed, for many Brexiters it was – and to some still is – an article of faith that Brexit would precipitate just that, by blazing a path that other member states would take, thus destroying the EU. In fact, almost from the outset Brexit was regarded in other countries as an inexplicable folly, and none of them have shown the remotest sign of wanting to emulate it.

## THE FIRST BREXIT WHITE PAPER

Having easily secured MPs' approval to trigger Article 50, but prior to sending the notification to the EU, the government embarked on the process of developing its approach to Brexit, with the publication of a white paper in February 2017. The headlines of that had been prefigured by the Lancaster House speech, but the white paper also made it clear that the UK would seek, via a trade agreement, to take in elements of the single market in certain (unspecified) areas, and to maintain a great deal of regulatory harmonisation with the EU across a very wide range of areas. This opened up significant questions, from a Brexiter point of view, about the extent to which the UK would have to comply with future changes to EU regulations over which it had no say. The plan also made it clear that the UK would leave ECJ jurisdiction, but posited some form of dispute resolution system with the EU, and there was also brief reference to some form of 'civil judicial cooperation'.

On the interrelated issue of the customs union, the white paper indicated that the government wanted an agreement which exempted the UK from the common external tariff and would allow it to have an independent trade policy, but which continued to allow tariff-free trade with the EU and which retained the same rules of origin (i.e. what percentage of a good had to originate in the UK in order to be treated as a UK good and, therefore, be tariff-free). What all this seemed to amount to was the recreation of many of the features of single market membership but avoiding, at least in name, ECJ jurisdiction and – of course – free movement of people rules. There would also be no formal contribution to the EU budget, but 'appropriate payments' would be made to programmes the UK wished to participate in.

As subsequently became clear to all, much of this was unrealistic and had evolved little beyond a 'cakeist' approach. It implied several times that the EU would see this as in their best interests, in part on the basis of the familiar Brexiter trope that the UK had a trade deficit with the EU. A particularly revealing aspect of it was a proposition which, whilst not widely discussed in public, was amongst Brexiters the key reason why they believed a trade deal should be so easy to do. It was contained in the preface written by David Davis, Secretary of State for Exiting the European Union, who was to be the UK's chief negotiator:

> We approach these negotiations from a unique position. As things stand, we have the exact same rules, regulations and standards as the rest of the EU. Unlike most negotiations, these talks will not be about bringing together two divergent systems but about managing the continued cooperation of the UK and the EU.[41]

This was based upon a total misunderstanding, albeit one which persisted right to the end of the trade negotiations (see Chapter Six). Existing regulatory convergence could only be helpful in facilitating a trade deal that was about seeking convergence. But these trade negotiations, unlike any other in history, were going to be about *divergence* and therefore also, by definition, about making terms of trade worse than those existing before the negotiations started. They also differed from normal trade talks in that, if the negotiations failed, the outcome would not be a continuation of the status quo but a reversion to WTO terms.

By contrast, the white paper, almost in passing, *disconfirmed* what had always been the central and most important of all the Brexiter claims when it said: 'Whilst Parliament has remained sovereign throughout our membership of the EU, it has not always felt like that.'[42]

It was a truly astonishing statement because it meant that the central plank of the leave argument – that the UK had lost its sovereignty – was completely untrue. It was just 'a feeling' yet, to assuage it, Britain proposed to turn its economy and polity upside down.

## NORTHERN IRELAND COMES CENTRE-STAGE

With the white paper and the Lancaster House speech affirming that the UK was going to seek a hard Brexit, even if with considerable naïvety about what this would mean, the issue of the Irish border came to the central position it was to occupy for the entire Brexit process from then on.

It had been clear from the outset that Ireland would be the EU country most economically affected by Brexit because of its proximity and economic interconnectedness with the UK.[43] The then Irish Taoiseach, Enda Kenny, warned of 'an economic disaster'[44] for Ireland and as early as October 2016 his government had prepared a 'Brexit-proof budget' to begin to address this. But the far more politically potent issue was what Brexit would mean for the border between Ireland and Northern Ireland.

It was an issue with roots in centuries of complex history

which are well beyond the scope of this book. The border was drawn with the Government of Ireland Act 1920 which came into effect in 1921 to partition the island of Ireland in the creation of the six counties of Northern Ireland and what was subsequently to become the Republic of Ireland. As such, it was bitterly resented by Irish nationalists, and the disputed constitutional status of Northern Ireland was central to 'the Troubles', or 'Northern Ireland Conflict', from the late 1960s which led to the deaths of over 3,500 people. From the early 1990s, multi-party negotiations in Northern Ireland combined with a joint British–Irish approach ('as partners in the European Union') to resolving conflict to help create the conditions for paramilitary ceasefires. This resulted in the Good Friday (Belfast) Agreement of 1998 (GFA) and the ensuing peace process.

Like Gibraltar, the Ireland/Northern Ireland border was an issue which had featured in the referendum campaign, although with nothing like the prominence that – as subsequent events have proved – it should have done. In particular, John Major and Tony Blair, the two British ex-Prime Ministers who had worked on the process that led to the GFA, had warned of the risks of Brexit, including at a joint event in Derry/Londonderry in June 2016. This was because of the possibility that Brexit would lead to the need for a 'hard' border, including physical infrastructure and customs checks, which would pose direct challenges to the conditions which underpinned the peace process. The situation was all the more complex because families, communities and business supply chains spanned the Irish border and its numerous crossing points.

At the time and subsequently, some Brexiters argued that this was untrue since the GFA did not explicitly remove, or require the removal of, the hard border. But the economic openness of the border was, by that time, an already assumed context for the agreement. Much of the 'hardness' of the border for trade had already been removed by the UK and Ireland's common membership of the twin institutions of the single market and the customs union. The GFA, and the de-securitisation of the border, thus enabled the effects of EU integration to be experienced at the border. No party to the agreement ever imagined that the UK and Ireland would not be members of the EU. Moreover, their common EU membership was a large part of what enabled the compromises and creative ambiguities of that agreement, for it meant that Northern Ireland, whilst still a part of the UK, could also be, like Ireland, within the over-arching structures of the EU. As such, both the UK government and the EU recognised in the early stages of the withdrawal negotiations that Brexit posed direct risks to the conditions that underpinned the GFA and, with it, the wider peace process.

During the referendum campaign Brexiters dismissed these concerns as – yet again – Project Fear. More specifically, Boris Johnson said that the existing situation with the Irish border would be 'absolutely unchanged' by a vote for Brexit, a claim echoed by the pro-Brexit then Northern Ireland Secretary, Theresa Villiers.[45] This assertion was (explicitly) based on the fact that since the 1920s there had been a Common Travel Area (CTA) for the movement of British and Irish people between the UK and Ireland which therefore long predated even the existence of the EU. But what that either concealed or failed to understand was that the most pressing concern posed by Brexit wasn't about the movement of people but of goods, to which the CTA was totally irrelevant.[*]

---

[*] This is a much more serious parallel to the persistent Brexiter misunderstanding, mentioned in the last chapter, that because the Franco-Swiss border could be freely crossed by people this meant that the same was true for goods.

The only way that the border could remain relatively un-changed would have been the very softest of Brexits; one in which Britain remained in the single market *and* had a com-prehensive customs agreement with the EU. It would have to have been both since, as explained in Chapter One, each, in different ways, removes the need for borders – the single market removes regulatory borders and the customs union removes customs borders. So, in terms of Brexit models, this would mean what might be called 'Norway +'. By early 2017 the UK government had emphatically ruled this out. Yet it was a signatory to the GFA and, of course, had a deep strategic interest in the peace process. The contradiction between the two was to prove the most intractable and complex part of the Brexit process from then on.

Many Brexiters, even now, claim that that the 'Irish border problem' was a confection of the EU, and of Ireland in particular, designed to thwart Brexit. That is categorically untrue: it arose solely from the pursuit of hard Brexit because, by definition, that entailed borders between the UK and the EU – not just with Ireland, of course, but it was the Irish border which had such profound political, and not just economic, consequences.

It is an irony that one of the main Brexiter slogans was 'taking back control of our borders' whilst so many of them refused to accept these consequences. Behind that, as regards the Irish border, lay something other than an intellectual fail-ure. It also reflected an ignorance, and often contempt, when it came to Ireland. In 2016, the Brexit Secretary David Davis had apparently not understood that Ireland was a country, refer-ring to 'the internal border with Southern Ireland'.[46] Later, an anonymous 'Tory grandee', infuriated by the influence Ireland was having on the Brexit process, was reliably quoted as saying that 'the Irish really should know their place'.[47]

Even more astonishingly, it began to be suggested that Ireland would, or even should, leave the EU ('Irexit') in order to resolve the border question that Brexit had created. It was a fantasy, of course, because support for EU membership in Ireland is very strong, but one which reflected an underlying strand in Brexiter thinking that was completely detached from modern realities. That same strand was evident in periodic delusional calls for a post-Brexit CANZUK (Canada, Australia, New Zealand and United Kingdom) confederation or even single market, which had no connection at all with the contemporary nature of these countries. It was also evident in the idea that the Commonwealth might be reconstructed as a kind of post-Imperial Preference trading system. As with the way Ireland was spoken of, such ideas betrayed a world view which was only slightly less insulting than it was fatuous.

## SEQUENCING VERSUS PARALLELISM

The fantasies about Irexit, CANZUK and the Commonwealth were irrelevant to the EU, but the centrality of Northern Ireland for Brexit was certainly well-understood and of much concern, and this informed another of the ways in which the lack of planning for – or understanding of – what Brexit meant in practice came to haunt the process of leaving. It had widely been assumed, and sometimes explicitly claimed, by Brexiters that the entirety of the negotiations about both leaving and the future – especially trade – terms would be conducted within the two-year time frame of the Article 50 process. For example, in December 2016, Boris Johnson had claimed that eighteen months would be 'absolutely ample' for both.[48] Indeed, as noted earlier, the Vote Leave campaign had gone even further and had claimed, without any legal foundation, that the future terms would be agreed before Article 50 was even triggered.

The latter was always untrue, and the former mistaken. Article 50 specified only that after notification of its intention to leave, 'the arrangements for withdrawal' of the departing member would be negotiated, 'taking account of the framework for its future relationship with the Union'.[49] However, when the letter formally invoking the Article 50 process was sent by the UK government it contained within it the proposal 'to agree the terms of our future partnership alongside those of our withdrawal from the EU' (and invoked the mistaken idea that existing regulatory alignment made this viable).[50] Two days later, when the EU Council published its draft guidelines in response, as mentioned previously, these made it clear that there would be a 'phased' approach in which 'preliminary and preparatory discussions' of the future relationship could occur but only if (in the judgement of the EU) 'sufficient progress' had been made in agreeing the terms of exit.

This was in line with Article 50 and, if anything, was a concession compared with the EU's earlier and stricter position that exit terms had to be fully agreed before any future terms talks could start. Nevertheless, in insisting on sequential rather than parallel negotiations it was in direct contradiction to the UK's preference and this, according to David Davis, would lead to 'the row of the summer' when the talks began.[51] It was a phrase which came back to haunt him.

The significance of sequenced rather than parallel talks was considerable and, I would suggest, far more so than has been widely recognised because in one way or another it kept recurring throughout the whole of the Brexit process. Its specific meaning in 2017 was that the EU would not discuss trade and other future issues until it was satisfied with what had been agreed in three key areas: the rights of EU citizens in the UK, the arrangements for Northern Ireland, and the financial settlement between the UK and the EU. Brexiters – including Davis – were adamantly opposed to this, at least as regards Northern Ireland and the financial settlement.

They saw the arrangements for Northern Ireland as inseparable from the terms of future trade. As Davis put it in May 2017:

> How on earth do you resolve the issue of the border with Northern Ireland and the Republic of Ireland unless you know what our general borders policy is, what the customs agreement is, what our trade agreement is? ... It's wholly illogical.[52]

There might have been some value in that claim, had it not been for the fact that the UK had *already* set as a red line not being in the single market and, although the details were fuzzy, a customs arrangement that would, at best, be less comprehensive than the customs union. At heart, this was rooted in the persistent confusion, discussed in Chapter One, between single market membership and a trade agreement. For no trade agreement, however comprehensive, could ever do away entirely with the need for a border. Davis's continuing failure to understand this was apparent in another phrase from this period that came back to haunt him, namely in his statement to the House of Commons in January 2017 that (my emphasis added):

> What we have come up with ... is the idea of a comprehensive free trade agreement and a comprehensive customs agreement that will deliver *the exact same benefits* as we have, but also enable my right hon. Friend the Secretary of State for International Trade to go and form trade deals with the rest of the world, which is the real upside of leaving the European Union.[53]

This cannot be treated as a casual comment. It was made by the Cabinet minister responsible for negotiating Brexit at the dispatch box. But it was nonsense to anyone with any knowledge, so Davis saying it was indicative of the extent to which the government was seeking to put into practice things which were believed by Brexiters but had no basis in fact and so were impossible to deliver. Yet it had a long afterlife, to the extent that it was not formally and publicly acknowledged by any government minister that Brexit would inevitably entail new border controls until February 2020, by which time Britain had actually left the EU (see Chapter Six).[54]

As for the financial settlement, whilst the UK had acknowledged in the Article 50 letter that it would need to be discussed, the EU response envisaged not just discussion but agreement. The crux of the difference again went to what was, and still is, an enduring misapprehension amongst many Brexiters that the financial settlement was, or should be, a quid pro quo of the future trade deal. This was totally unrealistic since it related to the calculation of what was owed as a result of Britain's prior membership, which existed independently of the future relationship. Yet this misconception, too, persisted for many years afterwards and, even now, some Brexiters argue that agreeing the settlement should have been held back until after the trade negotiations. For that matter, some Brexiters believe that no money was owed or should have been paid in any circumstances.

**A thought experiment**
Inevitably, the Brexiter press was in full cry in denouncing EU 'inflexibility' and 'punishment' over sequencing and more generally. But one fruitful way of thinking about the difference between the UK and EU positions would be to imagine

a scenario where it was not Britain leaving the EU but one of the other member states, whilst Britain was remaining. In this hypothetical case, Britain's reaction would depend partly upon which country we imagine was leaving. In particular, suppose it was Ireland. Then, Britain would see as its key strategic interest the need to preserve the Northern Ireland peace process and to uphold the Good Friday Agreement. Central to that would be ensuring as a non-negotiable position that, whatever form 'Irexit' took, it would not create a hard border on the island. Britain would, undoubtedly, put maximum pressure upon the EU to hardwire this into Ireland's Withdrawal Agreement. It is difficult to imagine many British politicians arguing otherwise.

Whichever country was leaving, it is a reasonable assumption that a central British requirement would be to preserve the integrity of the single market. After all, Britain, starting with the Thatcher government, has been its strongest proponent. It was Margaret Thatcher in her 1988 Bruges speech, which ironically inspired a generation of Eurosceptics, who had talked enthusiastically of opening up the single market, berating other members for not doing so to a sufficient extent. Indeed, much of the basic architecture of the single market had been devised by the Conservative minister, subsequently European Commissioner, Lord Cockfield.

Successive British governments have done the same thing, championing the extension of the single market into new areas, especially services. As recently as the 2015 election manifesto – the same one that had promised a referendum – the Conservative Party had proclaimed 'we say: yes to the single market' and spoke of extending it further into new sectors like digital services.

So it seems certain that in this hypothetical scenario Britain would be arguing strongly that the departing member could not 'have its cake and eat it': it would have to either be in the single market, accepting all of its rules, or out of the single market and no longer enjoying its benefits. Britain would surely be saying that the available options were for the ex-member to have the soft Brexit of single market membership or the hard Brexit of a free trade agreement, but not a mix and match. If the exiting country would not agree to that, then it would have to leave without a deal and accept the consequences of that choice.

Moreover, it seems certain that those *most* strongly of this view would be British Eurosceptics, who would see any 'cherry-picking' as taking advantage of Britain by giving the departing member unfair access to its markets without paying budget contributions or accepting the rules. They would, surely, lambast the EU if it showed any sign of wavering on this. To do so, they would say, would show the EU at its very worst, doing shady, unprincipled deals rather than applying the rules properly and fairly.

Similarly, would Britain argue for the departing member to pay its outstanding financial commitments or to be let off? The answer is obvious, as is the fact that Britain would be furious were the EU to take a different line. In short, in such a hypothetical scenario Britain – and Eurosceptics especially – would be the staunchest advocate of precisely the position being taken by the EU towards Brexit.[55]

Needless to say, no such thought experiment was conducted by the British government or by Brexiters. As for Theresa May, it is unclear what her understanding of these issues was in this period. In a disputed report of a private dinner-meeting she held with Jean-Claude Juncker in April 2017 it is said that she, too, was insisting that trade talks must come first, and even that no financial settlement was due. Reportedly, immediately the dinner ended Juncker called the German Chancellor Angela Merkel to say that May was 'deluded' and 'living in a parallel universe'. Whether or not that is true, it is a fact that the day afterwards Merkel spoke in the German Bundestag and affirmed her view that the talks should occur in sequence.[56]

On the other hand, earlier that same month, and just a few days after triggering Article 50, in a little-noticed interview[57] with Faisal Islam, the then political editor of Sky News, May had for the first time said that, quite contrary to what Brexiters had claimed, any trade deal could only come *after* the completion of the Article 50 process. And although she didn't quite accept that parallel talks would not occur, her remarks did open up the previously denied possibility that there would be a transition – or, as she called it, implementation – period after the end of the Article 50 period, rather than such a deal being ready for immediate operation. There was the glimmer of realism here, though it was not clear how widely it had permeated for, as we will see, even by 2020 there was still much confusion about the distinction between the exit terms deal and the future terms deal.

## CRUSH THE SABOTEURS

Theresa May's recognition of the time constraints of the Brexit process had not daunted her from triggering Article 50 at the end of March, despite having only the flimsiest of plans in the form of the white paper. She had boxed herself into that date with her conference speech promise the previous autumn anyway, so even if she had been minded to delay she would have been savaged by the Brexiters in her own party. At the time, and even more since, it seemed obvious that doing so was a major mistake because, from that moment onwards, the relentless time pressure of the two years specified in Article 50 ratcheted up. For despite the talk of 'no deal being better than a bad deal', it was obvious that if the clock ran down it would leave the British economy perilously exposed to a 'cliff edge' of overnight change.

Despite this, May went on to make perhaps the most extraordinary and most ill-judged decision in modern British political history (unless that was Cameron's calling of the referendum). Having adamantly insisted ever since her enthronement as Prime Minister that a general election would 'not be in the national interest' she suddenly, and without any warning or prior rumour, announced on 18 April 2017 that she wanted a general election to be held on 8 June.

There have been numerous discussions of this decision, the election campaign, and its outcome which are beyond the scope of this book,[58] but in terms of the Brexit story several things stand out. One, picking up on my points in the last chapter about May's overall approach to Brexit, is how she framed the rationale for holding the election:

'At this moment of enormous national significance there should be unity here in Westminster, but instead there is division. The country is coming together, but Westminster is not.'[59]

It was manifestly untrue in that the country was highly divided, and had been made more so in part because of the decisions May herself had taken. It was also arguably untrue in relation to Westminster, given the near unanimity of the vote to trigger Article 50. But in presenting it in this way, May clearly positioned her way of doing Brexit as the only way and opponents of that way, or of Brexit itself, as illegitimate. In this sense, the election was all of a piece with the 'enemies of the people' narrative and, sure enough, the *Daily Mail* again provided the defining headline: 'Crush the Saboteurs', accompanied by a menacing-looking photo of May and reference to '"game-playing" Remoaners'. So much for a country coming together.

However, there was an alternative interpretation, which was that the real Westminster problem May faced was not the opposition parties but her own and, specifically, the Ultras mainly associated with the powerful ERG. They had been supportive of the Lancaster House speech, but the compromises implied by the white paper and the emergent recognition that there would be a financial settlement to be made, and a transition period beyond Article 50, would be likely to attract their ire. Given a majority of only fifteen, this could have had major consequences for May's government. Already some Brexiters, in line with their recurring practice of pushing in an ever-harder direction, had begun to call for leaving with no deal at all. But if she could increase her majority on the platform of the white paper version of Brexit and against UKIP, which would run on a 'clean break' Brexit platform (i.e. no deal), then she would be in a much stronger position to face them down. It may never be known if this was her intention, but it has some plausibility.

Whatever the motivations behind it, the most remarkable feature of the election campaign was how very little Brexit featured within it.[60] This was extraordinary not only because May had framed the calling of the election in terms of Brexit, but because, plainly, leaving the EU was the biggest national event since the Second World War – far bigger than the decision to join – and possibly the most unusual political event in any developed democracy in living memory. When else had such a country decided unilaterally to rewrite almost all its foreign and economic policy, and to seek to simultaneously detach and reattach itself on unknown terms to the global trade system?

In those circumstances, an intense debate about the ins and outs of what Brexit would mean and how it would be pursued might have been expected. It could hardly be said that this had been settled by the referendum, precisely because of all the questions which had since emerged about what, in concrete terms, it meant. Equally, it was by this time becoming clearer that the decisions about this would affect every single area of daily life, from air travel through to nuclear waste disposal, and every industry from fishing to computer game design.

So there were huge new, and urgent, questions for the country. What exactly did the government's white paper Brexit plan, endorsed in the Tory manifesto, mean? Was 'no deal better than a bad deal'? How would a 'bad deal' be defined? What did a 'no deal' scenario look like? Perhaps most glaring of all, where was the discussion of the costs of the Brexit plan? Every single other policy, from whatever party, in any election, is relentlessly scrutinised for affordability and for how it will be funded. But such scrutiny barely occurred as regards Brexit, even though in any realistic scenario that cost would be in the high billions of pounds and would also vary very substantially depending on exactly how it was put into practice.

This in turn suggested numerous other questions. What would the effect on employment be? How would the tax take be affected? What would the impact be on what had been the totemic issue of politics in recent years, the fiscal deficit? What about the balance of payments? Would the UK's credit rating be affected? Would sterling's status as a reserve currency be affected? And what about the value of sterling, anyway? Brexit had seen a huge currency depreciation which at any other time would have been a major election issue. Yet there was barely any mention of any these things.

Beyond the economics, there was also little or no discussion of what foreign policy would look like not just post-Brexit but, now, in the context of Trump's America. Nor, except for in Scotland, did the new issues posed by the referendum result for the union get much attention. For that matter, it might have been expected that the fate of the more than one million Britons who were living in the EU and were directly affected by Brexit would merit some significant debate – not least since some of them had a vote in the general election. But they, too, were hardly mentioned.

That this bizarre near-silence persisted was in large part because it suited the two main political parties. The Tories were content to let the only Brexit-related issue be which of May or Corbyn would be able to negotiate 'the best deal'. This framing was in line with the wider attempt, ill-advised as it turned out, to make May's 'strong and stable leadership' the defining issue of the election, but it gave no sense whatsoever of what that deal would be. Instead, the Tory manifesto reiterated the white paper commitments to a form of Brexit that was neither voted for in the referendum nor advocated by many leading leavers, and which stood no chance of being accepted by the EU. But there was no explanation of why this was the preferred approach, how it would work in practice even if achieved, nor what costs – financial or otherwise – it would entail. So, for example, the party's manifesto launch was dominated by discussion of social care funding, which (again ill-advisedly, as it turned out) they sought to make the central policy issue of the campaign. Yet the very viability of the care system, which was heavily dependent on EU workers, was in peril because of Brexit. The manifesto as a whole mentioned Brexit just fifteen times, and never with any detail beyond saying it would be 'smooth and orderly'.

As for Labour, they fought the election without a policy position on Brexit that made any sense at all. Their manifesto devoted a chapter to Brexit but gave very little detail beyond

wanting to retain the 'benefits' of the single market and customs union but without being members of either, which was
meaningless and, indeed, misleading. In particular, they affirmed that freedom of movement of people would end with
Brexit and so accepted the central tenet of hard Brexit, and yet
said they wanted to 'retain unrestricted access for our goods
and services' which was incompatible with it. Throughout the
campaign, none of the leading figures in the party showed any
sign of understanding this made no sense, apart from Brexit
spokesman Sir Keir Starmer, although his comments were so
strangulated by the official party line as to require endless de-
coding. Corbyn himself said very little about it and typically
spoke only of seeking 'tariff-free access' to the single market,
implying, if anything, something less than the manifesto commitment and conceivably less, even, than the 'deep and special partnership' that the Tories promised. Yet all of the issues
Labour did focus on would inevitably be hugely affected by
Brexit, and the form it took, the NHS being just one obvious
example.

What was most striking about all this was that the only
halfway intellectually respectable justification put forward for
Brexit was that it would mean that the British electorate could
choose and dispose of its political direction of travel via the
general election ballot box. But what was now in prospect was
the use of that ballot box to endorse a scarcely specified, barely
discussed and yet central, historic policy. Although many commentators remarked that this was the first election in recent
times where there had been a very clear ideological distinction
between the main parties, on the core issue of Brexit they were
both committed to something which, to the extent it could
be pinned down at all, was virtually identical in terms of sac-
rificing single market membership in order to accommodate

ending freedom of movement. Perhaps the only really significant difference was that the Tories argued that, in May's phrase, 'no deal is better than a bad deal' whereas Labour were clear that 'no deal' would not be an acceptable outcome. And even there, since May also said when launching the campaign that not getting the 'right deal' would be 'dire', what did that difference really amount to?

The vagueness of their plans mattered hugely because it repeated the very problem caused by the referendum itself – if either party won then it would be able to claim a mandate for a policy that was largely bereft of practical detail. It should also be said that even those parties which might have been expected to have the clearest position on Brexit offered confused proposals. UKIP did not accept that the Article 50 process should be followed at all, and argued that the UK should simply have left unilaterally. But whilst its manifesto suggested that such a course could still be followed it also seemed to imply that, now it was started, the issue was the terms of exit that would be negotiated under the process.

On the other side of things, the Lib Dems wanted a referendum on the withdrawal deal with the option of reverting to EU membership. But this was less clear than it seemed. Firstly, because at that time it was not clearly established whether or not Article 50 was reversible. And, secondly, even if it turned out, legally, to be possible, what would that mean politically? Could either the UK or the EU, at the end of a long, complex and very likely acrimonious set of negotiations, simply go back to the status quo ante of not just EU membership but all of the particular UK aspects of it (e.g. opt-outs from Euro and Schengen, and the budget rebate)? Arguably, the most detailed set of Brexit proposals of any of the parties came in the Democratic Unionist Party (DUP) manifesto. However, whilst wanting the 'particular circumstances of Northern Ireland with a land border with the EU fully reflected', these proposals showed no sign of understanding how this core issue could be made compatible with the party's advocacy of hard Brexit.

The outcome of the election is well-known. May's decision backfired horribly, leaving her leading a minority government dependent upon the DUP. For Brexit, it meant that far from the 'saboteurs' having been crushed, they had new hope that Brexit could be softened or even, perhaps, reversed. Conversely, the victimhood of the Brexiters had been re-confirmed and their ever-present fears of Brexit being betrayed much enhanced. In that sense, the culture war encapsulated by the 'enemies of the people' headline was primed to continue and even intensify.

Perhaps that culture war was inevitable, given the strength of opinion of the two sides and the almost fifty-fifty split of opinion. But it also arose from spectacular failures of political leadership and political institutions. By now, the UK had had not one but three opportunities for a realistic and practical national debate about its membership of the EU – the referendum, the post-referendum hiatus and this general election campaign – and had signally failed to take them. The first chance had been squandered by dishonesty and complacency, the second by wilful neglect, and the third for reasons of party political convenience. So even a year after the referendum campaign had started, quite basic issues such as what leaving the single market meant were still not widely understood by the public or, for that matter, by many politicians.

Article 50 had now been triggered and two months of its two-year period had already gone without negotiations having even begun because of the election. Britain now had to undertake an unprecedented national change, using an untried process, in a tight time frame, and would have to define and debate what Brexit meant at the same time as enacting it. That would have to be done by a country that was profoundly and angrily divided, and with a government which had no majority, was itself subject to vicious factional battles, and which was led by a Prime Minister who had shredded her political authority.

It was a recipe for chaos, which was precisely what now unfolded.

## CHAPTER THREE

# THE ROAD TO CHEQUERS

*From the 2017 general election to the Chequers proposal*

It might have been thought that her failure to win the 2017 general election would lead May to reappraise her Brexit policy. After all, it had not been endorsed by the electorate. But as the dust settled, a more complex picture emerged. On the one hand, some things pointed to a move in the direction of a softer Brexit than that of her Lancaster House speech. These included the appointment of former remainers, such as Damian Green and Gavin Barwell, to key positions and the effectively enforced resignations of her key advisers, including Nick Timothy who had apparently been so influential in formulating the Lancaster House speech and her whole approach to Brexit.

Against that, the appointment of Michael Gove, central in the Vote Leave campaign, to the Cabinet suggested a reaffirmation of hard Brexit, as did the appointment of ERG chair Steve Baker, one of the most hardcore Brexiters, to a ministerial position in DExEU. And then there was May's new reliance on the Democratic Unionist Party (DUP), but how that would play out was difficult to assess. Logically, they should have been able to see that hard Brexit would ultimately imperil their overriding priority of Northern Ireland remaining in the UK and yet they continued to support it.

The bigger political landscape was that the fragile truce within the Tory Party that had held since May's leadership election had now disappeared. From this time onwards the Brexiters leapt on every sign of 'backsliding' from hard Brexit, whilst the relatively small group of Tory remainers, soft Brexiters or just 'pragmatists' were emboldened to oppose her. Their figurehead emerged in the perhaps unlikely form of the Chancellor, Philip Hammond, who by the standards of just a few years ago would have been considered a Eurosceptic. One measure of how extreme politics became during the Brexit process is that within four months of the election there were calls from the pro-Brexit former Chancellor Nigel Lawson for Hammond to be sacked for 'sabotage'[61] whilst the influential Brexiter journalist and presenter Julia Hartley-Brewer said on national television that he should be 'tried for treason'.[62]

Such comments were part of the intensification of the culture war and the 'Brexit McCarthyism' discussed in the previous chapter, and it intensified in part because when May failed to win the election it reopened, far more vociferously and publicly, the debate about what Brexit should mean which she had hitherto been largely able to suppress. Business groups began to call far more forcefully than before for soft Brexit, and the idea that Brexit might not even happen at all began to gain ground for the first time since the referendum.

That position was being articulated by grassroots campaigns around the country, and was represented in Parliament by the Lib Dems, led from July 2017 by Sir Vince Cable. But Labour, the official opposition party, despite having exceeded expectations in the election, remained in a mess over Brexit. In particular, as a result of the way they had framed their manifesto (as discussed in the previous chapter), Brexiters were now able to claim that 80 per cent of electors had voted for parties that had endorsed hard Brexit and that 'therefore' hard Brexit had been democratically confirmed as the way that Brexit should be done.

It was obviously highly misleading, since most Labour voters were remainers, and was contradicted by opinion polls. There had never been 80 per cent support for Brexit, let alone hard Brexit. But it had been gifted to Brexiters by Labour's electoral stance, just as Labour support for triggering Article 50 had also been a gift to Brexiters. Yet perhaps it contained a glimmer of truth as regards how MPs might vote, since when Labour MP Chuka Umunna tabled an amendment to the Queen's Speech to the new parliament, calling for continued single market membership, Jeremy Corbyn ordered his MPs to abstain and sacked those Labour frontbenchers who supported it. It was one of many ways in which Corbyn acted as the Brexiters' en- abler, as demonstrated by Nigel Farage's endorsement of his actions for 'showing his true Brexit colours'.[63]

## THE ROW OF THE SUMMER

Though some of the events just mentioned came a few days later, it was against this general background that the Article 50 talks belatedly started in the middle of June 2017. The 'row of the summer' that David Davis had threatened before the election did not transpire, and the UK accepted 'sequencing' without demur. At the time, this was taken to be a sign that the election had weakened the government's hand in the ne- gotiations, although very possibly it would have happened anyway. However, the underlying issue of how the two stages of withdrawal terms agreement and future terms agreement differed continued to be the subject of confusion and, amongst Brexiters, resentment.

The defining image of the negotiations, whilst it may have

been unfair, became so because it expressed an underlying truth. It showed Davis and the UK negotiators as the talks opened sitting without papers across the table from Michel Barnier, the EU's chief negotiator, and his team with bulging files. The truth it expressed was that Britain was totally unprepared for the negotiations, and that in turn expressed the even deeper truth that Brexiters still had no real idea about how to undertake Brexit beyond having won the referendum. They had, to coin a phrase, sent Britain 'naked into the conference chamber'.

Actually, there *was* a row of the summer but it turned out to be a domestic one and, strangely, it was not about the terms of the exit agreement, which was what was being discussed in phase one of the talks, and nor was it really about the terms of the future relationship, which were to be discussed in phase two. Rather, it was about whether there should be a transition or 'implementation' period between leaving the EU and commencing that still unagreed relationship. Whilst the focus was a peculiar one in the circumstances, it had a political significance in that it was the first substantive encounter between the Hammond-led group of 'pragmatists', who wanted a lengthy transition of perhaps up to four years, and the Brexit Ultras who wanted a short transition or none at all.

In July it seemed that Hammond had won the argument, but in August he and Liam Fox co-wrote an article repudiating transition; thereafter the issue rumbled on in one form or another until 2020. The summer 2017 episode of this battle is now largely forgotten, but it serves to illustrate how much UK domestic politics was out of synch with the realities of the negotiations with the EU, how much of that politics was an internal battle within the Tory Party, and the way that key issues kept recurring until the passage of events made them redundant.

## MAKE ME AN OFFER

If these arguments about transition put the cart before the horse of what form the future relationship would take – in other words, what the transition would be *to* – the latter question continued to be a vexed one and throughout 2017, with successive rounds of talks, this became ever clearer. In press conferences Michel Barnier repeatedly called for clarity from the UK as to what it wanted, and Laura Kuenssberg, the political editor of the BBC, reported that within the British negotiating team there was frustration at the failure of politicians, up to and including the Prime Minister, to take the 'big decisions' that would allow the talks to make progress.[64] This refusal to face decisions seemed obvious at the time, if only because of the continuing suggestion that 'frictionless trade' could be achieved despite hard Brexit, but a few months later it was confirmed in an extraordinary story that emerged from the January 2018 World Economic Forum at Davos.

There, during a semi-private event, Angela Merkel summarised the series of conversations she had had with Theresa May, going back to 2016:

> Mrs Merkel said that when she asks Mrs May what she wants the shape of the UK's relationship with the EU to be, Mrs May says 'make me an offer'. To which Mrs Merkel says, 'but you're leaving – we don't have to make you an offer. Come on what do you want?' To which Mrs May replies 'make me an offer'. And so, according to Mrs Merkel, the two find themselves trapped in a recurring loop of 'what do you want?' and 'make me an offer'.[65]

This had more than a ring of truth and, in fact, throughout the whole Brexit process there was very often a sense of the

UK telling the EU what its red lines were and then expecting the EU to come up with a 'deal' which would accommodate these. This is the origin of what became an important and controversial document: the slide showing the so-called 'Barnier staircase' published in December 2017.[66] It depicted a variety of versions of Britain's future trading relationship with the EU, each denoted by a 'step' with the flag or flags of a country or countries which had such a relationship. Each of them was then tagged to one or more of the UK red lines to show why it had been ruled out. What it left was a free trade agreement, denoted by the flags of Canada and South Korea (the only other alternative being no deal, with trade on WTO terms).

There was nothing novel in this as it simply set out what were always the main options. Yet when the framework documents (of which the staircase was to be a part) leaked they were described as having 'dashed Britain's trade hopes'.[67] Similarly, when, a couple of months afterwards, Donald Tusk indicated that such a free trade agreement, which would be 'worse than the status quo after leaving the EU', was the only option in the light of UK red lines this was seen by Brexiters as outrageous. Liam Fox's response was typical: 'The idea of punishing Britain is not the language of a club, it's the language of a gang. We need to begin this argument by putting politics aside and do what is in the economic interests of the people we represent.'[68]

Of course, Tusk had not used the word 'punishment' or even 'argument'. But the strangest feature of the outrage about Barnier's staircase and Tusk's speech was that many of those most angry about them had, during the referendum and/or afterwards, championed a free trade agreement as exactly the form they wanted Brexit to take.

To understand this contradiction, it's necessary, first, to recall the persistent failure of Brexiters to understand the difference between a free trade agreement and single market membership (as discussed in Chapter One). It meant that some Brexiters simultaneously welcomed talk of a 'Canada-style' deal (i.e. a free trade agreement) but, because they confused it with single market membership, railed against it being described as a worse trading relationship than EU membership, which they took to mean 'punishment' when it was just a statement of fact. Relatedly, but slightly different, for other Brexiters there was, at least implicitly, a belief that the Barnier staircase had a missing 'UK model' step in which an agreement could be made whereby Britain was somehow outside but still in the single market. Moreover, that was seen as a straightforward ask and should be, in what became Liam Fox's notorious phrase of July 2017, 'the easiest deal in human history'.[69] This analysis was still based on mistaken beliefs about what the German car industry could and would do to force such a deal and about the supposed significance of existing regulatory alignment. As previously noted, this was a red herring in the context of an agreement about divergence.

## BREXIT *DOESN'T* MEAN BREXIT?

However, beneath this fantasy about models of trade lay a deeper and more peculiar feature of Brexit. Whilst being presented as a radical and necessary change, many Brexiters also seemed to think that in almost every respect things would carry on as usual. Often this was only implicit and found in assumptions about the way that 'of course' we'll still be able to, for example, travel by air as easily as before, despite this being bound up with the European Common Aviation Area and the European Aviation Safety Agency, and so continuation of their provisions after Brexit would only occur by negotiation.

These implications, by their nature, are hard to pin down but permeated the way Brexit was discussed. Sometimes, however, they were made explicit, as in Davis's assertion in April 2017[70] that the European Medicines Agency (EMA) and the European Banking Authority (EBA) could still remain in Britain, despite Brexit. This was always nonsense, as was demonstrated when, in July that year, the EU announced the competition for their relocation (ultimately, the EMA went to Amsterdam and the EBA to Paris). Their loss was undoubtedly a very serious blow to Britain's position in the two fields affected, and just one of the many huge costs of Brexit, but it was an outcome that was inevitable.

A similar example came in November 2017 when it was announced that British cities would not be eligible for consideration as European Capital of Culture 2023. The reason was that to be eligible cities needed to be in a country which is an EU, EFTA or EEA member, or aspiring to become an EU member. By 2023 none of these criteria would be met by Britain. This announcement led to a huge outpouring of anger from Brexiters, railing against the pettiness, spite and hostility of the EU.

Whilst in itself possibly the most minor effect of Brexit, the reaction to it was not just illustrative of a recurring theme, but also showed how the UK debate was stuck in a recurrent circle. Thus one MP objected to Britain's exclusion because, in the words of a common Brexiter slogan, 'we are leaving the EU, not Europe' as if that could alter the consequences of leaving the EU. Even more revealing was a spokesperson for the Prime Minister objecting that this was unfair since Norway, whilst not being a member of the EU, had been eligible (because Norway is in EFTA/EEA). This harked right back to the repeated invocations of the 'Norway model' by Brexiters before the referendum, a model which May had, since the Lancaster House speech, insisted was not acceptable as it would not satisfy the 'will of the people'. Yet now it was being invoked again, as if the difference between the soft and hard models of Brexit had not been understood, or the consequences of choosing hard Brexit had not been accepted.

And this episode also illustrated in a small way some of the big issues about Brexit. For it emerged that the government had allowed cities to make bids as 'part of our plan for a dynamic, outward-looking and Global Britain' following Brexit,[71] against the advice of civil servants who had realised that there would be a problem about eligibility, and that Foreign Secretary Boris Johnson, in particular, had wanted bids to be made. So this was a microcosm of Brexit. In pursuit of its post-Brexit global future the UK entered a competition for which it was not eligible because of Brexit, urged on by pro-Brexit politicians against the advice of the 'remainer' civil servants who actually knew it was impossible. And when that impossibility could no longer be ignored, Brexiters denounced the EU for excluding them from that which they had decided to exclude themselves.

As came to be a recurring motif, Britain kept having to be told by the EU, in an ironic invocation of May's early phrase, that 'Brexit meant Brexit'. The refusal to accept this was so is usually referred to as Britain wanting to 'cherry-pick' the advantages of EU membership, but it went deeper than this. It was as if Brexiters saw leaving the EU as a kind of symbolic act, which did not have real practical and legal consequences. Even more perversely, many of the debates and arguments of this period (and later) would have made more sense if, rather than having voted to leave, Britain was being forced to do so.

It is an interesting thought experiment to imagine that this were so, and if it were how Britain would respond. We could expect in those circumstances such things as: trying to argue that, even so, agencies like EMA and EBA could stay in London; paying the minimum possible financial settlement; seeking multiple opt-ins to the single market, and frictionless trade despite being ejected from the single market and customs union; and considerable anger with the EU and anyone in the UK seen to be 'siding' with the EU. In short, almost everything that Brexiters were saying in the circumstance of having chosen to leave would actually have made much more sense as a response to being forced to leave.

## BRITAIN'S BREXIT POSITION: OUT BUT IN?

It is within this context that two of the major developments of the late summer of 2017 should be viewed: the slew of government 'position papers' and 'future partnership papers' produced between late June and early September, and May's Florence speech in September.

The former included papers on citizens' rights, customs, the Irish border, goods trade, dispute resolution and many other things, though notably excluded was anything on the financial settlement, despite it being the subject of intensive domestic debate and central to the ongoing phase one talks with the EU. Equally absent from the public domain were the fifty or more Brexit impact assessments that the government was known to have undertaken but which it was refusing to publish.

It would be a huge task even to summarise the fourteen papers that were published – and a largely pointless one given that in so many ways they have now been superseded. But taken as a package they had four features, as many commentators at the time observed. These features have been prefigured by the analysis in this chapter so far, but now came into full view.

One was that they were very much domestically focused, and seemed more to do with creating some kind of consensus within the Tory Party than with the ongoing negotiations with the EU per se. Second, in many key areas the approach was to remain very close to the existing arrangements as a member, even though the viability of doing so was questionable in the light of the government's red lines and so could be regarded as 'cakeist'. There was, however, some hint in the dispute resolution paper of the possibility of a role for the ECJ, which might have implied some softening of that red line. Third, they rarely set out concrete proposals so much as general ambitions. This was particularly so for the papers on customs and, crucially, the Irish border. Fourth, and related, this gave them the character of setting out what the UK wanted, whilst leaving it to the EU to devise a mechanism for delivering it.

In all of these ways, the papers did not really advance matters so much as demonstrate how little progress had been made, in what was now over a year since the referendum, in coming to terms with the multiple complexities of the Brexit process and the choices they required. Moreover, in the many ways that the papers sought to retain or stay close to the status quo, they implied an obvious question: what was the point of leaving at all?

### May's Florence Speech

This was a question which seemed even more pointed when Theresa May gave one of her most significant speeches on Brexit, in Florence on 22 September 2017. The part that was most heavily trailed and attracted the most immediate attention was the willingness to continue to pay into the EU budget for a probable two-year transition period whilst staying in the single market and customs union. But this was not the 'open and generous' offer it was claimed to be, just the bare minimum in order to achieve that transition which was now, apparently, once more the agreed policy of the government.

The wider issue of the exit bill in terms of future liabilities for past commitments – for example, for pensions – was not mentioned beyond a vague statement that Britain would honour its existing commitments, which anyway seemed to pertain to the current budget rather than to accrued liabilities from the previous decades. As regards the other phase one issues, nothing new or useful at all was said about the Irish border, and on citizens' rights May continued to maintain the primacy of UK courts rather than the ECJ.

May also failed to explain in detail what the UK wanted the future relationship to be because, of course, the Cabinet and party had not agreed on that. The idea seemed to be a 'Canada +' deal, with the plus presumably being considerable coverage on services. If so, it would be unlike any other free trade agreement in existence, and would involve a high degree of ongoing regulatory harmonisation with the EU, whereas Britain wanted also to have scope for regulatory divergence. May appeared to have fallen hook, line and sinker for the Brexiter myth that existing harmonisation made for an easy agreement.

So there was very little said that addressed the recurrent questions from the EU about what Britain wanted, questions which had been re-posed by Michel Barnier in a speech in Rome the day before. Rather, it seemed to be another attempt to get the EU to solve the problems that Brexit created for the UK. Hence there was much talk of 'shared responsibility' and of an 'imaginative and creative' approach. Indeed, the backdrop slogans of 'Shared History, Shared Challenges, Shared Future' all seemed to point to this as the central message. What these coded – as with the UK position papers, and as Merkel's later

Davos comments revealed – was again the idea that the EU should come up with solutions to the hundreds of vexed issues and, moreover, to do so in a way that respected the UK's red lines. Since these red lines derived entirely from the need to appease the Brexit Ultras in May's party and outside it, once again the EU was being asked to accommodate the problems of UK domestic politics, as had occurred so often throughout Britain's membership. But accommodating an existing member was very different to doing so for a departing one.

Fundamentally, the Florence speech simply went around the same loop that Brexit had been stuck in for months. In essence, although May claimed otherwise, the idea was that everything stays the same and yet everything changes. Britain would keep everything the Brexiters perceived as benefits whilst dropping all those things they didn't like. There is no mystery as to why things kept going around this loop and kept getting the same result. It was squarely down to the refusal of Brexit Ultras to accept that they were living in a fantasy world. Whether May had now entered that world, or whether it was just that she was too politically weak to face down the Ultras hardly mattered. The effect was exactly the same. But with Article 50 triggered, despite having failed to deal with the Ultras, something extremely important had changed. Each time the UK went round the same loop, it got closer to the day it would become a 'third country' without anything remotely like a deal in place. That day was now scheduled to be just eighteen months away.

One thing that was distinctive about May's speech, and very different to the way that the Ultras talked about Brexit, was its notably conciliatory and friendly tone. She talked about how the UK and the EU shared values, history, security challenges and economic needs, and of how cooperation and partnership could and should arise from these. Yet anyone reading or listening to it could hardly escape the irony that almost everything she said constituted a case to join the EU rather than an explanation of why Britain was leaving it.

## THE PHASE ONE AGREEMENT: SUCCESS TURNED SOUR

Whilst much of the discussion in the UK in the second half of 2017 was about the nature of future trade terms and whether there should be a transition to them, the negotiations with the EU were still about the phase one issues settling the exit terms. There was a measure of agreement in relation to citizens' rights – that is, the rights of EU citizens in the UK and UK citizens in the EU. It should, however, be noted that this fell well short of promises during the referendum that their rights would be unaltered. In many key respects, including those relating to family reunification, it had already emerged that rights would be reduced or lost. Citizens in these categories had been treated, and sometimes referred to, as 'bargaining chips', and their lives thrown into turmoil. This could in no way be assuaged by any phase one agreement since, of course, there could be no certainty until a final Withdrawal Agreement had actually been signed. Even then, a particular concern, exacerbated by the Windrush scandal the following year, was the possibility of being inadvertently undocumented and being unable to prove residency rights. This remains unresolved to the present day, because EU nationals who have been granted 'settled status' have not been provided with paper documentary proof of this.

On the second of the phase one issues, by the end of November it was being reported that Britain had broadly accepted the need for a financial settlement and pretty much agreed a methodology for calculating it, which at the time was estimated to yield a figure of about £50 billion. Tellingly, however, many Tory MPs and some Cabinet ministers still talked of this as being contingent upon a future trade deal, and so still did not seem to understand the nature of the two-stage process. This was underscored by the way that the phrase 'nothing is agreed until everything is agreed' was consistently misused to suggest that both the exit terms and the future terms were part of one over-arching deal.

This had perhaps been encouraged by the terminology of there being two phases to the Article 50 negotiations, which obscured the fact that only the first phase would yield a legal treaty – on the exit terms – whilst the most that phase two could produce would be a 'Political Declaration' to inform what would potentially be a second agreement on the future terms. But it was more than a misunderstanding, in that it also reflected that Brexiters did not accept the outcome of the 'non-row' of the summer over sequencing and the deeper issue of there being two separate agreements.

That also impacted on the third of the phase one issues, that of the Northern Ireland border. Again, some Brexiters, including Liam Fox, were still maintaining that this could not be settled independently of the future terms of trade. But as noted previously that would only have been true whilst a (very) soft Brexit was a possibility. As with the 'Capital of Culture' row and the question of EMA/EBA relocation, the UK discussion continued to muddy the waters by opportunistically conflating different models of Brexit. Now the same thing was happening again, with Brexiters such as Labour MP Kate Hoey repeatedly proposing Norway or Switzerland as models for the Irish border.[72]

This was misleading for two reasons. One, obviously, was that by this time both these models had been ruled out by the British government in favour of something like the Canada model. The other was that, in any case, for reasons explained in Chapter One, there is physical border infrastructure for goods traffic between the EU and both Norway and Switzerland (and, for that matter, in contradiction of another Brexiter claim in relation to the Irish border, between Canada and the US).

To the extent that these objections were acknowledged by Brexiters, the response was to say that new technologies could be deployed so as to do away with the kind of infrastructure found at these borders. This was again misleading as there were (and are) no existing examples of such a border, but it was an idea that was to recur endlessly in the years to come (as I will discuss later).

In any case, all of these arguments missed the point. Even if a form of trade agreement were to be devised that could avoid the need for borders, and/or even if technologies could be developed that would make borders completely virtual and invisible, the purpose of the exit agreement was one of insurance. That is to say, it was to ensure that if these things proved impossible, or if there ended up being no trade deal at all, there would be no border reinstated between Ireland and Northern Ireland. Once again, the issue was the distinction between the exit deal and the future terms deal: because the first preceded the second, it needed to contain provisions for Northern Ireland, as it was not known what, if anything, the future terms deal would consist of.

In early December 2017 it was announced that an agreement on phase one had been reached, in the form of a Joint Report. This was the basis on which phase two talks could start and was also intended to be the basis of the eventual exit agreement. On the key issues of citizens' rights and the financial settlement, the earlier leaks were confirmed and these two aspects remained essentially unchanged right through to signature of the final Withdrawal Agreement in January 2020. But on the Irish border issue matters were far more complicated, and remained so in one form or another even after Britain completely left the EU.

The Joint Report was a fudge in that whilst establishing that there would under no circumstances be a border between Ireland and Northern Ireland it glossed over the question of how this would be achieved. The possibility of the future trade agreement, or some other solution proposed by the UK, doing so was agreed but, in the absence of either, there would be full alignment between the UK and the EU on those aspects of the single market and customs union necessary to ensure the absence of such a border. It thus secured the EU's key objective but without fully and formally specifying how it would met.

It should be borne in mind that the pressure to reach an agreement on phase one came entirely from the UK government. Having failed to secure parallel talks on exit and future terms, it wanted to get to the future terms phase as quickly as possible. In this sense, the fudged wording to secure that outcome was very much in line with that desire. Yet within days of it being agreed it was called into question by remarks made by David Davis in a TV interview, when he said that the agreement was merely a 'statement of intent' and was not legally binding.[73]

Whilst it was true that it was not legally binding, and would not be until such time as there was a final Withdrawal Agreement, it was understood by the EU to have been much more than a 'statement of intent'. Rather, it was seen as an undertaking that the British government had fully accepted and endorsed. Davis tried to 'clarify' what he had meant, but the damage had been done. Almost equally damaging was the fact that Theresa May also told Parliament that the financial settlement was conditional upon there being a trade deal, again failing to understand, or perhaps to accept, the difference between the two agreements that needed to be made.

In retrospect, this was a pivotal moment in the Brexit process. Prior to that, there had been a sense that the EU regretted Brexit, was bemused by it, and was frustrated by a lack of clarity as to how the UK wanted to enact it. But Davis's cavalier dismissal of the phase one agreement introduced for the first time an element of serious distrust that began the process of souring the negotiations. It was also perhaps the first time that it became clear to the EU, and more widely, that under the grip of Brexit and with Brexiters like Davis in key roles, the British government was no longer operating according to the normal rules of diplomacy. That realisation was to grow in the years to come.

The immediate consequence was that although the text of the Joint Report was agreed and the EU accepted that 'sufficient progress' had been made to move to phase two of the talks, it also decided to immediately draft the planned Withdrawal Agreement in legal text. This had not been the original intention and was a direct result of the mistrust engendered by what Davis and May had said.

When this draft was completed in February 2018, it made explicit what by then was called the Northern Ireland 'backstop'. Under this, Northern Ireland would, in effect, remain within the EU customs union and within the single market as regards goods, including agriculture and foodstuffs (these being significant as they give rise to 'sanitary and phytosanitary' checks). This, of course, would only come into force if the UK's preferred methods of ensuring there was no border (i.e. some unspecified form of trade agreement and/or technological solution) failed to materialise, hence the term 'backstop'.

But if it did ever come to be used then it would entail an 'Irish Sea border', meaning a customs and regulatory border between Great Britain and Northern Ireland.

Although this was consistent with the phase one agreement, and it was apparent within that agreement that this was what the fallback would be if no other solution could be found, Theresa May immediately declared that 'no UK Prime Minister could ever agree to' this proposal because it would threaten the 'constitutional integrity of the UK'.[74] No doubt one reason for this was her reliance, since the election fiasco, on DUP votes because for unionists something which put barriers between Northern Ireland and the rest of the United Kingdom was unconscionable.

## PHASE TWO STARTS IN DISTRUST AND CONFUSION

As a result of all this, by the beginning of 2018 a very strange state of affairs existed. Notionally, phase one of the Article 50 negotiations was over but, in fact, one of the central issues, and the most contentious issue at that, remained unresolved and disputed. On the other hand, as regards phase two of the negotiations on future terms, what Britain wanted to achieve remained highly unclear.

The two aspects of this situation were interlinked, and they reflected the intractable problems that lay at the heart of Brexit. The implication of the phase one agreement was that, if the EU's Northern Ireland-only backstop was ruled out, the whole of the UK would remain within the customs union and at least within the single market for goods. However, that was not consistent with the UK government's desire to completely leave both of these. Yet it also wanted frictionless trade, which could only be achieved through those institutions.

There was no way of resolving these incompatible desires except by giving one of them up. There could be the softest of Brexits – in the single market and a customs union – and that would deliver frictionless trade and solve the border problem as neither a land nor a sea border for Northern Ireland would be necessary. That was unacceptable to Brexiters, and they were not alone in thinking that such an outcome would make leaving the EU totally pointless. Actually, that was not quite true, because it would have removed the UK from the ambit of EU foreign and defence policy, and could also have enabled Britain to leave the common agriculture and fisheries policies. But even if, conceivably, Brexit could have taken that form in 2016, by 2018 the commitments May's government had given made it entirely impossible. That being so, there had to be a border somewhere, but the GFA precluded it being a land border and, apparently, the integrity of the UK meant it could not be a sea border.

There was no solution. But the difficulty was that the Brexiters would not accept that and May was certainly in too weak a position to make them do so. Those inside the Tory Party had (just about) gone along with the phase one agreement but they were really only doing so because many still believed that, somehow, it would all be overtaken by the future trade agreement and that accepting it was simply a tactical ploy to move the EU on to the phase two talks so as to get around its insistence on sequencing. This was the significance of Davis's comment about the phase one agreement not being binding. It may well have reflected his own belief but, even if it hadn't, it was necessary to keep the ERG and other Brexit Ultras on board.

The necessity of that was to do with the long-term civil war over Europe within the Tory Party, compounded by the lack of a parliamentary majority. Moreover, within the wider Brexit movement, represented especially by Nigel Farage, the phase one agreement had already been denounced as a humiliation and a complete capitulation to the EU. So whereas the basis of holding the referendum had been to manage these battles within the Tory Party, and to hold off the threat of what was then Farage's UKIP, what had been unleashed was a new and far more toxic battle which now involved pretty much the whole country.

There was now apparently no way in which the fantasy of a borderless hard Brexit could be dispelled. Rationality and facts no longer had any purchase, because the culture war which had developed meant that these were now dismissed as a remainer ploy, designed by the elite to deny the 'will of the people'. But that did not make facts go away, so what followed was an extraordinarily repetitive process in which, over and over again, attempts were made to resolve the irreconcilable desires of Brexiters and, over and over again, these attempts foundered on the realities of this irreconcilability.

## THE SEARCH FOR SOLUTIONS TO AN INSOLUBLE PROBLEM

Almost inevitably, this led to an upsurge in what had been present for a while, namely the demand to cut through the tangle and simply leave without a trade deal and, if necessary, without a Withdrawal Agreement either. This would entail severe economic (and other) consequences, since it meant trading on WTO terms as explained in Chapter One, the meaning of which Brexiters persistently misunderstood or misrepresented and the consequences of which they continued to denounce as Project Fear. But, crucially, it still didn't solve the problem of the Irish border since this would also be needed in a WTO scenario. Whatever Brexiters may have believed, or wanted to believe, the need for a border between customs areas and between regulatory areas was not an invention of the EU (still less of Ireland). Rather, it was the EU customs union and single market which had removed the need for such a border between its member states. The only answer that they had to this was to continue to talk of technological solutions which did not, at least as yet, exist.

Throughout most of 2018 the government was therefore caught in a trap. It was too weak to challenge the fantasies of the Brexiters inside and outside Parliament, and its own previous decisions had made that even harder. In any case, some of its key ministers, including Johnson, Davis and Fox, shared those fantasies. But it also faced the relentless time pressure of the Article 50 process, which at this stage was taken to mean that a text of the Withdrawal Agreement and of any Political Declaration about the shape of the future terms would have to be ready by about October 2018 in order to allow ratification in time for the scheduled departure date of 29 March 2019.

Nor was this the only pressure, because there was a growing movement in the country, as well as a more vociferous business campaign, against Brexit. And parliamentarians, including some rebels within the Tory Party, were finally beginning to assert themselves against the increasingly chaotic situation that Brexit was causing. As regards the latter, there had been an early indication of it during a vote on the EU Withdrawal Bill in December 2017. For the first time, the government lost a vote on Brexit with the passing of Amendment 7 to the Bill, which provided for a 'meaningful vote' on the final terms of Britain's exit from the EU. This amendment came to have a massive significance for the Brexit process, as will be discussed in the next chapter. For now, the point is that it showed how vulnerable the government was to both wings of the Conservative Party. It also showed that, despite the tremendous hostility and threats the rebels faced, some MPs were no longer willing to be cowed by the 'Brexit McCarthyism' that had influenced the vote to trigger Article 50.

Clearly any such meaningful vote was a long way off, since the negotiations were still ongoing. But for the reasons described above, that negotiation was still largely not with the EU at all, but an internal one within the UK and, to a large extent, within the Conservative Party and its partner the DUP. Thus through the first half of 2018 numerous strangely named schemes were developed. Each of them tried to solve the insoluble contradictions of hard Brexit and the Irish border or, in some cases, conceded on one or other of the incompatible demands of the Brexiters but did so in a formulation they might swallow.

Variants of this included 'ambitious managed divergence', also known as 'managed divergence' or 'the three baskets' approach, the 'customs partnership' or 'hybrid model', and 'maximum facilitation' or 'maxfac'. There is very little point in recounting the details of what each contained or the debates around them, except to say that each of them provoked divisions both within the government and amongst Tory MPs. A non-binding vote in April suggested there might actually be a parliamentary majority for being in a full customs union with the EU. This was Labour policy and, unlike all the other models for customs, was one which was realistically negotiable with the EU. However, apart from being loathed by Brexiters and incompatible with May's stated policy, whatever merits it may have had it would not in itself solve the Irish border issue, because there would still be the issue of the regulatory border entailed by being outside the single market.

The question then became whether there might, now, be a parliamentary majority not just for a customs union but for single market membership as well. For despite the hard Brexiters' 'will of the people' rhetoric, this was, according to opinion polls, the public's preference. It was a question given concrete form when in May 2018 the House of Lords voted to amend the EU Withdrawal Bill so as to require the government to stay in the single market via EFTA. However, because this was against Labour's Brexit policy, when the Bill came back to the Commons in June, Corbyn whipped his MPs to reject it (there was also some pointless chicanery of introducing a different amendment which talked of 'full access' without specifying EFTA).

It will never be known for sure, but had he not done so then there might have been enough Tory rebels – as had been shown by the Amendment 7 vote and the non-binding customs union vote – to have carried it. What would then have happened is unguessable, but it was one of the pivotal moments in which a rear-guard parliamentary action might averted hard Brexit, and in which Corbyn once again acted as the hard Brexiters' enabler.

## GO WTO, ALTERNATIVE ARRANGEMENTS AND GATT XXIV

As these various political and parliamentary manoeuvres continued, the wider Brexiter narrative was splitting in two contradictory directions, although each shared a common feature. As mentioned, one was the growing call to leave the EU with no deal and, as the emerging slogan had it, to 'Go WTO', and the other was a growing insistence that there was an easy solution to the central problem – that of the Irish border – in the form of 'alternative arrangements', meaning technological and administrative systems.

What both shared was what might be called 'simplism': that is, the idea that complex, almost intractable problems actually had a simple solution. It was an approach in line with that of the leave campaign in the referendum and it had an obvious public appeal. Perhaps the more interesting thing was that at the same time as this simplism, the calls to 'Go WTO' and for 'alternative arrangements' for the Irish border both deployed what could sound like 'expert' technical jargon and ideas (this also revealed that Brexiters did not entirely disdain experts; rather, that they were happy to deploy expertise but in a highly selective and misleading way).

As regards a no-deal, WTO terms Brexit, Brexiters suddenly made 'GATT Article XXIV' the central part of their argument. It became their constant reference point in the following years, but the first high-profile time it was referred to was in a television interview with Jacob Rees-Mogg on the BBC's *Daily Politics* show in May 2018. His claim was that this meant that under WTO rules the UK could just go on trading with the EU on its existing terms for ten years, during which time a trade deal could be negotiated.

Delivered in Rees-Mogg's characteristic lofty drawl, this might have sounded to the average viewer like an authoritative pronouncement. In fact, it was drivel, in multiple ways. For one thing, it referred to the time period to implement a deal, and it would require both parties to agree, whereas Rees-Mogg was using it to claim that no deal or agreement was needed. For another, even if it were true that trade could continue on existing terms in the meanwhile, that would imply the UK being in a ten-year transition period, whereas for Rees-Mogg such transition entailed 'vassalage' to EU rules.[75] Actually, it meant virtually nothing, and certainly nothing like what Brexiters claimed for it. As leading trade expert Peter Ungphakorn put it, all that saying we want to use GATT Article XXIV means is 'we want a free trade deal in goods that complies with WTO rules'.[76]

As regards the Irish border, the Brexiters' go-to text was what they widely, but erroneously, referred to as an EU report (in fact, it was a consultant's report to the European Parliament).[77] This was by no means drivel, but nor was it the magic bullet claimed by the Brexiters, especially in relation to food and livestock traffic. It was predicated on drawing together a wide range of technologies which were in current use in various parts of the world, or under development, and deploying them, for the first time, in conjunction. It may one day prove to be possible but that is not certain and, even if so, would take many years to develop and, even then, it might not completely solve the very particular political requirements of the Irish border. Given these uncertainties, it could not act as an alternative to the backstop. At very best it might, as the phase one agreement provided for, mean that the backstop would never be used or, if used, only temporarily.

In both these cases (and there are others), Brexiters regurgitated semi-digested factoids, often dug up by an ever-changing array of pro-Brexit think tanks, which they thought would enable them to wriggle out of the basic, factual conundrums of Brexit. I do not think that this was necessarily due to dishonesty so much as an ingrained certainty that what they wanted 'must' be possible. The consequence for the wider public was that these supposed solutions went quickly around social media so as to become established facts for, especially, leave-inclined voters. All of the detailed technical rebuttals and debunkings that followed had no chance of keeping up.

That was fine in terms of 'winning' the public debate, and no doubt contributed to a sense amongst the public that Brexit was only dragging on because of the incompetence or ill will of politicians in ignoring these 'simple' solutions. However, no government, no matter how committed to Brexit, could actually implement these solutions because they did not in reality exist, and could not be made to exist by force of belief. This was one of many ways in which civil servants, in particular, were put in the impossible position of being accused of 'remainer sabotage' because they could not make true that which was untrue.

## 'A PARALLEL UNIVERSE'

There were signs in the middle of 2018 that Theresa May was beginning to realise this, and also to understand the practical problems of the hard Brexit she had embraced in the Lancaster House speech. This seems to have been partly because of the influence of Olly Robbins, the civil servant who in September 2017 had moved from being Permanent Secretary at DExEU to being May's personal Brexit adviser at the Cabinet Office, and effectively the leading civil servant in the Brexit negotiations.* He was to become for Brexiters one of several civil service hate-figures, of whom Sir Ivan Rogers had been the first.

It is also the case, perhaps because of Robbins's influence, that May had meetings with senior business figures during this period, who explained to her the intricacies of international supply chains. Moreover, it seems that in this period she also came to recognise what hard Brexit would mean for the security situation in Northern Ireland. It seems plausible that just as her experience as Home Secretary had predisposed her to be hostile to freedom of movement, so had it sensitised her to

---

\* It is beyond the scope of this book, but there is much that could be said about the relationship between DExEU and the Cabinet Office in the Brexit story; most notably whether DExEU should ever have been created in the first place.

security matters.[78] If so, what is surprising is that she had not realised the implications for these of her hard Brexit stance. My own belief is that she simply hadn't understood them at the time of the Lancaster House speech.

Whatever the truth of this, as the second anniversary of the referendum came, Britain was no closer to having a settled view of what Brexit should mean, still less one that could be put to the EU. On the customs issue, when, in June, the EU Withdrawal Bill returned to the Commons, the ongoing debate was papered over by agreeing to an unspecified 'customs arrangement', which could have meant anything up to and including a customs union, and a new 'meaningful vote' amendment was not carried. What this latter illustrated was that, with a few exceptions, the Tory anti-Brexit or soft Brexit rebels simply did not have the ruthlessness of the ERG Brexit Ultras and, unlike the Ultras, could be swayed by appeals to party loyalty.

In terms of the wider debate, multiple models of Brexit continued to be discussed in the media and elsewhere, ranging from the familiar Norway, Canada and WTO ones to Ukraine (Association Agreement) and Jersey (goods-only single market). The extraordinary and crucial thing to recall is that this domestic debate was all happening whilst the UK was actually *in negotiations with the EU* about their future relationship, yet the UK had no agreed position on which to negotiate. As Tony Connelly, the Europe editor of Ireland's RTÉ, who had emerged as one of the best-informed and most insightful journalists covering Brexit, reported, 'the view from Brussels and Dublin is that Westminster is quite simply in a parallel universe'.[79]

But although Westminster politics was important, there was a different political force emerging in the form of the People's

Vote campaign, founded in April 2018, which was demanding another referendum on whether to accept the terms of any Brexit which might be agreed. On the second anniversary of the original vote, it held a march in London which the organisers estimated to have attracted at least 100,000 people. Meanwhile, politics aside, there were almost daily reports of companies relocating or deferring investment decisions.

## CHEQUERS PROPOSAL: CHAOS BECOMES CRISIS

As July 2018 started, not only was it more than two years since the referendum but it was also just eight months until Britain was due to leave the EU and, on what was still expected to be the timescale, about three months until the exit deal was needed to be ready for ratification. It seems even more extraordinary to record this in retrospect than it did at the time.

Finally, the government came up with a plan for what it wanted – the Chequers proposal.[80] In essence it proposed that the UK remain in the single market for goods (via a 'common rulebook') and have a 'facilitated customs arrangement' whereby there would be a 'combined customs territory' with the UK setting its own tariff rates on UK trade with the rest of the world (except the EU) but maintaining EU tariffs for trade with the EU and collecting tariffs on its behalf (quite how this would ever have worked in practice remains unclear). It is important to understand in view of what came later that this was, indeed, a proposal for the future relationship and, as such, would not form part of the Withdrawal Agreement. Nor did it change the nature of the Northern Ireland backstop which would be in the Withdrawal Agreement. However, aspirationally at least, it meant that if this were to be the form that the future relationship agreement took then the need to implement the Northern Ireland backstop would never arise.

It was hokum but, in one way and one way only, it made sense. It was an attempt to operationalise the Brexiters' idea that everything would change and yet things would continue to be the same. There was scarcely a single commentator who thought it could possibly be accepted by the EU, since it was only a sophisticated version of 'cakeism'. Its only purpose was to try to get the Brexiters to accept something which might then, in some form, be negotiated with the EU. But that proved to be an entirely vain hope. Almost immediately, David Davis, who had been threatening to resign for weeks, did so. Boris Johnson followed, as did Steve Baker, the DExEU minister.

In the years since, it has often been claimed that, with her Chequers proposal, May put forward a compromise that, had remainer MPs supported it, would have been the basis for a workable 'soft Brexit'. This is categorically untrue, for several reasons. First, it was not soft Brexit. Second, it was not workable as it would never have been acceptable to the EU, not least because the basic features of the customs arrangement were too complicated to implement. Third, it was scuppered first and foremost by the Brexiters. And whilst it is true that it was a compromise of sorts, it took the form of trying to create an institutional fudge, whereby everyone could think it meant what they wanted it to mean, rather than an agreed consensus, so it wouldn't have been durable.

The Chequers proposal was doomed from the start and, although May's premiership limped on, it marked the moment when any residual chance that she could deliver Brexit disappeared. It was a failure which was both honourable and dishonourable. Honourable, because she had dutifully tried to take all the hard Brexiters' contradictory promises, confusions and downright lies and turn them into some kind of policy, at which point they turned on her. Dishonourable, because she had failed to challenge the hard Brexiters when she had a chance and had, instead, promised to deliver what they wanted despite it being literally impossible.

As July 2018 ended, it was no longer clear whether the UK had a functioning government as regards Brexit. The Chequers proposal was the basis of a new white paper, but virtually everyone knew it would not be agreed by either the EU or the Brexit Ultras. Boris Johnson, in a predictably dishonest resignation speech, denied that the Irish border problem existed. The new Brexit Secretary, another Ultra, Dominic Raab, denied that any financial settlement was due. Parliament was paralysed, and neither the government nor the opposition had realistic plans for Brexit. In the media and on social media the debate was increasingly angry, and people were increasingly taking to the streets.

It is vital to restate that none of what was happening was remotely like what had been promised by the Vote Leave campaign and its heirs. It had been promised that Brexit would be quick and easy. It had been promised that, irrespective of Brexit, Britain would be 'part of a free trade zone stretching from Iceland to the Russian border'. It had been promised that Brexit had no implications for the Irish border.

These promises had all been fantasies, and the attempt to turn those fantasies into policy was now leading to a national crisis.

# CHAPTER FOUR

# PARALYSIS

*From the Chequers proposal to Theresa May's resignation*

The half-in, half-out nature of the Chequers proposal re-flected the underlying structural paradox that Brexit posed for any government trying to implement it. By definition, at least according to any reputable independent forecast, it was a policy which contradicted the more general political pressure on any government not to make the country poorer and weaker. Whilst the Vote Leave campaign had denied any such problem, that was not a luxury that a pragmatic government could indulge. But May's government had already rejected the most obvious way of minimising the damage – soft Brexit – and in that sense had endorsed the idea that real Brexit meant hard Brexit.

The Chequers proposal was an attempt to split the differ-ence by somewhat softening hard Brexit, but in doing so pro-posed something which pleased no one, including the Brexit Ultras who up to this point had (first enthusiastically, later grudgingly) supported Theresa May. For remainers it was still Brexit, and hard Brexit at that. Nor was it acceptable to the EU, although it initially received a polite reception if only be-cause it was the first time in two years that the UK had come up with a concrete plan for how to undertake Brexit.

In consequence, the story of the remaining months of May's

premiership is mainly characterised by three things: negotiating with the EU on how to get from the Chequers proposal to a Withdrawal Agreement and Political Declaration; the determined opposition of Brexiters to anything which that negotiating process might yield; and the growing pressure from remainers to further soften or to altogether abandon Brexit.

## PARLIAMENT MIRRORS THE NATION

The latter two aspects played out both in Parliament and outside it, in campaigns and demonstrations, and in media and social media discussions and arguments. These were linked in that, perhaps by chance, the vagaries of the British electoral system had with the 2017 election delivered a parliament which was, as in a sense it should always be, the mirror image of the country it represented, which is to say hopelessly split. In consequence, arcane parliamentary processes became the focus of national attention, whilst scenes of extraordinary drama in the House of Commons were matched by noisy and often angry pro- and anti-Brexit demonstrations outside it, all witnessed by the world's media which set up a semi-permanent encampment of broadcasting tents on College Green, adjacent to Parliament. So in recalling how the parliamentary events unfolded, it should not be forgotten that they were not occurring within 'the Westminster bubble' but were a vivid embodiment of this wider national convulsion.

In Parliament, the ERG MPs, who by now had become virtually an independent party within the Conservative Party, suddenly discovered the virtues of scrutiny and rebellion. Before the Chequers proposal, they had vociferously condemned such actions as 'tying the hands' of the Prime Minister and as 'undermining Britain's negotiators'. But that was when they thought things were going their way. Now that that was not so, they had no such compunction and availed themselves of every opportunity to do so.

The first example came when, in July 2018, they proposed amendments to the Customs Bill which directly contradicted the core of the Chequers proposal/white paper (e.g. as regards collecting tariffs for the EU on EU-bound goods entering the UK, and as regards any scenario in which Northern Ireland was in a separate customs territory to Great Britain). Knowing it would lose if a vote were held on them, the government accepted these amendments.

What this again illustrated – and it was a theme to be endlessly repeated – was that even as it negotiated with the EU the government was engaged in a parallel negotiation with its own MPs. In this case it had a particularly bizarre character because it meant that the government was making proposals in Brussels which it had already conceded to those MPs would not be implemented. If this were not topsy-turvy enough, by the end of July Michel Barnier had, for the first time, stated in terms what had always been obvious about the Chequers proposal, namely: 'The EU cannot – and the EU will not – delegate the application of its customs policy and rules, VAT and excise duty collections to a non-member who would not be subject to the EU's governance structures.'[81]

Thus the central plank of the UK's proposal had been unequivocally rejected by the EU and ruled out by the ERG's amendments to the Customs Bill which the government had accepted – and yet the government's official position remained that it was the non-negotiable basis for a Withdrawal Agreement with the EU.

## THE CONUNDRUM OF NO-DEAL PLANNING
As these events played out, throughout the summer and autumn of 2018 there was increasing discussion and development of government planning for there being no deal (i.e. no

Withdrawal Agreement). This was largely to satisfy the demands of Brexiters, who claimed that doing so would persuade the EU that Britain was willing and able to leave without a deal, which would in turn pressure it to accept Britain's demands. However, it revealed a glaring contradiction which was to recur continually over the months and years to come. If Brexit was such a good idea, and all talk of costs, problems or disruption was simply Project Fear, then how could that be squared with making preparations for, for example, disruptions to food and medical supplies?

That question couldn't be answered by saying that leaving with a deal would not be disruptive, only leaving with no deal. That was partly because in that case no-deal preparations could hardly be a negotiating lever with the EU (because it revealed how damaging no deal would be for the UK) but mainly because some of the very people advocating ramping up no-deal preparations were also actually advocating no deal as a desirable outcome.

Again, Brexiters outside government could ignore these obvious contradictions, but the burden of them fell on those in government who were obliged to present no deal as a terrible outcome in order to garner support for its unpopular proposals for a deal. This became acutely obvious in August 2018 when one of the Ultras, Dominic Raab, as Brexit Secretary, released the government's technical papers on how to cope with no deal. In doing so, he had to claim simultaneously that it would be a calamity (to persuade MPs to support the government's deal) and that it would be easily dealt with (to rebut Project Fear). Similarly, a few weeks earlier, he had glumly promised that even if there was no deal the government would ensure that 'there is adequate food supply'.[82] It was hardly a ringing endorsement of Brexit.

## THE ROLE OF SECOND WORLD WAR NOSTALGIA[83]

Admittedly, there was a segment of the leave-supporting population for whom the privations of no deal were actually rather appealing. In the run-up to the referendum, it was widely remarked upon that one significant strand of the leave campaign channelled the British fixation with, and often mythologisation of, the Second World War. For example, Peter Hargreaves, the wealthy businessman who donated millions to the leave campaign, funding a leaflet to every household in the country, enthused that 'it will be like Dunkirk again'.[84] How big a part the Second World War played in the outcome of the vote is impossible to say, but it seems plausible that it was a factor amongst the demographic that voted most strongly for Brexit, the over 50s. This would be not so much people who remembered the war – by now a relatively small number – but the generation or two who grew up in its shadow.

Whatever role it may have played in the referendum, invocations of the war permeated the years that followed to an extent that they became clichés. Hence, for some, suggestions that no deal might bring shortages, queues or rationing might have a kind of nostalgic appeal. Indeed, this nostalgia fed into the growing demands from the Ultras to leave with no deal in broader ways. As the outgoing German ambassador to Britain had remarked earlier that year (and for which he had been pilloried by Brexiters for 'mocking' them), it had two components.[85] One was the idea of Britain 'standing alone' as in 1940, and the other a narrative that linked, as Boris Johnson had explicitly done, Nazi Germany's attempt to subjugate Europe with the present-day EU's actions. Such references took on a new life in the aftermath of the Chequers proposal, with Johnson cultivating his supposedly Churchillian image as Prime Minister-in-waiting, insisting in his resignation speech as Foreign Secretary that the Brexit dream 'is dying, suffocated through needless self-doubt'.

To these two components could be added others, including references to 'the Blitz spirit' and, quite often seen on social media in particular, the idea that Europe owed Britain a debt of gratitude from the war that ought to be repaid by accepting all its negotiating demands and by waiving the financial settlement. Unlike other European countries which had managed to get over defeat and occupation, Britain, it seemed, could not get over having – all alone, as it was often presented – been victorious.

Whilst being partly about invoking an idea of British stoicism in the face of privation, these wartime references also fed the more destructive development of what had now become an ingrained narrative of EU 'bullying' and 'punishment'. This was almost invariably accompanied by invocations of German aggression and sometimes of French duplicity. It was pernicious in its blackguarding of the EU but also in what it said about Britain. This was not so much because it relied upon a highly partial picture of the war but because it presented an entirely unrealistic picture of Brexit. Britain, through its vote and its government's actions, had chosen to leave the EU and to do so in the form that entailed losing all of the benefits of the single market. It was not 'bullying' or 'punishment' to be expected to face the consequences of that choice. This was not 1940. Britain had not been forced by foreign aggression to 'stand alone': it had chosen to do so.

## THE GROWING DEMAND
## FOR ANOTHER REFERENDUM

Even if wartime motifs played well with a certain kind of leave voter, they only served to re-enforce the argument of remainers that what was in prospect was a calamity. Their concerns had been not just ignored but mocked ever since the referendum, and this, along with the growing chaos, fuelled a more organised movement. The People's Vote campaign which, as noted in the previous chapter, had been launched in April 2018 and had already staged one large demonstration, was increasingly active and attracting growing support. In July, the former Education Secretary Justine Greening became the first high-profile Tory MP to publicly propose a 'second' or 'confirmatory' referendum, although there were ongoing difficulties in defining what question would actually be asked in such a referendum.

The most common idea, and that advocated by the People's Vote campaign, was a vote between whatever exit deal was negotiated (i.e. the Withdrawal Agreement) and not leaving at all, but other ideas included having 'no deal' on the paper as well. This would have entailed some way of ranking options or transferring votes between options, which clearly would have been more complex. Another difficulty arose from the perennial issue of the distinction between the exit deal and the future terms deal: until any future terms deal was made, there could be no vote on what Brexit actually meant in practice, but once the exit terms deal was done there could be no way of remaining in the EU. Thus a vote that gave a genuine choice between a fully defined Brexit and remaining in the EU was impossible.

The arguments for another referendum, however the question was to be framed, were quite muddled, and the People's Vote campaign suffered accordingly. These included the long-standing one that the original vote had legally been only an advisory one, and the fact that the majority won originally had only been of those who voted, not the electorate as whole. As I suggested in Chapter One, these had very little political traction. Other arguments included the complex claims and counter-claims about funding irregularities and misuse of data by both official and unofficial leave campaigns in the 2016 referendum, and about possible Russian interference in that referendum. Whilst some remainers passionately believed – and still believe – that these were key issues, their wider political traction was, again, limited. That was partly because there was never a definitive 'smoking gun' moment to support these claims, and partly because it helped to fuel resentment amongst leave voters that they were being belittled and that remainers were 'bad losers' seeking to overturn a democratic vote.

Such arguments muddied the waters of what was otherwise a perfectly coherent and certainly not undemocratic case: the original vote had been on whether or not to leave, but there had never been a vote on the particular way of leaving. That indeed lay at the heart of all the problems that had followed. Therefore, once the way of leaving became specified (even if the full details of the future terms had still to be negotiated) it was entirely legitimate to ask the electorate whether or not this was what they wanted. Someone had to decide, so why not the public rather than MPs? It would not have been a re-run of the 2016 vote and could certainly not be called undemocratic since if the majority of voters still wanted to leave then they would be able to choose to do so. So although Theresa May and the Brexiters would undoubtedly have resisted another referendum anyway, the case for it would have been stronger if couched solely in such terms.

However the case was made, the growing support for it was undeniable. Towards the end of October 2018, the People's Vote London march attracted some 700,000 demonstrators, compared with the 100,000 at the June event. Their cause received a small boost when, at its annual conference, the Labour Party inched towards supporting another referendum in certain circumstances. It was already the unequivocal policy of the Lib Dems, Green Party, SNP and Plaid Cymru. It received an even bigger boost in December, when an ECJ ruling confirmed that it would be legal for the UK to revoke its Article 50 notification. This meant that, for the first time, it was undeniable that if another referendum resulted in a vote to remain in the EU then this would be legally possible to implement so long as it happened before the end of the Article 50 process.

## 'HUMILIATION' AT SALZBURG

As the domestic conflicts continued, the government had been engaged in negotiations with the EU over the Chequers proposal. However, any lingering idea that it would be adopted had been destroyed at the Salzburg summit towards the end of September, when the EU made it abundantly clear that it would not accept it. This was widely reported in the UK press as a 'humiliation' for Theresa May and for Britain, feeding the narrative of 'punishment'. Both she and the media spoke as if the EU's rejection of the proposal had been an 'ambush' with 'no reasons given'.

This was nonsense in both specific and general ways. The specific reason was that ever since the Chequers proposal was announced, and certainly since Michel Barnier's statement at the end of July, quoted earlier, it had been known that the EU would not accept it and why. The Salzburg rejection certainly didn't come out of nowhere. The more general point is that, for all the talk of being 'humiliated', the fundamental truth was that Britain had been humiliating itself, with May's facilitation. That was due to the refusal to face the realities of what Brexit meant and, in particular, the refusal to acknowledge the binary choice between single market membership and non-membership. This had been evident in every twist and turn of the government's position – quite as much (albeit in different ways) in the Lancaster House approach, which Brexiters supported, as in the Chequers proposal, which they didn't. These, and all the other variants that had been discussed in between, sought in some way to mix and match elements of membership with elements of non-membership.

It was quite misleading for the government to say, as May did again after Salzburg, that this binary choice was being forced upon Britain by the EU. In the run-up to the referendum it was precisely these two (plus a no deal, WTO option) which had figured as the forms that Britain's post-Brexit trading relationship could take. This had been clearly evident in, for example, the Treasury's modelling of these three options prior to the vote. It had also long been known that the form Brexit took would have profound implications for Northern Ireland.

The basic parameters of the choices available had been clear for months, stated over and over again by Barnier and others in the EU, and obvious to informed commentators in the UK. Every time, the response from both the government and the Brexiters had been either to ignore them and press on regardless, or to rail against these statements – which were invariably couched in polite, diplomatic language – as grotesque insults showing a lack of respect. These narratives, combining the self-pitying victimhood and bellicose nationalism which characterised Brexit throughout, reached a new crescendo in the fall-out from Salzburg. The dishonesty of the domestic debate had finally come into a head-on collision with objective reality. What was 'humiliating' was the refusal of the Brexiters and of May's Brexit government to be honest and realistic with themselves or with the British people.

Equally humiliating was May's response to what had happened in Salzburg, which was to call for the EU to come up with a form of Brexit which was acceptable to Britain. As noted in the previous chapter, this had been a recurrent feature of her approach to Brexit, as if it were a problem for the EU to sort out rather than a choice that Britain had made and was responsible for. Moreover, it was asking the EU to resolve the ever more polarised divisions within Britain which its own politicians, May included, had so notably failed to do. So, far from taking back control, she was left demanding that the EU 'show us some respect' whilst saying that 'we now need to hear from the EU what the real issues are and what their alternative is'.[86]

## THERESA MAY'S WITHDRAWAL AGREEMENT

Within a few weeks the EU had spelt this out, leading to the publication of a text for the draft Withdrawal Agreement in November. Many of its provisions had already, in form or in substance, been present in the phase one agreement, such as those relating to the financial settlement and citizens' rights. But on the core, contentious issue of the Irish border backstop there was a provision whereby, in the absence of any other agreement being reached in the future, the whole of the UK would remain in a single customs territory with the EU, whilst Northern Ireland would also remain in regulatory alignment with the single market.

As for reaching a different agreement that would avoid the backstop, this would be undertaken within the framework of the accompanying Political Declaration. Unlike the Withdrawal Agreement which, if ratified by both sides, would form a legally binding international treaty, the Political Declaration was a non-binding statement of intent about what the future terms agreement might contain. It was fairly vague in setting aspirations for 'an ambitious, broad, deep and flexible partnership' which would encompass both trade and security, and incorporated, at least by implication, some of the Chequers proposal ideas about a free trade area for goods. At the same time, it noted that the UK objectives included an end to freedom of movement of people and the ability to pursue an independent trade policy. Thus, hard Brexit remained the objective for the eventual outcome.

The timetable for creating the future terms agreement was to be that after leaving the EU on 29 March 2019 there would be a transition period in which the UK remained within the single market and customs union and other EU institutions – albeit with no political representation – until the end of December 2020. The transition period was, however, extendable if both sides agreed by the end of June 2020. As will become clear in Chapter Six, this timetable, set out in November 2018, was to prove significant in the very different circumstances of 2020.

The new backstop arrangements represented concessions by both the EU and the UK. The EU had moved from its proposal of a Northern Ireland-only backstop. This was a vital point to the UK government (at the time) because Theresa May had said that it would have violated the constitutional integrity of the United Kingdom. The UK had compromised by accepting that, if used, this backstop would not be 'time-limited' – that is, it would only cease if both sides reached an agreement which rendered it obsolete. This was a vital point to the EU because had it been time-limited or unilaterally revocable then it would have ceased to act as a cast-iron guarantee against there ever being a hard land border between Ireland and Northern Ireland.

In mid-November, the Cabinet endorsed the agreement – as well it might, since the government had negotiated it with the EU – but Brexiters denounced it as a 'betrayal'. Dominic Raab immediately resigned as Brexit Secretary, citing, in particular, the backstop, and its unlimited and unilaterally irrevocable character, as his reason. So too did some other government ministers. As with Davis, Johnson and Baker before them, when given the power to deliver something they regarded as 'true' Brexit, Brexiters were never able to actually do so. The Brexit they believed in remained something which could only exist as a utopian theory – any attempt to actually operational-ise it proved elusive in the face of practical realties, but rather than recognise that they called the operationalisation a 'betray-al' and retreated to the sidelines, where they could cling on to the utopian theory.

Apart from constitutional issues, Brexiters were also unhap-py because the backstop, if implemented, would preclude the UK undertaking its own trade deals, since it would still be in a customs territory with the EU and so, in effect, in the customs union. Equally unhappy were the DUP, because although the revised backstop was apparently enough to satisfy May that the integrity of the union was preserved, they pointed to the fact that it would mean a different regulatory regime for Northern Ireland. This seemed slightly bizarre since on many matters dear to them, such as abortion rights and same-sex marriage, they wanted to maintain different regulations. As we will see, in the light of what was eventually to happen it was not just bizarre but spectacularly ill-judged.

As with the Chequers proposal, just because the draft Withdrawal Agreement was unacceptable to the Brexit Ultras, that did not mean it was palatable to remainers, or even to softer Brexiters. For whilst being condemned by the Ultras as not being Brexit at all, or being Brexit in name only (BRINO), that was far from true. As the Political Declaration made clear, the eventual outcome sought by the UK was still hard Brexit, in the sense that the intention to end free movement of people precluded single market membership and the intention to have an independent trade policy precluded a customs union.

This is a crucial point because, later on, it came to be said (as it was of the Chequers proposal) that May's deal was a compromise solution which foundered on the refusal of both remainers and Brexiters to accept any compromise. But it was far from being a compromise. It was very much tilted towards the Brexiters in that it was hard Brexit. Remainers received nothing from it in the way that could have been said had soft Brexit been pursued. The reason Brexiters disliked it wasn't because it was a retreat from hard Brexit but because it was what hard Brexit looked like when translated from fantasy into policy. In particular it showed what hard Brexit meant once the realities of the Irish border and the Good Friday Agreement were accepted.

## THE BREXITERS' SEARCH FOR ALTERNATIVES

The fact that hard Brexit in practice ended up looking like BRINO and betrayal to the Brexiters was the backdrop to their persistent attempts to articulate how it could be otherwise. These had been rumbling in the background for many months, but gained momentum in the wake of the Chequers proposal. Both the ERG and the many groups and think tanks associated with them produced a string of reports in the summer and autumn of 2018 to try to break out of the remorseless reality that the Brexit negotiations had forced upon May's government.

These were invariably repetitions of the same basic set of ideas: either versions of 'Canada-style' Brexit or of 'WTO Brexit'.* The Canada model was often appended with a '+' or

---

\*   For basic descriptions of these models, see Chapter One and for more detailed discussion of the different meanings of a 'Canada-style' Brexit deal, see Chapter Six.

even a '+++' to indicate it would be more extensive than the Canada–EU deal. WTO Brexit was sometimes called the 'WTO deal' to avoid the negative connotations of 'no-deal Brexit', though misleadingly so since it was not a deal but the absence of one.

In whatever variant or using whatever terminology, there were persistent flaws or confusions in all these proposals. One reflected the recurring conflation of the two deals that needed to be done. So sometimes the Brexiters' proposals were presented as alternatives to the Withdrawal Agreement, but sometimes as possibilities for the future terms agreement. If the former, then the problem was that in the absence of a Withdrawal Agreement there would be no future terms agreement.

In other words, a Canada-style future terms deal (or any variant thereof) was not going to happen without first agreeing exit terms, and it was now abundantly clear, if it had not always been, that this would require agreeing on the core issues of the financial settlement, citizens' rights and Northern Ireland.

Perhaps the most peculiar version of this position was articulated by David Davis shortly after the publication of the Withdrawal Agreement. Arguing that a Canada-style deal would be the best outcome, he suggested that 'if we need to leave with no deal and negotiate a free trade agreement during the transition period, so be it'.[87] But the transition period would only exist if there was a deal, so this was simply absurd and, coming from someone who had been immersed in the Brexit process for two years as Brexit Secretary, truly outlandish.

As for a WTO Brexit, this might mean one with no exit agreement and no future terms agreement, or with an exit agreement but no future terms agreement. However, most Brexit Ultras insisted that the latter combination was unacceptable, not least since they still viewed the financial settlement in the exit agreement as conditional on a trade deal. So, at this time, in practice what the Ultras meant by WTO Brexit was both no exit agreement and no future terms agreement.

However, having no exit agreement would mean such massive disruption not just to trade but to things such as air travel that some Brexiters (though not the most hard-line) came up with the idea of a 'managed no deal'. This would mean that whilst there was no comprehensive exit agreement, the UK and EU would negotiate a series of mini-agreements to mitigate disruptions in specific areas. It was something of a non-sequitur, as it entailed a deal (or deals) without a deal and without, apparently, recognising the legitimacy of the EU's three core exit demands.

In any version of WTO Brexit there would be considerable damage to UK–EU trade (some Brexiters denied this, whilst others said it was a price worth paying) and, of course, the WTO would provide nothing in relation to non-trade issues, such as security. But the more fundamental problem was that all variants of WTO or Canada-style Brexit did not resolve the Irish border question because, as explained in Chapter One, that was a consequence of leaving both the single market and the customs union which was common to all of the variants of hard Brexit (i.e. Canada-style, WTO and 'managed no deal').

Whilst some Brexiters persisted in claiming that this was a non-problem invented by the EU, others recognised its validity and, as outlined in the previous chapter, proposed that various administrative and technological solutions existed, or could be developed, that would solve it. However, apart from the difficulties previously discussed, this approach contained within it a fundamental logical flaw. If it were the case that such solutions did, or would, exist, then the backstop would never be needed, or would come to an end as soon as they were developed. That was written into the Withdrawal Agreement. If and when the solutions existed, there was no possibility of the UK being 'trapped indefinitely' in the backstop. Given that, there should have been no basis at all for Brexiters not to back May's deal.

In fact, May's deal was precisely premised on the idea that there would be something like a Canada +++ relationship in the future terms agreement (it was certainly envisaged in both the Chequers proposal and the Political Declaration as being an extensive one and, moreover, as having a substantial non-trade component), and that the UK would develop alternative arrangements for the Irish border. This was exactly what the Ultras said they wanted. So the only basis on which they could fail to support it was either because they actually wanted an even harder (WTO) Brexit rather than 'Canada-style' or because, whatever they wanted the future terms to be, they knew that alternative arrangements and technological solutions were *never* going to exist and that their claim to the contrary was dishonest.

Notwithstanding this obvious flaw, the Brexiters continued to regurgitate the same arguments in the final months of 2018 and these eventually coalesced into what came to be called the 'Malthouse Compromise' of January 2019. As we will see shortly, it effectively drew together several of these ideas into a series of proposals. It was a 'compromise' not between the UK and the EU but between the factions within the Tory Party. The reason such compromise was needed was the extraordinary outbreak of open warfare between those factions when the Withdrawal Agreement came to the House of Commons in December 2018.

## THE FIRST MEANINGFUL VOTE

If it was ironic that the ERG had now discovered the virtues of rebelling against the government's Brexit legislation when before they had called it treachery, even more ironic was the fact that they were now in a position to vote down May's deal in its entirety. For this only arose because of the actions of the Amendment 7 rebels who in December 2017, as discussed in the previous chapter, had forced the provision of a 'meaningful vote' on the Withdrawal Agreement. At the time they were lambasted by Brexiters for their perfidy. Now it was the Brexiters' lifeline.

This meaningful vote was scheduled to take place on 11 December 2018, and as that date approached it became ever clearer that the government would be defeated. Labour (and the other opposition parties) would of course vote against it. Labour's position remained an ambiguous one in that it still advocated negotiating 'a strong single market deal', but without specifying what this meant in terms of the core issue of single market membership, and still advocated a permanent customs union apparently without recognising that this didn't solve the Irish border issue. Even so, they would clearly vote against the government's proposal. So would the unequivocally anti-Brexit parties.

Additionally, there were widely signalled rebellions in prospect from Tory MPs on both wings of the party. That meant the ERG and those of similar views, but also those who favoured another referendum or who advocated a variety of soft Brexit positions including, in some cases, members of the emergent 'Norway +' (later called 'Common Market 2.0') group. If this made for a strange assortment of rebels, those set to support the deal were equally mixed, comprising not only some Brexiters but also veteran Europhile Ken Clarke, who had been the only Tory MP to vote against triggering Article 50.

Apart from the fact that the deal agreed pleased almost no one, May's tactics in trying to sell it were counterproductive. Both in Parliament and in a slightly peculiar national tour, as if this were an election campaign rather than the prelude to a parliamentary vote, which was clearly intended to reprise the 'people versus Parliament' theme of the ill-fated 2017 election, she insisted that the only alternatives to her deal were no deal or no Brexit. The problem with that message was that in attempting to warn both sides of the dangers of opposing her deal, it gave each side a reason to do so. Many Brexit Ultras would be very happy to see no deal, whilst remainers would be very happy to see no Brexit.

This is another reason why the subsequent claims that remainers or soft Brexiters had been foolish to reject May's 'compromise' when it was on offer are mistaken, or, at best, rely on hindsight. For at the time it really did seem – and May herself was saying so – that all outcomes remained possible. It therefore made perfect sense for anyone who wanted a different outcome to May's deal to oppose it.

Not only were all outcomes still in play but there was an increasingly febrile debate about different processes through which they might be reached. Apart from another referendum, these included a Tory Party leadership challenge (either forced upon May, or provoked by her resignation), another general election, a national government of some sort, or a parliamentary vote to revoke Article 50 notification.[*]

Against this background, the parliamentary debate began. All the well-rehearsed arguments were out in force. Some of

---

[*] The latter idea gained a following after the ECJ ruling on revocability, referred to above. Strictly speaking, this hadn't been made before the meaningful vote debate began, but a pre-ruling had trailed it, and the final judgment was published whilst the debate was in progress.

the criticisms of May's deal were unfair or based on misunder-standings, in particular the suggestion made by both the Brex-iters and by Jeremy Corbyn that it was a flawed 'blind Brexit' because it did not include the deal on future trade terms. Of course, it was never going to do that. The demand of the Ultras was to 'drop the backstop', something repeated by Boris Johnson, who also called for half of the financial settlement to be made contingent on a future trade deal. None of this was remotely realistic and yet again, whether as a result of misun-derstanding or political opportunism, showed the perpetual confusion between exit terms and future terms.

A key moment came when the government lost a vote on a cross-party amendment led by Dominic Grieve, the Tory former Attorney General, who had also tabled the original Amendment 7 rebellion that had led to the meaningful vote itself. Its immediate significance was for what would happen if the government lost the vote on May's deal. Under the terms of the EU Withdrawal Act, the government would have twenty-one days to present a motion to MPs on what it planned to do. Grieve's amendment, which was comfortably passed, meant that such a motion would itself be amendable, meaning that MPs could vote on whether to add to it some requirements (such as: to hold another referendum). This was actually the third vote the government lost that day, one of the others being an historic one in finding the government in formal contempt of Parliament for refusing to publish legal advice relating to the Withdrawal Agreement. That was a literal example of the many ways that in a metaphorical sense Parliament got treated with contempt by the government during the Brexit process.

The wider significance of the Grieve amendment was that it marked the beginning of a period in which several back-bench MPs – including Grieve and Sir Oliver Letwin on the

Tory side and Yvette Cooper and Hilary Benn on the Labour benches – were to play a pivotal role. As we will see, this often involved using complex or obscure parliamentary procedures. Crucially, in the context of a hung parliament, they mobilised cross-party coalitions and, often, provided greater political leadership than came from either front bench.

### Postponement of the meaningful vote

With it now abundantly clear that it would lose the meaningful vote itself, after just three of the scheduled five days of debate the government suddenly took the unusual step of ending the debate and announcing that the vote would be deferred to an unspecified date. It was described by the Speaker of the House of Commons, John Bercow – who was to play a significant role in the months to come – as 'deeply discourteous' to MPs. In the meantime, the government committed to go back to the EU to seek 'further reassurances' on the central issue of the backstop.

Two days after postponing the meaningful vote, Theresa May faced another vote, this time one of no confidence in her leadership amongst Tory MPs, instigated primarily by the Brexiters. But it was a miscalculation on their part in that she won it fairly comfortably. Under the party's rules, this meant that she could not be challenged again for another year, and so somewhat strengthened her position.

Two days after *that*, May was in Brussels at an EU summit where she was told that there would be no further changes to the Withdrawal Agreement. In a recurrent motif, Jean-Claude Juncker was reported as saying 'there is an impression in the UK that it is for the EU to propose solutions. But it is the UK leaving the EU.'[88] There might be further warm words and 'clarifications' but no changes of substance, and in particular no agreement to put a time limit on the backstop. That should have been obvious, since nothing could change the fact that, to be a backstop, it could not be time-limited, and it was an issue that had already been discussed and agreed.

So as 2018 ended, all the familiar problems remained, with some new ones added. They ultimately rooted back to the fact that the referendum hadn't defined Brexit and that, whatever Theresa May thought, that vote in itself didn't provide the political basis for the form of Brexit she had devised. There had to be some political consensus built and by embracing hard Brexit she had failed to build it. Yet even as she continued to mouth the slogans of the hard Brexiters, thus making it impossible to bring anyone but them into a consensus, they themselves had disowned her.

In addition to that long-standing problem, as I have been at pains to stress, as the Brexit process had unfolded there had developed a nearly universal confusion in the UK between the exit part and the future terms part of that process. That arose in part because every Brexit model ever discussed was in fact a model for the end state, and not for the exit process. That had been latent in the row over sequencing versus parallelism, and was now overt in the parliamentary debate about the Withdrawal Agreement, and the Political Declaration about possible future terms.

For whilst much of the focus of that debate was on the Northern Ireland backstop in the Withdrawal Agreement, it failed to recognise that the backstop was an aspect of the relationship between that agreement and the future terms. So every time Brexiter MPs stood up in Parliament to demand that the government negotiate a Canada-style deal instead of the Withdrawal Agreement, they were ignoring the fact that such a deal could not be done until after the Withdrawal Agreement. They were also ignoring the fact that if by 'Canada-style' they meant something less than the more extensive agreement on goods trade implied by the Chequers proposal then the backstop would be necessary. Their proposed solution to what they so disliked was, in fact, its cause.

By the time the first meaningful vote was eventually held in January 2019 it was inevitable that the government would lose. Perhaps the only surprise was the scale of the defeat, which at 230 was the largest in modern history. Yet the following day, the government survived a no confidence motion. Thus a truly bizarre situation now existed in which Parliament apparently had confidence in the government whilst overwhelmingly rejecting not only its central and pretty much only policy, but a policy which concerned the entire shape of the country's economic and geopolitical strategy. Belatedly, May proposed to 'reach out' to the opposition parties to try to forge some consensus, but at the same time made it clear that her existing 'red lines' were non-negotiable.

## THE AFTERMATH OF THE
## FIRST MEANINGFUL VOTE

The parliamentary gridlock was now a matter of widespread public debate and could be heard discussed on trains and in pubs as much as in newspaper columns. As in Parliament, that discussion had become even more sulphurous because the culture war between leavers and remainers had now morphed into a series of factional disputes in which any and every position could be, and was, denounced by others as a 'betrayal'. The most obvious manifestation of that was that pro-Brexit supporters of May's deal were denounced for betraying 'true Brexit', whilst 'true Brexiter' opponents of her deal were denounced for betraying Brexit in one or both of two ways. Firstly, they stood accused by some Brexiters of opening the door to another referendum and the potential abandonment of Brexit. Secondly, they were accused of creating the possibility of no deal, in contrast to the promises of the leave campaign.

That situation had been inherent in the Brexit project as a whole, since any actual delivery of it would not satisfy all, or even most, Brexiters. But 'betrayalism' had now spread much further, with bitter infighting between People's Vote advocates and 'Norway +' supporters (both of whom were, of course, in turn regarded as traitorous by the May deal Brexiters and by the Brexit Ultras).

All this was still mainly at the level of vicious words, insults and threats, but at the end of January Britain's most senior counter-terrorism officer Neil Basu warned that the febrile atmosphere of the debate was in danger of fuelling far-right terrorism. Given that the Labour MP Jo Cox had been murdered by just such a terrorist during the referendum campaign, it was hardly a warning to be taken lightly. Meanwhile, some Brexiters were talking openly of the possibility of civil unrest were another referendum to be held. It said much for how things had developed that the prospect of a democratic vote in a democratic society could now be regarded in such a way.

In Parliament, a string of strange votes was held in January and February. In one, MPs resolved that they wished to avoid a no-deal Brexit. But that would happen by default if nothing else was done (e.g. seeking to extend the Article 50 period), and yet they voted against an amendment that would have created a mechanism to avoid that default. So the original vote against no deal was a peculiarly meaningless gesture.

In another vote, in a plot worthy of *Yes Prime Minister*, Theresa May instructed her MPs to support the 'Brady Amendment' (named after Graham Brady, the Brexiter MP who proposed it), which rebelled against her previously stated policy that the

Withdrawal Agreement could not be renegotiated, to the effect that the Northern Ireland backstop should be renegotiated so as to be replaced by 'alternative arrangements'. So here the government was committing itself to a position that had already been rejected by the EU and abandoned by the government itself.

The day after that vote, in a very rare public statement, Sabine Weyand, the EU's deputy Brexit negotiator and trade specialist, pointed out that, as regards alternative arrangements and technological solutions for the Irish border, UK negotiators had tried and failed to identify these. But, she pithily observed, this was not their fault, since such solutions 'do not exist'.[89] She also pointed out what should have been obvious, that the negotiations over the Withdrawal Agreement were now closed. The passage of the Brady Amendment was perhaps the most glaring example to date of UK domestic politics proceeding in a vacuum, as if Parliament voting for something imaginary could make it true.

## The Malthouse Compromise

As these votes progressed, a new, somewhat related, Brexit rabbit hole was opened up. The grandiosely named 'Malthouse Compromise', named after housing minister Kit Malthouse and more prosaically called 'Plan C' consisted, confusingly, of a Plan A and a Plan B.[90] As mentioned above, there was nothing new about either of them. They were retreads or amalgamations of various documents that had been circulated by the ERG and allied groups for several months. But, significantly, this initiative had the support of some of those on the more remain wing of the Tory Party, such as Nicky Morgan who had been one of the Amendment 7 rebels. That significance, again, was a purely domestic one – it was designed to broker a compromise, or shared position, between these two wings. That is to say, the Malthouse Compromise was not a proposal for a compromise between UK and EU positions but between the factions within the Tory Party.

Malthouse Plan A was effectively the existing Withdrawal Agreement with the backstop ripped out, to be replaced by 'alternative arrangements'. So, essentially, the Brady Amendment. If Plan A failed then Plan B was effectively the 'managed no deal' canard, whereby there would be no Withdrawal Agreement but, nevertheless, an agreed transition period and various side deals on security and so on. Implicitly, as with Plan A, the envisaged future trade relationship was Canada +++, but Plan B also invoked the more recent ERG factoid, GATT Article XXIV (discussed in the previous chapter).

All these ideas had been endlessly debunked by a series of experts yet, whilst not going so far as to endorse it, May called the Malthouse Compromise 'a serious proposal that we are engaging with sincerely and positively'. Given that, by virtue of the Brady Amendment, she had committed to go back to Brussels again to try to amend the backstop she had more or less embraced Malthouse Plan A. And there could be little doubt that what most of the 'Malthousers' wanted from that was for it to be removed altogether. Otherwise, presumably, most of them wouldn't support any amended deal when it came to the 'second meaningful vote'. Then, the pressure would be on the government to adopt Malthouse Plan B as the pre-ordained direction of travel from Plan A. As so often, May was unwilling or unable to confront her backbenchers with reality.

A useful way of thinking about all this is to imagine the converse situation. Suppose that the EU had, at this late stage, announced that despite what had been agreed in the negotiations it would only be by, say, increasing the financial settlement and changing the backstop back to being Northern Ireland only that it would be possible to secure sufficient support from the European Council and Parliament. The outrage of Brexiters can easily be guessed at, and the UK response would almost certainly have been a flat refusal.

## A 'special place in hell'

In the absence of such insight, events continued to go round in circles. In February, pointing to the core reason for this, Donald Tusk spoke of there being a 'special place in hell' for those who had led the campaign for Brexit with no plan for delivering it.[91] This provoked much manufactured outrage from Brexiters (strangely forgetting the far more vicious comments they had made about the EU) that 17.4 million leave voters had been insulted, although it had very clearly been aimed at the leaders, not the voters.

Tusk's remark had a deeper significance than restating (albeit colourfully) the obvious fact that the Vote Leave leaders had not had a plan for Brexit. He made it clearly knowing that, as Irish premier Leo Varadkar pointed out to him when he did so, the British press would have a field day. It was a demonstration of the fact that the EU leadership were simply no longer interested in trying to mollify Brexiters or to tread carefully around British political sensibilities. That was important given that many British commentators and politicians were urging the EU to do exactly that. But whilst the British polity had danced to the Ultras' tune for so long, and continued to do so, the EU would no longer try to accommodate them. Expectations to the contrary were another example of the self-contained nature of UK domestic politics.

Equally, Tusk's remarks were revealing of something else which was far more uncomfortable for remainers, for all that they may have agreed with his diagnosis of the Brexiters' irresponsibility. What he had said was clearly unhelpful to their cause – for example, if there were to be another referendum it would be quoted endlessly by Brexiters claiming that it showed that EU leaders were arrogant and disrespectful to British leave voters – and anyway, as he also made clear in his statement, he now regarded that cause as a lost one.

Thus, the dynamic of the relationship between the EU and the remain campaign had changed decisively once the Withdrawal Agreement was drawn up. From then on, for the EU polity, Brexit was effectively a done deal. Remainers might be pro-EU, but the EU was no longer pro-remain. That didn't mean, of course, that there were not plenty of individuals, including politicians, in the EU who still hoped that Brexit might be reversed. But the institutional logic had now shifted, and Tusk's remarks were a reflection of this.

## THE SECOND MEANINGFUL VOTE

As February gave way to March, the political chaos in Britain continued. A new Independent Group of eleven MPs – mainly Labour but some Tories – left their parties. They were all remainers, or supporters of the softest of Brexits, and their defections exposed the deep splits within the main parties, as well as further complicating the arithmetic of parliamentary votes.

Perhaps of greater significance was that, in the face of the near certainty of a vote forcing it upon her if she did not accept it, Theresa May conceded that if she lost the second meaningful vote then there would be a vote on whether to seek an extension to the Article 50 period, something she had adamantly refused to countenance in the past. Meanwhile a slew of alternative ideas was under discussion, of which arguably the most coherent was the Kyle–Wilson plan, whereby MPs would support May's deal subject to it being put to the electorate in a referendum. This at least had the merit of addressing the actual choice that had to be made, but, mainly due to lack of support from the Labour front bench, it failed to make progress.

Separately, the Attorney General, Geoffrey Cox, came under sustained pressure to give legal advice to the effect that the UK could unilaterally leave the backstop were it to come into force. This could have given the Brexiters sufficient reassurance to vote for May's deal. Whilst himself a staunch Brexiter, Cox, to his credit, refused to give such advice. To do so would have been nonsensical as it would mean the backstop was no longer a backstop, and would certainly have meant the EU would not sign the deal. (This brief episode in the Brexit process was to be echoed later, in more significant ways, in 2020, when the government proposed unilaterally breaking the terms of the successor to the backstop, as discussed in Chapter Six).

Unsurprisingly, when the second meaningful vote was held on 12 March 2019 the government again lost, albeit less heavily than the first time. In the following days, further votes confirmed that MPs did not want no-deal Brexit (but again without specifying how to avoid it) and, of passing interest, a vote on pursuing the Malthouse Compromise was lost. This should have marked its death, but it was to reappear, zombie-like, several more times in the months to come. More importantly, the amendment on whether to seek an Article 50 extension was passed.

This, certainly at the time, seemed to be a huge moment. For almost two years Theresa May had repeatedly and almost robotically insisted that, come what may, Britain would leave the EU on 29 March 2019. Suddenly, with just two weeks to go until that date, that apparently impregnable dam had been breached. Admittedly, the extension to be asked for was only until 30 June – this being the last date before which, if the UK had not left, it would be necessary to hold elections for the European Parliament. And, in the event, the extension offered by the EU was only until 22 May (if the UK ratified by 28 March) or 12 April (if it did not). Even so, it was a threat to Brexit happening at all and, correspondingly, provided a boost for remainers.

## A 'NATIONAL EMERGENCY'

Britain now faced a 'national emergency' according to a highly unusual joint statement by the heads of the CBI and TUC. A military planning team was activated in the Ministry of Defence in preparation for no deal (bizarrely, in a nuclear-proof bunker, which sounded like Project Fear by any standards). Other preparations were subject to hundreds of government gagging orders. Whether this was to prevent alarm at how far-reaching the plans were or ridicule of their feebleness was, by definition, impossible to know.

The phrase 'Bercow's bombshell' joined the list of Brexit jargon. It referred to the ruling by Speaker John Bercow that MPs couldn't be asked to vote twice on the same proposition, which therefore precluded a third meaningful vote. This was widely reported as resurrecting some arcane rule from the 1700s. In fact, it merely confirmed what had been custom and practice since then.

What was noteworthy was that Theresa May had sought to break with custom and practice. Noteworthy, but not surprising. May's actions and Bercow's ruling occurred against a background in which May had repeatedly sought to evade or downgrade the role of Parliament. That went right back, of course, to her ill-fated attempt to prevent a vote on triggering

Article 50, and her efforts to prevent the meaningful vote on the final deal (these two things are sometimes, wrongly, conflated), as well as the many other ways in which she had been both literally and metaphorically in contempt of Parliament. So although Bercow was inevitably denounced as a remainer (and from his public statements this would seem to be true), his conduct throughout this period is better understood by his commitment, which long preceded Brexit, to defending the rights and privileges of the legislature against the executive.

The consequences of Bercow's bombshell were difficult to interpret. One reason for that was the utter confusion amongst Brexiters about May's deal. Since it was represented by different pro-Brexit factions as delivering Brexit *and* as betraying it, it is not surprising that some saw Bercow as their saviour and others as a saboteur. Remainers, meanwhile, scented an opportunity. As for May herself, she made a quite extraordinary televised address to the nation.

Even at this distance of time, it is difficult to overstate what an appalling travesty it was, and how inadequately it spoke to a country in such a deep crisis. Despite all that had occurred, she still refused to speak seriously and honestly about what was happening and why. Instead, replete with all her trademark awkwardness – repetitious clichés, a liverish and slightly spiteful tone – and her peculiarly unpleasant stare, she presented herself as the tribune of the people against the machinations of MPs.

This was dishonest, dangerous and ill-judged. The dishonesty came from the obvious fact that much of the delay and most of the division in Parliament arose from her own decisions on the timing and nature of the Brexit process. Far worse was the explicit pitch of the people versus MPs. This was a direct affront to the notion of representative democracy and deeply irresponsible at such a febrile and unstable time. It ramped up the populist betrayal narrative. She did not quite use the 'enemies of the people' and 'crush the saboteurs' language, but that was the message.

For a Prime Minister to spit out the words 'motions' and 'amendments' as if the basic mechanisms of parliamentary democracy were appalling perversions was shocking. But, of course, it was all of a piece with that long history of contempt for Parliament. Later she claimed that her tone was due to 'frustration' but it was part of a pattern of behaviour and, anyway, quite out of place in the context.

In any case, her message was incoherent in its own terms. She must have known that 'the people' were as divided as the politicians. There was no unitary 'people' for whom she could purport to speak, and to imply otherwise was, indeed, to embrace populism. And it was tactically ill-considered. Most obviously, it was far more likely to alienate the MPs whose votes she needed than to bring them on board. Additionally, the only audience to whom her message of being protector of the people's will against treacherous politicians would appeal was that which had already written her off as 'Theresa the Remainer'. In many ways that one short TV appearance was a microcosm of her premiership.

## INDICATIVE VOTES AND THE COOPER ACT

With a third meaningful vote apparently ruled out, and shortly after the biggest march and rally yet by the People's Vote campaign, towards the end of March 2019 MPs embarked on a first round of 'indicative votes'. Whilst non-binding, the purpose of these was to try to establish whether there was any one Brexit policy that commanded majority support. If so, this might be a basis for government policy (though quite what government would then enact it was unclear, given the circumstances). This again was an innovative procedural device, developed on backbenchers' initiative in the face of government opposition. But the outcome was inconclusive, as no single proposal commanded a majority. The nearest to do so was a proposal to be in a customs union with the EU.

This was the point at which the divisions between the various groups opposed to hard Brexit became glaring and very much deserving of criticism. I've suggested that the subsequent criticism of them for not supporting May's deal is misplaced, because that was still hard Brexit, but in the indicative votes they had an opportunity to decisively shift away from that with votes on EFTA membership, on Common Market 2.0, and on a version of the Kyle–Wilson plan which would have led to a referendum. The following week, in the second, and as it turned out final, round of indicative votes they again had the option of Common Market 2.0 or of the actual Kyle–Wilson plan, amongst others. They failed to support any of them, as not enough adherents to each of these ideas were willing to vote for the other, close but different, proposals. If there was a moment at which soft Brexit finally died, along with any lingering possibility of an outcome that most of the population could – arguably, at least – have lived with, it was this.

Crucially, between the two rounds of indicative votes, a third meaningful vote had been held, avoiding the Bercow ruling by voting just on the Withdrawal Agreement not, as before, on the Political Declaration as well. Once again, the government lost substantially, although by a smaller margin than before. Partly because of their growing fear that Brexit might be abandoned entirely, partly because of Theresa May's promise to resign if she got her deal approved, some of the Ultras, including Boris Johnson, this time voted in favour despite all the opprobrium they had heaped on it. But the self-styled 'Spartans', the most hardcore of the ERG, did not.

The first week of April 2019 provided some of the most incredible scenes ever seen in the House of Commons, including naked protesters in the public gallery (this was nothing to do with Brexit, but a demonstration about climate change) and a flood of what was initially reported to be sewage, though later turned out to be water, in the chamber. A very unusual move saw MPs take control of the business of the Commons so as to propose legislation (rather than it being proposed by the government) in order to also control decisions about further extensions to the Article 50 period, leading to the 'Cooper Act' being passed, named after Yvette Cooper, the Labour MP who proposed it. Along the way, an amendment led to a tied vote which was lost on the basis of an, again, unusual Speaker's casting vote, adding to the drama.

The Cooper Act was, however, rendered redundant because before it had passed Theresa May had sidestepped it by requesting another extension from the EU, this time to 30 June. The process through which that Act had arisen, though, proved significant in developments later in the year.

I have only sketched the parliamentary dramas of spring 2019 lightly, ignoring many of the sub-plots and complexities. No doubt they will be the subject of many far more detailed analyses in the coming years. Even so, it should be stressed just how significant they were, not so much because of all the procedural intricacies, but because they were a direct reflection of the wider debates and disputes within the country. For all that May and many others railed against these 'political games', and for all that they engendered an atmosphere of uncertainty and crisis, they were in fact laudable in that Parliament was doing its job. The crisis was not because of any defects in Parliament but because the job it had been set was so divisive and so poorly specified.

## MAY'S DEMISE

In the event, the EU decided to extend the Article 50 period until the end of October 2019,[92] with Donald Tusk advising Britain 'not to waste this time'. It was advice that went unheeded. May's premiership staggered on, and she held further talks with the Labour Party. But, again, these were doomed to failure due to her insistence on her own red lines. In any case, despite their obvious ideological differences Corbyn and May were quite similar at a personal level – stubborn, humourless, intellectually unimaginative – so their meetings were unlikely to achieve much. There was talk of a fourth meaningful vote or of further indicative votes, but it came to nothing. It was clearly only a matter of time before she would resign, and on 24 May 2019 she did so, setting in train a leadership contest in the Tory Party to determine who would be the next Prime Minister.

The consequence of the Article 50 extension was that Britain would now hold elections for the European Parliament. Some Brexiters, infuriated that leaving had been delayed, spoke of doing all they could to disrupt the business of the EU whilst still a member. They seem to have had no idea – or, more likely, simply did not care – about how much damage such statements did to Britain's reputation or to the prospects of future negotiations with the EU. And the European elections now gave a fresh platform for Nigel Farage and the motley collection of candidates standing for his new Brexit Party to inject even more poison into the already toxic situation. Those elected proceeded to drag the country's reputation further into the mire with childishly insulting stunts in the European Parliament that many British people found embarrassing and shameful.

## The Tory leadership election

As for the Tory leadership contest, even had the candidates not been minded to do so, it involved pandering to a small and generally elderly party membership which was now virulently pro-Brexit. So with the honourable exception of one of the candidates, Rory Stewart, it became a bidding war to take the most extreme positions. It was a sign of just how polarised the Brexit debate had become in the previous three years that Stewart – who in the leadership contest embraced leaving the single market and customs union – was described as an 'ultra-remainer'. What might, conceivably, have been a fresh chance to sensibly debate the realities of Brexit was squandered and, instead, all the old saws about GATT Article XXIV and 'alternative arrangements' for the Irish border were out in force.

Boris Johnson was always the favourite candidate, and in a contest rewarding whoever could shrug off practicalities and espouse hard-line rhetoric without regard for its consequences he had obvious advantages. In the end, what emerged were four key requirements that party members demanded of their next leader: to renegotiate the backstop, to rule out further extensions to Article 50, to embrace no deal as an outcome if necessary, and to be ready to prorogue Parliament.

The first three of these were by now the boilerplate positions of the Brexit Ultras. Ironically, they had also been held by Theresa May. She had found that the backstop couldn't be renegotiated, and had had extensions forced on her, but the Ultras believed that, despite her having said that 'no deal was better than a bad deal', she had not truly believed it and the EU knew it. That, in turn, they saw as being because she did not truly believe in Brexit. Therefore, they reasoned, a different Prime Minister, who was a true believer, would have the leverage to renegotiate the backstop. This would mean no more extensions were needed or, alternatively, that Britain would leave with no deal – as many of them would actually have preferred anyway.

There was perhaps a certain naïvety in thinking that Johnson was such a true believer – he had famously equivocated about whether to campaign for Brexit or not and, anyway, was not exactly well-known for strong attachment to principle. But the committed Brexiters knew that he did have a strong attachment to his own advancement and so felt confident that he would be bound to deliver their agenda. Moreover, they believed that he was an electoral asset who could see off both the newly rejuvenated Farage and the threat of Jeremy Corbyn.

The fourth of the leadership tests, prorogation, was something new. Prorogation, the process of suspending Parliament, had first been mooted in January 2019 by Jacob Rees-Mogg as a way of thwarting MPs' attempts to prevent a no-deal Brexit. It was actually a rather strange suggestion for him to make since, had Theresa May been minded to, it could also have been a way of forcing through her deal, to which Rees-Mogg was adamantly opposed. In any event, no one took it very seriously at the time. But during the leadership contest, willingness to prorogue emerged as a Brexit virility test of the candidates and, unlike Jeremy Hunt, his rival in the final vote amongst the party members, Johnson repeatedly refused to rule it out.

To no one's surprise, Boris Johnson was elected as party leader and on the afternoon of 24 July 2019 became the new Prime Minister. Within hours it became abundantly clear that something else had happened. Just over three years since the referendum result, and with a scheduled three months to go until Britain left the EU, the Vote Leave campaign had now, in effect, become the British government.

## CHAPTER FIVE

# BREXIT REDUX

*From Theresa May's resignation*
*to the 2019 general election*

The advent of Boris Johnson's premiership marked at once a new beginning for the Brexit process and a re-run of much of what had already occurred. In some ways it was as if the previous three years had been expunged, and all the reasons that had led to Theresa May's deal taking the form it had were forgotten. This enabled all the same old claims to be made about how quick and easy a deal with the EU could be, and Johnson's early speeches remained very much in the mould of campaigning for Brexit rather than facing up to the practicalities of delivering it.

In consequence, the months between Johnson becoming Prime Minister in July 2019 and the general election of December often seemed like a re-run, at higher speed, of many of the debates and dilemmas of the previous years. This was not least because the same brutal realities of parliamentary arithmetic remained for Johnson as they had for his predecessor, with his MPs split on Brexit and his government dependent upon the support of the DUP. Similarly, the starkly polarised divisions within the population as a whole, and between the constituent nations of the United Kingdom, were unchanged.

This background conceivably presented Johnson with the

opportunity to reset the entire approach to Brexit and, during his leadership campaign, some had wondered if this might happen. In particular, he might have sought to create a more consensual, less economically damaging, softer Brexit. This was sometimes expressed by comparison with 'Nixon in China' – a reference to the way that US President Richard Nixon had created a rapprochement with communist China during the 1972 visit – the point being that Nixon could only deliver this domestically because of his impeccably anti-communist credentials. In the same way, since Johnson, unlike May, had been the leading campaigner for Brexit, he had more credibility to take a softer line. Plus, if anyone could get away with a 180-degree revision of positions he had held just a few days before then, surely, some commentators argued, it was Johnson.

This was probably never a realistic idea, if only because of the hardness of Brexit sentiment amongst the Tory Party membership that had just elected him, and instead a very different Nixon comparison became relevant. This was the 'madman' approach. In Nixon's case it meant convincing the Soviet Union that he was 'mad' enough to trigger a nuclear war, thereby assuring that deterrence would work. In the present context it meant that Johnson was totally prepared to leave the EU with no Withdrawal Agreement at all and would thereby be able to force an exit deal on his terms.

## A 'HARD BREXIT COUP'

It became immediately clear that Johnson was going to go down the second of these 'Nixonian' routes when he purged the Cabinet of almost all who did not support hard Brexit, and demanded that all support the position that the UK would leave the EU on 31 October, with or without a deal. At the same time, a whole swathe of former members of the Vote Leave campaign were brought in as special advisers, most notably Dominic Cummings who, as Johnson's closest adviser, was given an unprecedented degree of power whilst disdaining conventions of traditional political conduct.

Cummings was to be a pivotal figure in the coming months. Widely supposed to have been described by David Cameron as a 'career psychopath', his abrasive and fanatical personality had served the Vote Leave campaign well. But that contributed to the way that, as will be shown, the administration was to operate far more as a campaign than as a government. Cummings also notoriously alienated many MPs and Cabinet ministers, including many committed Brexiters, whom he often treated with contempt (for example, he had described David Davis as 'thick as mince').[93] He had similar, if not greater, scorn for the civil service. He seems to have had an excessive regard for his own intelligence, which was fed by media lionisation of his supposedly Machiavellian skills. Yet again and again during his time in Downing Street he made tactical and strategic errors, so that the phrase 'classic Dom' became shorthand amongst journalists and commentators for a seemingly clever ruse which immediately, and spectacularly, backfired.

Overall, the new government had a distinctly 'cultish' feel about it in which nothing mattered other than commitment to the most extreme approach to Brexit, including legal and constitutional conventions. One commentator described it as 'a hard Brexit coup',[94] invoking the image of the Jacobins of the French Revolution. It was an image that had been used by others seeking to capture the political psychology of the Brexit Ultras, in which revolutionary purism led in ever more extreme directions, ever more ruthlessly pursued, and accompanied by dramas of loyalty and betrayal.[95] Now that psychology had moved from the fringes to the centre of government. This, combined with Cummings's political maladroitness, almost immediately led to chaos and crisis, to a degree that eclipsed even the worst moments of May's administration.

The initial situation the new government faced was that its critics were considering a whole array of different scenarios that might avoid a no-deal Brexit. The febrile parliamentary atmosphere that had characterised Theresa May's final months had by no means abated during the summer recess. MPs and commentators discussed possibilities including a vote of no confidence in the new government and the formation of a government of national unity. But what most spooked Johnson and Cummings was the possibility of MPs again taking control of the business of Parliament, as had happened with the Cooper Act, so as to force the government to seek another extension to the Article 50 period.

It was a totemic issue for Johnson that such an extension would not happen, for two reasons. One was, simply, the 'do or die' commitment he had given to that date during his leadership campaign, a commitment reinforced when, in early September, he said he would rather 'be dead in a ditch' than extend. The other, related, reason was the belief that he and other Brexiters shared: that only by sticking to that date would the EU take seriously the threat of no deal. Their belief remained that if the EU had believed this of May then it would have given her a better deal, a better deal being defined now primarily in terms of the removal of the Northern Ireland backstop. This, as explained in the previous chapter, had emerged as the Brexiters' central objection to May's Withdrawal Agreement, and its removal had been a key issue within the party leadership election.

## THE PROROGATION OF PARLIAMENT

Faced with the possibility of Parliament preventing this approach by removing the possibility of no deal, Cummings's preference for confrontation and Johnson's attraction to risk and gesture-making coalesced to bring the idea of prorogation to the fore. Suddenly, what had been discussed as a bare possibility during the leadership campaign was being talked about as an imminent prospect. And hardly had such talk begun than, at the end of August, the Queen's assent was sought and obtained to prorogue, or suspend, Parliament with effect from 9 September until 14 October 2019.

It is difficult to overstate the extent of the political shockwaves this created. Governments rule by virtue of their ability to command a majority in Parliament, so for a government to suspend Parliament for fear it did not command such a majority was to strike at the heart of parliamentary democracy. There was also particular alarm because prorogation brought the Queen into political conflict in a way that was at odds with her purely ceremonial role. Ministers sought to argue that prorogation was just the standard practice in the circumstances of a new Prime Minister, but in truth its length and purpose were unprecedented.

Indeed, the whole situation was, at least in its particular combination of circumstances, an unprecedented one. Changing Prime Minister between elections was by no means new, flowing from the nature of the British parliamentary system, but as political reality had become increasingly 'presidential' in recent decades, so too had the legitimacy of such leadership changes declined. Formally, of course, it was (and is) still the case that electors vote for MPs and the government is formed by whichever party can command a majority, with that party free to change its leader at any time. But, with elections dominated not just by parties but by their leaders, in recent years an informal question mark had come to hang over such changes. This was all the more so given that Johnson did not command a majority in the parliament he was now intending to suspend. Moreover, he was doing so in order to potentially enable a no-deal Brexit that was not mandated by any election, nor by the referendum result.

Brexit Ultras did not see it that way, of course, since they claimed that the referendum mandated any Brexit outcome, including no deal, regardless of Parliament and, moreover, claimed that the parliamentary vote to trigger Article 50 (though it was a vote they had opposed in the first place) meant that MPs had already endorsed no deal as a possible outcome. That partly reflected the inherent problems of inserting the direct democracy of a referendum vote into a system of representative democracy. Yet, even if it was believed that the referendum vote trumped Parliament, the same old problem remained that that vote had not specified what form Brexit should take. The Brexiters' position was therefore flawed, because they themselves regarded certain forms of Brexit as not being real Brexit – specifically, this had been their view of May's deal. So it could not now make sense to deny Parliament a vote on the way that Johnson proposed to undertake Brexit. Nor could it make sense to say that by voting for Article 50 MPs had endorsed any outcome of the Article 50 process, since May's deal was also one such outcome, yet they had considered it perfectly legitimate for Parliament to reject that.

In sum, the Brexit Ultras – and, now, this meant the British government – had come to regard Parliament entirely opportunistically as a tool to be used to prevent a form of Brexit they did not like in the name of *representative* democracy, or to be dispensed with, if it seemed likely to prevent a form of Brexit they did like, in the name of *direct* democracy. In parallel, they claimed the referendum result, which had not endorsed any particular form of Brexit, as having been a vote endorsing their preferred form. This had long been incipient, but prorogation brought it all to a head, creating a near-revolutionary situation in which Brexit mattered to them more than parliamentary democracy (or any other institution) and, in consequence, Brexit had become not just about leaving the EU but about the very nature of the British constitution.

That diagnosis can in no way be undermined by the related Brexiter claim that this was a 'remainer parliament'. For one thing, unless they really envisaged the end of all parliamentary democracy, it had been elected since the referendum, and so even if it was a remainer parliament then it had been voted for by the same electorate as had voted in the referendum and had a legitimacy of its own. In any case, that parliament had rejected May's Brexit in large part because of Brexiters voting against it rather than because of remainer opposition, and, indeed, many erstwhile remainer MPs had voted for it. So the situation was hardly one of remainers having thwarted Brexit.

## The reaction to prorogation

The announcement of prorogation led to demonstrations across the country, and legal action,* initially in the Scottish Court of Sessions but ultimately to end in the Supreme Court, to have it ruled unlawful. Meanwhile, Parliament returned on 3 September and immediately embarked on precisely the course of action Johnson and Cummings had wanted to avert. Namely, in a similar way as had happened before with the Cooper Act, a motion tabled by the Conservative MP Sir Oliver Letwin

---

* There had already been some anticipatory legal action but it now continued.

enabled the House of Commons to propose its own legislation to avoid a no-deal Brexit.

This was supported by twenty-one Tory rebel MPs, all of whom lost the party whip (another, Phillip Lee, defected to the Liberal Democrats) although ten of them were subsequently to have it restored. It was a draconian response. It also meant that at a stroke the government lost its majority, even with DUP support. The twenty-one included very senior parliamentarians such as Kenneth Clarke and former Chancellor Philip Hammond, and it is worth recording the fact that many of them sacrificed their political careers on a point of principle. Subsequently, two government ministers, one of them being Jo Johnson, the Prime Minister's brother, resigned in protest at the rebels' treatment.

The Letwin motion paved the way for the Benn Bill, led by Labour MP Hilary Benn, the key provision being that if there was no Withdrawal Agreement in place by 19 October then the Prime Minister would be obliged to apply to the EU for an extension to the Article 50 process until 31 January 2020. The Commons comfortably passed this on 4 September and on the same day refused to endorse an attempt by Boris Johnson to force a general election.

Despite an attempted filibuster in the House of Lords, the Benn Act received Royal Assent on 9 September. On that same day MPs also – by use of an obscure mechanism – forced the government to release documents about the prorogation and about 'Operation Yellowhammer', the plans to deal with the consequences of a no-deal Brexit, which revealed just how dire those consequences would be (Brexiters inevitably dismissed it as the work of 'remainer civil servants').

A few hours later, in the early morning of 10 September, amid angry scenes in the House of Commons, Parliament was prorogued. It was a shameful and – as it turned out – illegal moment in British political history.

## THE IMMEDIATE AFTERMATH OF THE FAILURE OF PROROGATION

The illegality of prorogation was definitively confirmed by the Supreme Court on 24 September. It was a judgment of huge significance, not least for the calm, rational and – naturally – judicious manner in which it was delivered by Lady Hale, the President of the Court. That was a symbolic reminder that for all the rhetoric, high emotions, lies, insults and threats of the Brexit process there was still a bedrock of protection for civilised and ordered society.

The sober tone was in keeping with the content of the ruling. For all the furore it provoked, it was at heart unremarkable. No great legal knowledge was needed to see that if a government were able to suspend Parliament whenever it wanted and for whatever reason, or for no good reason, then parliamentary democracy would be meaningless. What was on display was the British constitution working as it should, with the judiciary playing its role in maintaining the separation of powers that underpins democracy.

If the judgment was unremarkable in confirming the basic principles of parliamentary democracy, what was truly remarkable was the forensic dismissal of each and every part of the government's case, with the unanimous agreement of all the judges. It was a damning and unequivocal demolition of what the government had done and the justifications it had provided for doing so, to the extent of confirming that, in fact, it had in a legal sense done nothing – that is, prorogation had not, as a matter of legal fact, occurred.

This made the reaction of Johnson, when Parliament resumed

the day after, all the more out of place. Like an insolent school-boy, his mealy-mouthed 'acceptance' of the judgment – as if, somehow, he was making a concession – was immediately followed by the claim that the judges had got it wrong. On what grounds? Simply the repetition of the argument that had been totally discredited by the judgment, namely that this had just been a normal prorogation for a Queen's Speech and had been nothing to do with preventing MPs debating and voting on Brexit.

But to that was added the inevitable, dangerous line that this judgment was all about blocking Brexit, inviting Brexit supporters to fill in the unspoken inference of judicial anti-Brexit bias which had already been made explicitly in the media. It was a line that harked back to the 'enemies of the people' calumny of 2017 but, that apart, it was ludicrous even in its own terms. If Johnson was being truthful in saying that it was just a normal prorogation for the Queen's Speech and nothing to do with attempting to prevent Parliament intervening in Brexit, then how could ruling prorogation unlawful be an attempt to derail Brexit? His very critique of the judgment of his case was based on the acknowledgement that his case was a lie.

This was not the only way in which Johnson's reaction to the failure of prorogation was to further intensify the bitter divisions within politics and wider society. Repeatedly, he jabbed at what he insisted on calling the 'Surrender Act' – meaning the Benn Act on seeking extension if there was no deal – with its connotations of treachery and lack of patriotism, sneeringly dismissing objections and even pleas not to use this term. Even when an MP, in tears, told him how such language linked directly with the death threats she and many others were receiving, he persisted.

Shortly afterwards, Dominic Cummings all but condoned

abuse and threats against MPs by saying they were 'not surprising' and resulted from the failure to 'respect the result' of
the referendum and from MPs being disconnected from real
people outside London.[96] This was nonsense at every level given
the ambiguity of what respecting the result meant (largely due
to Cummings's own tactics in the referendum campaign) and
the fact that Brexiter MPs featured prominently in preventing
May's deal going through. It was also as absurd to depict the
nine million who live in London as 'unreal' as it was to portray
the rest of England, still less the UK, as a seething mass of
hardcore Brexiters. But, illogical as it was, it gave tacit licence
to intimidation.

Similarly, during this same period an anonymous Cabinet
minister warned of riots if another referendum were to occur.
By failing to make the obvious point that such riots would be
totally unjustified, such comments were less speculation about,
than implicit threat of, violence. Such politicians were, like
Cummings and Johnson, always very careful to avoid explicitly endorsing threats and violence but, rather like business
minister Kwasi Kwarteng's remarks about how 'many people'
(though not, naturally, him) believed judges to be biased
against Brexit, the dog whistles were loud enough for the deaf-
est mutt to hear.[97]

## THE COMFORT ZONE OF CAMPAIGNING

Much of this was the familiar culture war territory of the previous three years, but it had a new significance for two reasons.
One was the battle with Nigel Farage, now revivified by the
success of his Brexit Party in the European Parliamentary
elections. So in a re-run of the cleavages of the referendum
campaign itself, Johnson and Cummings were again in vicious
personal and political conflict with Farage and – if there were

to be another general election – would be competing with the Brexit Party for a similar pool of voters. Ramping up the culture war was useful for that, as well as keeping Johnson and Cummings in their preferred 'campaigning' comfort zone.

The second reason showed the limitations of staying in that comfort zone. Stoking the culture war was easy for Johnson and Cummings whereas their first couple of months in power had shown just how inept they were at government. The smash and grab approach favoured by Cummings, in particular, had spectacularly backfired. The 'nuclear button' of prorogation had been pressed, but the missile had failed to detonate. On the contrary, it had contributed to the growing sense, especially abroad, that the UK had a government which was contemptuous of the rule of law and was becoming increasingly unpredictable and untrustworthy.

Thus Helene von Bismarck, a well-known German historian specialising in British politics, argued that with prorogation Johnson had badly miscalculated how it would be regarded by the EU, and that it had done nothing to improve his reputation for being untrustworthy.[98] That reputation was partly a personal one to do with his years of writing anti-EU articles and his role in the leave campaign, but it now exacerbated the way that, especially since reneging on the phase one agreement about Northern Ireland (see Chapter Three), the UK polity as a whole was acquiring a reputation internationally for dishonesty. It was a reputation which was to worsen in the coming months, but already as sober a figure as Chris Patten, former Chairman of the Conservative Party, was warning that with prorogation, and other Brexit-related developments, Britain was risking a decline into being a 'failed state'.[99] The failure of prorogation did not remove its stain, with Johnson's bellicose reaction reported as causing 'despair' within the EU.[100]

But, beyond the damage to Britain's political culture and reputation, the prorogation manoeuvre had not just failed in its own terms but made matters worse. If it had been intended to prevent MPs from passing legislation to prevent no-deal Brexit it had, on the contrary, provoked and hastened them into doing so by passing the Benn Act. Moreover, in the process, the government had jettisoned its majority and massively inflamed divisions amongst Tory MPs by the savage treatment of the rebels. So it had even less control of the Commons, but could still not hold an election because MPs would not agree to that and, under the terms of the Fixed Terms Parliament Act, Johnson could not call an election without such agreement.

It was, indeed, 'classic Dom', but there was no sign that he or Johnson had learned the lesson, for, even now, Johnson was refusing to confirm whether or not he would comply with the Benn Act. And there was talk of yet more procedural chicanery, this time that the government might try to use an Order of Council to suspend the Act until after 31 October in order to force no-deal Brexit through.

## THE EMERGENCE OF 'JOHNSON'S DEAL'

Throughout the period of prorogation, there had been continuing discussions with the EU about renegotiating the Withdrawal Agreement even though, formally, the terms of the Article 50 extension precluded any such renegotiation. Indeed, the fact that these discussions were occurring was held up by Johnson as proof that his critics were wrong in saying that renegotiation was impossible.

But, as usual, this was disingenuous. There was no possibility of a renegotiation if it meant, as Johnson insisted it would, simply removing the backstop, but from mid-September leaks suggested that what might be in prospect was a reversion to a

Northern Ireland-only backstop. In other words, the revival of what had initially been agreed in phase one of the Article 50 negotiations but subsequently repudiated by Theresa May.

Johnson maintained in public that no such arrangement would be acceptable, but there was no sign that he really understood the nature of the problem which Northern Ireland posed for Brexit. Some reports suggested that he was flirting with the idea that a solution could be simply for Northern Ireland to stick to EU rules on food and livestock, until in a meeting with Jean-Claude Juncker he finally understood the magnitude of what customs and regulatory checks when outside the single market and customs union actually meant.[101] It wasn't exactly a surprise that Johnson was not on top of detail but it was indicative of how, even now, many of the leading architects of the Brexit project didn't understand even in a general way what it involved.

Perhaps as a result of the meeting with Juncker, the so-called 'SPS solution' (i.e. because it only involved sanitary and phytosanitary [SPS] checks on food and livestock, not other regulatory or customs checks) gave way to a formal proposal from the UK government for yet another model – the 'two borders solution'. Published at the beginning of October, this would have involved a customs land border (but not 'at the border') between Northern Ireland and Ireland, and a regulatory (i.e. single market) sea border between Northern Ireland and Great Britain. There would also be a periodic consent mechanism for the Northern Ireland Assembly (which at this time had not sat for two years).

This was supposedly the UK's 'final offer' but in fact gave rise to further negotiations during a very confused two-week period, during which some of the ugliest events of the entire Brexit process took place. Now, perhaps, forgotten – though not, I suspect, in Ireland – there were various statements about how the UK could bribe or alternatively bully Ireland into accepting these proposals. At the same time, a Downing Street 'contact' (widely assumed to be Cummings, though it was impossible to be certain) warned that, if the UK were obliged by the Benn Act to apply for an Article 50 extension, the government would regard any EU state agreeing to the application as being guilty of hostile interference, with consequences for security and other cooperation.

Again, as with prorogation, the use of such 'hardball' tactics did nothing for the ever-declining international reputation of the UK. In passing, it is worth recalling that at this period Brexiters misguidedly pinned much hope on Hungary, in particular, vetoing any extension request. And one of them, Tory MP Daniel Kawczynski, actually lobbied the Polish government to do so.[102] It was an example of just how extreme Brexiters had become that, having campaigned to 'take back control', one of them now sought for a foreign government to subvert what would be, if it happened, a decision of the British Parliament. It was all the more perverse given the government's warning against such interference were it to be in the direction of supporting extension.

The 'two border' proposal was never going to be accepted by the EU, because it still failed to recognise what the avoidance of an Irish land border actually meant. Suggesting that physical checks would be at designated places away from the border (at customs clearance sites, though the practicalities never got spelt out) misunderstood that the issue was not simply checks 'at the border' but one of border checks per se. Indeed, far from meeting the fundamental EU red line, deriving from the Good Friday Agreement, of there being no Irish land border, a leading customs expert was quoted as saying that this latest suggestion was 'the hardest border the UK has proposed'.[103] Moreover, the proposal also relied upon the still unproven possibilities of technology to minimise the extent of physical checks.

However, shortly after publishing the proposal, Boris Johnson held an impromptu meeting with the Irish Taoiseach, Leo Varadkar, following which it was suddenly announced that there was a 'pathway to a deal'. In the coming days this emerged in the form of yet another model, the 'dual customs solution'. What it meant in effect was that Northern Ireland would remain in the EU single market for goods and in the customs union (the 'dual customs' aspect being that goods moving from Great Britain to Northern Ireland would be differentiated from those destined to go on from there into Ireland and, hence, the single market). In practice, that would lead to both customs and regulatory borders being across the Irish Sea, hence this, which became the agreed solution, has since been referred to as the Irish Sea border. This solution also incorporated a consent vote to be held periodically in the Northern Ireland Assembly.

## THE SIGNIFICANCE OF JOHNSON'S DEAL

There were – and still continue to be – considerable uncertainties about how the very complex practicalities of this would actually work. But the essence of what had been agreed had two significant features. One was that, as had been trailed in the leaks of early September, the new agreement which emerged on 17 October was, indeed, to a very large extent the old phase one Northern Ireland-only backstop which had been rejected by Theresa May because it undermined the integrity of the United Kingdom.

It was for this reason, rather than being some great

negotiating triumph on the part of Johnson, that the EU accepted it, for it was what they had already negotiated almost two years before. Equally, in terms of domestic politics, like its original version it was a solution which was completely unacceptable to the DUP.

The second feature was more complicated, and insufficiently understood by many politicians and commentators at the time and some since. For, unlike either that initial phase one plan, or May's subsequent deal, the Irish Sea border solution was in fact no longer a backstop. The idea of a backstop was that it would come to be used *only* if no other means of avoiding an Irish land border could be found in the course of the future terms negotiations. But what Johnson had proposed in the 'two borders' solution and accepted in the Irish Sea border agreement was a 'frontstop' – that is, the *final* form of the arrangements for Northern Ireland *regardless* of the future terms negotiations.*

As noted in the previous chapter, many Brexiters had treated May's backstop as if it were the final form of the arrangements for Northern Ireland, and they regarded that as unacceptable. That was strange in itself since they claimed to believe in the viability of 'alternative arrangements' (technological and administrative solutions) which, were they to exist, would under May's deal have avoided any border at all. Yet Johnson had now agreed, in perpetuity, to an Irish Sea border. It was especially strange for members of what was formally known as the Conservative and Unionist Party.

---

\* It was and remains unclear what would happen if the Northern Ireland Assembly were to withdraw consent in the future. There would be a two-year period after that for the Joint (UK–EU) Committee to propose an arrangement which would protect the Good Friday Agreement. But the consent mechanism is complex and this situation may never arise.

It seemed highly likely at the time, and subsequent events have appeared to confirm it, that neither Johnson nor many of the Brexiters actually understood what it was the UK had agreed to. For Johnson, in particular, his lack of interest in detail and overwhelming desire to proclaim that he had successfully 'renegotiated' May's deal and 'removed the hated backstop' seem to have led him simply to agree the new deal regardless of the consequences. Moreover, he was at this point still committed to leaving the EU at the end of October and so, as so often in the Brexit process, the pressure of time led to making commitments which – as with the original phase one agreement – were either not understood or did not command genuine consensus. As we will see in the next chapter, what got hurriedly put together in these few weeks of October 2019 was to have major ramifications.

Whilst the main difference between May's deal of 2018 and Johnson's of 2019 was in the shift to the frontstop – overall, well over 90 per cent of the text of the two agreements was the same – this entailed two other important differences as well, one explicit and the other implicit. The explicit difference was that May's deal had included in the Northern Ireland Protocol commitments to maintaining a 'Level Playing Field' (LPF) with the EU on regulatory standards relating to labour, the environment, social rights, business taxation, and competition and state subsidies. Under Johnson's deal, these were moved to the Political Declaration.

The significance of this again relates to the recurring underlying issue of the Article 50 process, and of the sequencing of the Article 50 talks. To reprise, the process meant that there would be a legally binding treaty governing exit arrangements, consisting of the Withdrawal Agreement, including the Northern Ireland Protocol, but a non-binding Political

Declaration setting a framework for a potential future trade and other future terms agreement. In Johnson's deal, LPF lay – as Brexiters had always argued it should – within the domain of future terms, and should not be agreed to in the absence of a trade deal.

This, too, was to have major consequences in the coming months. So was a particular complexity within it, namely that one aspect of LPF – state subsidies for business – also resided in the (binding) new Northern Ireland Protocol and, indirectly, this could affect how such subsidies would operate in Great Britain. The consequences of this will be discussed in the next chapter but, for now, the point is just that in the rush to get his 'renegotiated' deal, Johnson left hanging many complex and difficult threads that would return to haunt the Brexit process.

In addition to the explicit differences between the May and Johnson deals there was also an important implicit difference, little remarked upon at the time. Throughout May's tenure in office there had been repeated promises that the eventual outcome would be 'frictionless trade'. It was never clear how this could be achieved once she had embarked upon hard Brexit, but remained her claim. And, indeed, it was partly for this reason that it made some kind of sense to claim that the backstop would never need to be used. It's possible, for example – we will never know – that in the end, the ideas for the future relationship contained in the Chequers proposal would have morphed into some form of soft Brexit, if only in order to avoid the backstop.

At all events, what happened in the early months of Johnson's premiership was the quiet acceptance that frictionless trade was impossible for the Irish border – hence, the frontstop, which was an acknowledgement that as that border could not be on land it had to be on sea, but that a border there must

be. But if that was true for the Irish border then it must be so
for other borders as well. In other words, there would not be
frictionless trade at Dover, or Harwich, or Holyhead, or Hull,
or any other part of the border between Great Britain and
the EU single market and customs union. It was the first, and
much belated, time that some Brexiters had accepted, if only
implicitly, that Brexit meant borders (though as will be seen in
the next chapter, others continued to deny it).

Hence, too, the government began to issue preparedness
advice for British exporters from which it was officially clear
for perhaps the first time that, just as critics of Brexit had long
warned, there would be substantial extra bureaucracy needed
to trade with the EU. Certainly, the ludicrous claim that David
Davis had made about having found a way for the UK to have
'the exact same benefits' as it had enjoyed as a member of the
single market and customs union by means of a future trade
agreement had been discredited. However, it would not be
until months later that any government minister publicly acknowledged the inevitability of border friction.

## THE FINAL PARLIAMENTARY DRAMAS

So Johnson had got his deal which, predictably, he pronounced
to be a great one. But he faced the recurring problem that
any particular form of Brexit, once defined, was invariably
denounced as insufficient by the most extreme Brexiters. In
particular, Farage and the Brexit Party insisted that it was a
betrayal of Brexit. Farage was bound to do so since, at this
point, his position was that any 'treaty' with the EU would
be a betrayal. This in effect meant that no deal was the only
true Brexit because any deal would take the legal form of a
treaty. He had no MPs, of course, but, as had been shown for
many years, plenty of influence both on Tory MPs and party

members. And then there was the DUP: committed Brexiters – indeed committed hard Brexiters – but with this new deal very abruptly discarded.

One of the most puzzling features of the Brexit story is that the DUP failed to see that anything other the very softest of Brexits was likely to be disadvantageous to their core interest of preserving Northern Ireland's union with Great Britain, the more so once the referendum result had showed that a majority in Northern Ireland did not want Brexit at all. The threat to that core interest was now abundantly clear. Johnson's deal would not just put an economic barrier across that union but it would also create a distinctive regulatory and customs connection between Ireland and Northern Ireland. That would tend to make, at least in due course, Irish political reunification more likely than it might otherwise have been.

Against this background, on 19 October 2019 the House of Commons held a highly unusual Saturday sitting – dubbed 'Super Saturday' by the media, as if it were some sports tournament – whilst on the same day the People's Vote campaign held what may have been its largest London march. That confluence serves as a reminder that, as throughout 2018 and 2019, the parliamentary dramas had as their counterpart (or were the counterpart of) a wider politics of contestation taking place in demonstrations, newspaper columns, social media and even in family and workplace debates and arguments.

The date of the sitting was significant, and explained the urgency, because it was the one specified in the Benn Act as the deadline for Johnson to send a letter requesting an Article 50 extension if a deal hadn't been agreed. Of course, a deal *had* in principle been agreed – with the EU. But there was a problem, arising from the near-total breakdown of trust between the government and Parliament that had developed both under

May and, even more, under Johnson, and which was exacerbated by the now well-established ruthlessness of the Brexit Ultras.

For there was a loophole in the Benn Act which meant that if MPs approved Johnson's deal then its provisions would be satisfied, and no extension would need to be sought. But if the subsequent domestic legislation needed to implement the deal was then collapsed – perhaps by the ERG, perhaps even by the government itself, given Johnson's avowed position that the Benn Act was illegitimate and that he would thwart it by all means possible – then so too would the deal with the EU collapse before it had been formally signed. But, if so, by that time the provisions of the Benn Act would have lapsed because the date of 19 October it specified would have passed. Thus a no-deal Brexit could still occur, despite the Benn Act which had been designed to prevent it.

To forestall this possibility, yet another backbench amendment, again led by Sir Oliver Letwin, was put down, withholding agreement to Johnson's deal until the necessary domestic legislation had been passed. This motion was passed, not least because of the votes of those erstwhile Tory rebels who had lost the whip over the Benn Act and those of the DUP. In turn, the government abandoned their plan to vote on Johnson's deal that day.

So, over and over again, the actions of Johnson – like May before him – had provoked the circumstances of greater mistrust, greater suspicion and greater acrimony that thwarted his plans. And how did the government react to Saturday's defeat? By Jacob Rees-Mogg, now the Leader of the House, using the device of a point of order (which meant he did not have to answer questions about it) to announce that on Monday there would be a new 'meaningful vote' – that is, a vote on whether to accept Johnson's deal or not, the same question as the motion that had not been voted upon because of the Letwin Amendment. And, as points of order were made in response, Rees-Mogg arrogantly walked out of the chamber of the House of Commons.

It was, yet again, contemptuous of Parliament and, perhaps most foolishly, of those on his own benches who had just supported the Letwin Amendment. It could also only increase the suspicions about the government's intentions which had led them to do so. For, if held and passed, the Monday vote would mean the extension letter being withdrawn, and the possibility of no-deal Brexit (via the loophole just described) would be reinstated.

Two immediate questions now arose and were quickly answered. The first was whether Johnson would, as required by the Benn Act, send the extension request letter to the EU. It was in a way extraordinary that this was in doubt, since not to have complied would have involved him breaking the law. But there had been persistent rumours, stoked by Johnson's own evasive statements, that he would either refuse to send the letter or send it along with another one negating the first. The eminent legal commentator David Allen Green wrote that even the suggestion that a British Prime Minister might defy the law was in itself to undermine the principle of the rule of law, and noted that it was 'a sign of how extreme and toxic the political atmosphere has become in Britain that the unthinkable has become plausible'.[104]

In the event, very late that Saturday evening, Johnson sent the letter, albeit petulantly dispatching an unsigned photocopy of the legally prescribed text, along with another letter which, whilst not countermanding the first, indicated his displeasure at having to do so. It was another example of how self-defeating for his own and Britain's standing it was to make threats that he could not deliver on, and in particular the emptiness of the idea that he could treat the law with disdain. And whilst the damage would certainly have been greater had he refused to send the letter, some had been done anyway, as Green had said. There was now an established pattern that could only intensify the sense that the Brexit process in general, and Johnson's leadership in particular, was pulling the country ever further from the norms of liberal democracy and the rule of law.

The other immediate question was whether Speaker John Bercow would allow a fresh meaningful vote on Johnson's deal to be held on Monday, as Rees-Mogg had stated. Or would this, as had happened with Theresa May, be treated as an attempt to get MPs to vote twice on the same motion? The answer turned out to be the latter, to the outrage of Brexiters in Parliament and the country. Yet, as before, it was not an unprecedented decision and, for all that the Brexiters deemed it anti-Brexit, was consistent with Bercow's long-standing commitment to championing the powers of the legislature against the executive, whether on the subject of Brexit or anything else. Indeed, as at least some backbench Brexiters acknowledged, Bercow had over many years been intensely supportive of their voices being heard.

## The Withdrawal Agreement Bill

The consequence of Bercow's decision was to leave as the government's only option the introduction of the domestic legislation needed to implement Johnson's deal (i.e. because this would satisfy the Letwin Amendment such that MPs would not ratify that deal prior to the passing of that legislation). This set the stage for what would turn out to be the last of the great parliamentary Brexit dramas.

The legislation in question, the Withdrawal Agreement Bill (WAB), did pass its 'second reading' by a majority of thirty. This represented a degree of success that had eluded Theresa May and might have been the basis for Johnson to have achieved Brexit. The problem was his insistence on an extremely curtailed timescale for debate of the WAB, as well as a refusal to provide an economic impact assessment of his deal. This in turn was driven by his continued implacable desire to leave the EU on 31 October despite having had to send the Benn Act letter seeking extension.

The timescale represented another instance of Johnson, like May, treating Parliament with disrespect, and as an inconvenience. It was a totally unnecessary provocation: even if the WAB had passed in this compressed timescale, then the 31 October date would all but certainly have been breached anyway, if only to allow European Parliament ratification. If the concern was 'wrecking amendments' it was pointless, as such amendments could have been laid anyway. As so often, with Johnson (and, presumably, his adviser Cummings) it was posturing. And, again as so often, it proved to be a tactical error, since MPs voted by a majority of fourteen against the motion setting the WAB's timescale.

There were three features of the October 2019 introduction of the WAB that later in the Brexit process were to become significant. First, during the debate, speeches by some of the most hard-line Brexiters suggested that they felt no joy in what had been agreed, and although they were willing to support it did not regard it as the Brexit they had really envisaged. More generally, the impression given was that the government had something to hide in seeking to ram it through so quickly. It was no good saying, as some did, that Parliament had had years to discuss every aspect of Brexit. The fact was that, after all those years, it was the first time that anyone had seen in precise, detailed, legal terms what Brexit (at this stage) meant. In the next chapter, we will see how some of those MPs who had voted for it came to repudiate it, and some who had said there was no need for more discussion subsequently claimed that the lack of discussion had meant they did not understand what they had voted for.

Second, it became clear as the WAB was debated by MPs (initially, it seemed, to the surprise of the Brexit Secretary himself) that the new arrangements for Northern Ireland would involve new customs processes and other controls for goods travelling between Great Britain (i.e. England, Scotland and Wales) and Northern Ireland. This further underscored the reasons for the DUP objections to the deal for, indeed, it showed how transactions between the two parts of the same country were going to be pretty much on a par with trading goods between separate countries. There could hardly be a greater affront to Northern Irish unionism.

This, along with the different regulatory arrangements for Northern Ireland, exposed the stark truth at the centre of Johnson's deal, which was that after Brexit the UK would no longer be a single market for goods. Expressed in that way it is quite remarkable. There had been long debates about whether or not the UK could and should remain in the (European) single market after Brexit. Never was it envisaged that, in order to leave that single market, the UK's single market would be brought to an end.

Third, and most surprisingly, in that it was not entailed by Johnson's deal with the EU and so had not hitherto been known, the WAB deprived Parliament of the right to force the government to seek an extension to the transition period in order to prolong post-Brexit trade talks, should that be necessary. This was significant to what would happen – and very soon – after Brexit day, if and when it came, because a potential new cliff-edge would arise if there was no trade agreement in place by the end of the transition period at the end of December 2020 and if the UK had not asked for an extension by 1 July 2020 (something Johnson had already said he would not do).

Thus, just at the moment when Parliament had thwarted no-deal Brexit in the meaning of 'no Withdrawal Agreement', it was being invited to set up the possibility of no-deal Brexit in the new and different meaning of 'no future terms agreement'. Moreover, by that point there would be no 'revoke Article 50' option available as a conceivable final defence against the new version of no deal, because it would come after the end of the Article 50 period, so Britain would have left the EU.

For all of these (and other) reasons, it was clear that there was plenty to debate in the WAB, and much that MPs might want to amend, hence their refusal to agree to the government's timescale. Brexit was once again in a kind of limbo. But it did not last long. On 28 October MPs finally acceded to Johnson's request – his third – for a general election, to be held on 12 December. The next day, the EU once again extended the Article 50 period, this time to the end of January 2021. For remainers, Brexit had again been averted and, perhaps, might yet be avoided altogether. For leavers, the prize had just slipped tantalisingly out of their hands, but was still in sight.

It was more than three years since the referendum but the UK's future still hung in the balance.

## THE 2019 GENERAL ELECTION

There remains to this day considerable controversy about the decision by the opposition parties to allow the 2019 election.

That controversy goes well beyond what it meant for Brexit but certainly includes that. In particular, many remainers believed both at the time and since that it was a massive error by those parties and MPs who were pro-remain. Yet, at the time, there were good reasons to think otherwise. On the one hand, the fact that the WAB had passed its second reading reasonably comfortably made it more than likely that, if Johnson relented on the timescale, it would eventually pass. On the other hand, it had repeatedly been made clear that the House of Commons was not going to pass a vote for another referendum, which was the only politically viable way of preventing Brexit (a point I will return to shortly).

In these circumstances, the only realistic route to remaining in the EU was via a Labour administration, perhaps especially a minority one reliant on SNP and perhaps Lib Dem support (though they were ruling out a pact with Labour), and perhaps some other small parties. It's true that Labour's Brexit policy remained a contorted one, but it was clear enough in supporting a referendum on the deal that it would renegotiate with the EU, with the other option being remain (the contortion lay in the kind of deal they envisaged, but, in terms of remainers' hopes, that was neither here nor there). So although with the benefit of hindsight it was, from a remainer perspective, the wrong decision, it was at the time a justifiable risk.

In some ways, again at the time rather than with hindsight, the bigger risk was for the Tory Party and for the Brexiter cause. For if the writing was on the wall for remain after the WAB passed its second reading, it seemed wiser for Johnson to push on, agree a revised timetable, get his deal passed and then hold an election having 'delivered Brexit' after which, assuming he won a decent majority, he could drop any amendments that had been forced upon him to get the WAB through. Going for broke with an immediate election looked like the familiar pattern of Cummings's aggression and Johnson's risk-taking, which had ended so badly for prorogation.

It was true that the Tories had a lead in the opinion polls, but most commentators agreed the outcome was highly unpredictable, and the 2017 election had shown how fragile an early poll lead could be. Moreover, there was some doubt as to how well Johnson would stand up to the scrutiny of a general election, despite his reputation as a campaigning maestro. General elections throw up unpredictable encounters with the public, probing interviews with tough inquisitors and, perhaps, awkward televised leadership debates. Plus, with Johnson, there was the omnipresent possibility of some personal scandal emerging. It was telling that during the Tory leadership campaign his 'minders' had been at pains to keep him in the background. There was a reason for that – they knew his capacity to implode. For very different reasons, he might prove no more effective on the stump than had Theresa May. Equally, as in 2017, Jeremy Corbyn might surpass expectations.

Beyond his own character and abilities, Johnson was politically vulnerable on two fronts. One key question was the extent to which remainers would make remain their sole priority to the extent of voting tactically for whoever was the most conducive candidate in their constituency (this would also be likely to make national opinion polls misleading). There was no formal 'remain alliance', but various websites made it quite easy for voters to work this out. The other key question was what Farage's Brexit Party would do. Johnson's Achilles heel amongst leavers was having failed to deliver on his repeated, high-profile, central pledge to have left the EU, 'do or die', on

31 October. If Farage ran a full-on campaign against the Tories for having 'betrayed Brexit' then he could hurt them badly, losing them seats even without gaining many, if any, himself.

For various reasons none of these risks eventuated. This is not the place to analyse the election campaign as a whole.[105] But, in brief, although it is certainly arguable that Johnson didn't campaign well, and avoided most debates and interviews, he did prove persuasive to, especially, some traditional Labour voters in hitherto safe Labour 'red wall' seats. And remain voters were not as single-minded as might have been expected. In some cases (e.g. Tory remainers) this may have been because they were more averse to voting for Labour under Corbyn than to Brexit; in others (e.g. Labour remainers) because the memory of Lib Dem support for austerity was more important than avoiding Brexit.

One particular issue was that the Lib Dems – who might have expected to have reaped the same kind of reward from remainers for their anti-Brexit stance as a decade previously they had from opponents of the Iraq War for their resistance to that – had adopted a policy which even some of the most committed remainers found indefensible. This was to revoke the Article 50 notification without a further referendum if they were to form the next government. It was totally pointless in itself, since no one could seriously believe they would win the election, although their leader, Jo Swinson, insisted that she did. But, aside from that, it had a clear problem of legitimacy: surely, only another referendum could annul a previous one?

The issue here wasn't one of legality – for revocation without referendum would have been perfectly legal – nor was it one of democracy, for it is certainly arguable that if enacted by a government elected with that central to its manifesto, revocation would be democratic. But legitimacy is ultimately a matter of widespread public perception rather than legal and political theory. And although it is true that some leave voters would have regarded another referendum as lacking legitimacy, they would surely do so in greater numbers and with much greater reason in the case of revocation, and would be joined in that by at least some remainers.

In any case, just suppose that the Lib Dems had won and enacted revoke. Then, what would stop a subsequent Tory government deciding, without any referendum, to leave the EU? For if Parliament alone could decide on revocation, why not on Brexit Mark 2? Whether or not that possibility ever came to pass, it also pointed to the question of exactly what kind of member of the EU would the UK be after revocation. The only way that would be good for both would be a wholehearted recommitment (or, one might say, for the first time a wholehearted commitment) by the UK to the EU. How could that possibly be achieved on the back of a revocation which even if undertaken by a majority government would, very likely, only have had the backing of a minority of voters given the first past the post system? Especially in the toxic politics and culture that obtained, it would have been a recipe for disaster for both the UK and the EU.

It was no good saying, as some revoke advocates did, that since the 2016 referendum was deeply flawed in its set-up, conduct and interpretation there was no need to be finicky about how to annul it. For, as discussed earlier in this book, that argument only had cut-through with those who already held that view. The previous three years had shown that it had no traction at all with those who saw the referendum result as inviolate, even if they recognised its flaws, which many did not and were never going to. Legal reality and political reality aren't the same.

Of course, something doesn't have to be good as a political principle to be good as a political tactic. But although it offered a clear and distinct political positioning for the Lib Dems, it was quite hard to see what kind of voters, not already committed to voting Lib Dem, would now change their minds. Revoke was a policy for their core vote, and any swing voters attracted by it were likely to be offset by those uneasy about or even hostile to it. And, inevitably, it made an easy target for journalists and political rivals who could paint it as 'undemocratic'. So almost every interview and debate involving the Lib Dems in the election campaign got hijacked by that accusation. The Lib Dem revoke policy, far more than their support for holding the general election, was a massive error.

As for the threat to Johnson from the Brexit Party, initially Farage declared, as expected, that Johnson's deal was not 'real Brexit' and was virtually the same as staying in the EU. Hence he threatened to stand a candidate in every seat unless Johnson agreed a pact whereby the policy became one of 'clean' – in other words no-deal – Brexit. As his campaign launch speech made clear, Farage's proposal rested on the endlessly discredited proposition that it was possible to tear up the Withdrawal Agreement and 'invoke' GATT Article XXIV (see Chapter Three). It was a nonsense in the strictest sense of the word because, stripped to its core, it meant 'we don't need a deal because we can have a deal'.

Admittedly, it wasn't very long ago, during the Tory leadership campaign, that Johnson himself was blustering about the 'GATT XXIV option', but since becoming Prime Minister he had ceased to do so. Presumably, his civil servants had managed to explain to him its utter fatuity. But, even if that were not so, there was no way that he was going to accept the Farage 'offer', for two reasons. One was the well-documented antagonism between Farage and Dominic Cummings. The other was that Johnson's central challenge was – like David Cameron's in calling the referendum – to remove Farage (whether as UKIP or Brexit Party) from the political board. That couldn't be done by forming a pact with him.

In the event, Farage caved in, and only contested seats not won by the Tories in 2017. The reasons he gave – that Johnson had committed not to extend the transition period and to seek a 'Canada-style' deal – were unconvincing, as those commitments had already been made before Farage's change of heart. Conspiracy theorists suggested he had been bought off with the promise of a peerage but, like most conspiracy theories, that was untrue and has since been proved so. More likely, it was due to pressure from his supporters and allies who perceived that splitting the leave-supporting vote would risk Brexit not happening.

For these and other reasons Johnson's key message held sway. It was the deeply dishonest one that he had an 'oven-ready Brexit deal' so that voting for him would 'get Brexit done'. That appealed, for obvious reasons, to committed leave voters but also to many others who, regardless of how they had voted in the referendum, were by now heartily sick of the seemingly interminable Brexit process. Sick, indeed, of the very word Brexit. But it *was* dishonest, because as had so often been the case, it conflated the Withdrawal Agreement deal with the future terms deal. Johnson did have the first deal 'oven-ready', if MPs voted for it, but the second had still to be negotiated with the EU.

Throughout the campaign, this basic truth was obscured by Johnson, but he was aided and abetted by Corbyn who, in a televised leaders' debate, talked of the trade deal he would do with the EU which would then be put to a referendum.

But not only did he still, after all these years, show no under-standing of the difference between single market membership and a free trade agreement, he also, like Johnson, confused or concealed the fact that any such trade deal would not be the subject of the Withdrawal Agreement but of the future terms deal. This meant that it could not, as Corbyn said it would, be put to a referendum alongside a remain option because, by then, the UK would have left the EU. As with Johnson it was either profoundly dishonest or, equally likely, reflected his ignorance of, and lack of interest in, what the Brexit process actually involved.

It was the final illustration of Corbyn's inadequacy and in-competence in engaging with the major political issue of the period of his elevation to front-line politics. Not just in the elec-tion, but in the hung parliament of 2017–19, when he could have had a decisive influence on Brexit, he failed to do so in large part because of his barely concealed sympathy for 'Lexit'. Effectively, he abdicated leadership on Brexit and left it to Labour back-benchers like Hilary Benn and Yvette Cooper to do what they could to prevent the inevitable damage that Brexit would do to the ordinary workers Labour was created to represent.

As a result of this and other factors – including the fail-ure, for the most part, of the media to ask sufficiently tough questions or to challenge false or misleading assertions[106] – this final chance for the UK to have a serious public debate about the practicalities of Brexit was lost in favour of slogans and misinformation, and by the desire of both main parties to cam-paign as if Brexit were not the central issue facing the country, impacting on every other policy area. It had not happened in the referendum, nor in the post-referendum flux, nor the 2017 election, nor the 2019 leadership election. Now it had been squandered again.

So in December 2019, when Johnson's Tory Party won a thumping eighty-seat majority and with almost all of the potential rebels amongst his MPs expunged, the die was cast. There was no longer any possibility whatsoever that Britain would remain in the EU, even though almost all opinion polls since the referendum had shown the majority were against leaving. The Brexiters had comprehensively won.

Yet there was still no certainty as to what being out of the EU meant.

## CHAPTER SIX

# BREXIT GETS REAL

*From the 2019 general election to the*
*end of the transition period*

**W**ithin days of the 2019 election, Boris Johnson's Withdrawal Agreement Bill was passed, with minimal debate or detailed scrutiny, by a large majority. There was no opposition from his own MPs, for all the dissident voices within the Tory Party had disappeared or gone into deep hiding. The likes of Oliver Letwin and Dominic Grieve, who had led previous rebellions, were no longer in the Commons but even if they had been this was no longer the hung parliament of 2017 to 2019.

Even so, beneath the surface, there were mutterings which would later become important. The ERG and similarly minded Tories, stronger than ever numerically, were almost bound to support Johnson's deal, not least since they had just been elected on that platform. But whereas they had backed it before the election on the basis that Brexit might be lost altogether if they did not, they were now obliged to so despite regarding it as the unloved product of May's deal (to which it was in many respects similar) and the circumstances of what they regarded as the previous 'remainer parliament'. It was likely that in due course this lack of enthusiasm would come out into the open.

Once the domestic legislation was enacted, as it was in January 2020, the way was clear for the UK to sign the Withdrawal Agreement and Political Declaration with the EU and, in turn, for the UK to leave on 31 January 2020. It did so with little in the way of fanfares or jubilation, except from a small number of the most committed, and certainly wasn't generally greeted as some great day of national liberation. In fact, Britain left without Brexit having had majority support in the opinion polls for almost the entire period since the referendum.

Polls also showed that 56 per cent thought that it would be economically damaging, and only 21 per cent that it would be economically beneficial.[107] Small wonder as, earlier in the month, a study by Bloomberg Economics calculated that it had already cost the UK £130 billion, and estimated a further £70 billion before the end of the year.[108] Indeed, throughout the year there were to be ever more desperate warnings from businesses and others about the economic damage that Brexit was already causing, and what worse damage was in prospect. But the comment allegedly made by Boris Johnson in June 2018, 'fuck business', seemed to have now virtually become government policy.[109]

Unsurprisingly, at the time of leaving there was on all sides of the debate within the UK a flurry of reassessments of what Brexit meant, and repetition of long-familiar arguments. There was certainly little sign of any national unity about the direction the country had taken. Abroad, too, there was much commentary, but here there was more consensus, with an editorial in the *Irish Times* recording that 'no state in the modern era has committed such a senseless act of self-harm'[110] being typical of the overseas media.

## WHAT DID 'GETTING BREXIT DONE' MEAN?

One reason why these debates continued to rage was that, despite Johnson's claim at the election and when signing the Withdrawal Agreement, Brexit had not been completely 'done'. So it was quite ludicrous of him to try, as he did in January 2020, to insist that the term 'Brexit' should no longer be used because it was now over and, although some Cabinet ministers heeded him, the attempt inevitably failed. Certainly, the UK had left the EU, but the future terms, especially the future terms of trade, had still to be agreed during a transition period set to expire at the end of 2020.

This also meant that it was misplaced for Brexiters to mock the predictions that had been made for the impact of leaving the EU when, on 1 February, very little, at a practical level, changed. For that was because during the transition period the UK was still in the single market and customs union, albeit without being part of the political structures of the EU. Brexit had happened, but the main economic changes had still to be made.

In principle, and certainly as a matter of law, Brexit having happened meant that the mandate of the 2016 referendum had been discharged in full, since the instruction to leave the EU had been complied with. It also, as with the referendum itself, left open what was to come afterwards. This could, and should, have meant that no more would be heard of 'the 17.4 million' and the 'will of the people', since their will had now been done. However, the distinction between 'leaving the EU' and the agreement of future terms remained as little understood as ever, not least because Johnson had obscured it with his 'oven-ready deal' election claim. Because of this, confusingly, 'no-deal Brexit' had now shifted from its 2019 meaning of 'no Withdrawal Agreement' to that of 'no future terms, including trade, agreement' in 2020.

## The many meanings of a 'Canada-style' deal

As noted in the previous chapter, Johnson had only ever talked in very vague language about the future terms, so it was still unclear what the government intended them to be. The recurrent phrase of a 'Canada-style' deal was vague and ambiguous, and was to remain so throughout 2020. Hardly had the Brexit day celebrations ended, such as they were, than Johnson was reported to be 'infuriated' that the EU had 'reneged' on its promise to strike a 'Canada-style' free trade deal by now insisting on 'Level Playing Field' (LPF) requirements in terms of state aid, workers' rights, environmental standards and so on. But this had been the EU's clearly stated position since April 2017 and, perhaps more importantly, was set out in the text of the Political Declaration that Johnson himself had signed in January.

In fact, it soon emerged that the UK intended to regard that apparent commitment as redundant, and was able to do so because the Political Declaration was not legally binding. That caused a further deterioration in trust with the EU, which had regarded it, not unreasonably, as a serious statement of intent on both sides and not the irrelevance that Johnson was treating it as. But, in any case, it did not make the demand for LPF go away.

The EU position remained that since the UK was a large, geographically close and deeply interconnected economy this meant that the terms of a trade agreement could not be identical to those which it had agreed with Canada, and it believed that the UK had accepted this. In short, the issue was that the UK was *not* Canada, not least for the obvious reason that Canada had never been a member of the EU. This basic fact was compounded by the EU's concern that, as at least some Brexiters wanted, a post-Brexit UK would seek to become 'Singapore-on-Thames', meaning a deregulated, low-tax competitor on the EU's doorstep, undercutting its standards.

In a sense, the issue hinged on the word 'style' in 'Canada-style deal'. What that meant was not a deal 'identical to Canada' but – as had been implied by the Barnier staircase with its 'step' showing the Canadian and South Korean flags – a deal in the general category of free trade agreements, rather than that of single market and customs union membership (see Chapter Four). However, the situation was more complicated than this. Despite what the government seemed to think, CETA, Canada's deal with the EU, did include some LPF conditions, albeit less stringent than those the EU sought from the UK, and also it did not provide the completely zero-tariffs deal which the UK sought.

Thus, even if 'Canada-style' were taken to mean identical to CETA, then it would not mean the zero-tariff deal with no LPF that some Brexiters said it would. Moreover, many Brexiters, including Johnson, had frequently stated that their aim was a 'Super Canada', 'Canada +' or 'Canada +++' deal, implying one more extensive than CETA. And indeed, as became clear, the UK was seeking something more extensive in the negotiations – for example, in terms of mutual recognition of professional qualifications, which was important for British services businesses. For that matter, the future terms deal envisaged in May's Chequers proposal, with its close alignment for goods trade, could reasonably be described as 'Canada +'. As with 'style', it was really a question of what was denoted by the '+' sign.

So the debate was one of constant confusion because, at times, 'Canada-style' was used by Brexiters to imply a 'basic' or 'bare bones' trade agreement and at other times to denote a comprehensive 'best in class' deal. To the EU it meant a deal of the broad category of CETA, but adapted to the specific situation of the UK. To muddy the waters further, when the EU had first spoken of a 'Canada-style' deal, some Brexiters had been outraged and denounced it as 'punishment' because it was described, accurately, as meaning worse terms than EU membership (see Chapter Three). Beyond all that, CETA could not serve as a template for the entire future terms agreement anyway, because that was to be about a range of UK–EU cooperations, including security, which went well beyond a trade deal.

## DID THE UK AGREE WHAT HAD ALREADY BEEN AGREED?

Thus, even before the future terms negotiations began in March 2020, there was a lack of clarity and a lack of trust between the UK and the EU. Perhaps more problematically, there were already signs that the UK government either had not understood or was not content with what it had signed up to in the Withdrawal Agreement, in particular as regards the Northern Ireland Protocol. As foreshadowed in the previous chapter, this may have partly been because of the rushed manner in which the 'frontstop' had been agreed, itself in part because of Johnson's desperation to agree to anything which would satisfy his promises to remove the backstop and to leave the EU at the end of October. That had since been compounded by the rush to pass the agreement after the election so as to meet the new end of January departure date.

Whatever the reasons, within just forty-eight hours of the UK leaving the EU it was reported that Dominic Raab, the Foreign Secretary, was denying that the Withdrawal Agreement meant customs checks on goods moving from Great Britain to Northern Ireland,[III] and later in the month the newly-installed Northern Ireland Secretary, Brandon Lewis, denied that an Irish Sea border had been agreed.[112] Then, towards the end of February, it was reported that Johnson was seeking ways to 'get around' the Northern Ireland Protocol, so as to evade the sea border checks.[113]

This mattered a lot more to the EU even than reneging on the LPF agreements in the Political Declaration, because it threatened a legally binding international treaty and, moreover, one of its central red lines since the beginning of having a stable solution for Northern Ireland which was consistent with the Good Friday Agreement. The apparent refusal of the UK government to understand or to be truly committed to what it had agreed alarmed the EU, especially on top of the earlier episode of discarding the phase one agreement on Northern Ireland and the general sense from the prorogation that Johnson had little regard for the rule of law. It was an issue that was to become increasingly vexed later in the year, and its roots went deep. At heart, it was another manifestation of the refusal of some Brexiters to accept what Brexit meant for Northern Ireland and, indeed, for borders in general even though, as noted in the previous chapter, this had been the implication of having agreed the Irish Sea border frontstop.

## SOVEREIGN EQUALS AND THIRD COUNTRY PRECEDENTS

The other significant piece of background to the commencement of the future terms negotiations was the publication of the UK negotiating approach which, along with a major speech by David Frost, now the UK's chief negotiator, marked a new phase in how the UK was to conduct its relations with the EU. Central to it, in a phrase that was to become so ubiquitous as to be a cliché in the coming months, was the concept of 'sovereign equals'.

At first sight, this might be taken as just another outing for Brexiter sloganising about 'taking back control', but it coded a much deeper shift in how the UK was approaching Brexit under Johnson. Throughout May's Article 50 negotiations, the frequent accusation was that Britain was trying to 'cherry-pick' the advantages of EU membership, whilst avoiding the constraints and obligations of such membership (otherwise referred to as 'cakeism'). Both the EU and many UK commentators remarked that this failed to understand that, after Brexit, the UK would be a third country with respect to the EU. At the same time, many Brexiters were suspicious of such an approach, believing that in practice it would keep the UK tied too closely to the EU's orbit.

In the new approach, the government flipped this criticism around so as to constantly emphasise that what it sought was a series of arrangements which were in line with precedents from other third countries' relationships with the EU. The precedents varied, according to what aspect of the future relationship was being referred to, but in the negotiating approach document they included Canada, of course, but also Japan, Australia, New Zealand, South Korea, the US and Norway. The term 'precedent' or cognates of it appeared thirty times in the thirty-page document.[114]

The significance of this was two-fold. On the one hand, it was a message to the EU, but also to both pro- and anti-Brexit actors domestically, that the UK was neither asking for anything which was unreasonable for a non-member nor for anything which was in any way incompatible with Brexit. On the other hand, and here the notion of 'sovereign equals' was important, it implied that these arrangements were, or should automatically be, on offer to the UK since they were selected from the menu of what independent states were able to agree with the EU.

It was an approach which was at best naïve and at worst deliberately misleading. It seems to have derived from transposing the rules-based nature of EU membership onto the EU's external relationships. EU membership entails rights and obligations within a system of rules, since that is the only way of holding together a group of (indeed) sovereign, independent countries. It was that which precluded cherry-picking, which would fatally undermine such a rules-based system. Once the rules are bent, they cease to be rules. Hence the impossibility of being both a beneficiary and a non-member. What the government's new approach implied was that the same logic applied to third countries. That is, that they, too, have a certain set of rights, albeit different to those of member states. David Frost expressed this quite unambiguously in saying that the British approach was 'to claim the *right* that every other non-EU country in the world has' (emphasis added).[115]

If that were indeed so, then of course there would be no reason why the UK shouldn't have, say, a New Zealand-type veterinary agreement or a Japan-type agreement on financial services regulation, to give two examples envisaged in the UK negotiation approach document. In particular, to take the central and most contentious example, it suggested there was no reason why the UK should not have the same trade agreement as Canada, without the need for any additional Level Playing Field commitments. All of these were 'within the rules' for third countries, had 'precedent' and, therefore, the UK had a 'right' to them by definition.

One flaw in this was that whilst each particular 'ask' might have a precedent, as a package what the UK was seeking was unprecedented. However, the central flaw was that there were no such 'rules' or 'rights', and the quasi-legal notion of 'precedent' was all but irrelevant in this context. To the extent that the EU is, indeed, a 'sovereign' it can make whatever external agreements it sees fit, with or without regard for 'precedent'. What it would do in the negotiations would be based upon the calculation of its own interests, refracted through the internal negotiation of the differing interests of its own member states. In particular, what was at issue was the relative negotiating strength of the EU vis-à-vis the UK.

In the latter respect, 'sovereign equals' was a meaningless construct. Whilst sovereignty applies equally to all countries, that does not make them 'equal' with respect to what they can do with that sovereignty, including what they can achieve in trade or other negotiations. The US is the 'sovereign equal' of, say, Chad – but in any trade negotiation between them the US is clearly the stronger party, and it would be absurd to imagine that because the US has such-and-such a relationship with, say, Canada, it follows that this would be made available to Chad, and still more absurd that it would be made so as of 'right'.

The disparity between the UK and the EU is, of course, much less than in this example. But economically, especially, the differences in size between the two was enough to make the EU stronger. Yet, on the other hand, precisely because of the UK's economic size and proximity to the EU, it is unsurprising that, as noted earlier, the EU was not willing to offer what it had agreed with Canada without any additional preconditions and safeguards. In short, the UK was both too small to be able to dictate its own terms and too big to be granted them.

An alternative reading of being 'sovereign equals', and one which was found in numerous government statements, was that it simply meant that just as the EU would not accept or be bound by UK law, regulation and jurisdiction neither would the UK accept or be bound by that of the EU. This was important within the context of the negotiations because it emphasised, in particular, the idea that any role for the ECJ would be unacceptable to the UK.

But this version of sovereign equality was also naïve and misleading. The global economy relies upon transnational regulatory systems, of which those of the EU and the US are by far the most extensive and powerful, as well as upon global standards, such as those of the UN for vehicle manufacture. The UK is of course free to set its own standards, and to that extent is the 'sovereign equal' of any other country. But there is no possibility of the UK being an international 'rule-maker' and so to that extent it is bound to be a 'rule-taker' unless it retreats from international trade entirely. The Brexiter position on this was in any case contradictory given the enthusiasm they evinced for trading 'on WTO terms', which also meant being bound by WTO law, and for making free trade agreements which frequently entail Level Playing Field commitments and binding dispute resolution systems.

The outcome of the negotiations was therefore going to be a matter of realpolitik, not of a quasi-theological notion of 'sovereign equals', nor of a fantasy that some system of rules and rights governed what kinds of deals the EU must do. It was also quite irrelevant to talk, as Brexiters often did, of what the EU 'ought' to do if it had regard for their (the Brexiters') calculation of its (the EU's) interests, or those of its member states, or of their industries, as in the familiar 'German car makers' argument. That calculation was a matter for the EU, just as it was for the UK – in that sense, only, were they sovereign equals. Both could make their own decisions and, as it might be, their own mistakes.

At one level, the sovereign equals doctrine and the idea of rights and precedents were – as so often – aimed as much or more at a domestic audience as at the EU. Thus tabloids reported the government 'blasting' the EU for refusing to accept its own logic (i.e. a version of the 'precedent' argument). That was in part another example of how Brexit continued to be conducted as if it were still a campaign but also, of course, an indication of how, especially if no deal were done, it would be blamed on EU intransigence.

At another level, it reflected something which many remainers, especially, still fail to understand. Committed Brexiters really do believe their own propaganda and, in particular, really do believe that 'sovereignty' confers unconstrained freedom. In this sense, the fantasy of what being a 'sovereign equal' means as a non-EU member was the mirror image of their equally erroneous belief that sovereignty had been lost by virtue of being an EU member. And allied to that was the persistent paranoia that, as a member, the UK had been ruled by the EU and as a non-member was being punished by the EU.

There were also some more fiddly and detailed issues in play. First, during the May years, as it became progressively clearer how complex the realities of Brexit would be, Brexiters had developed the notion of 'managed no deal'. As discussed in Chapter Four it was a non-sequitur, for it entailed making deals without making a deal. But it lived on in the future terms negotiations. For whereas the EU approach was to seek a single deal, encased in a single governance architecture, the UK 'precedent' approach envisaged a series of mini-deals, modelled on this or that precedent.

There was some irony in this, since one could argue that the EU approach was to offer a 'bespoke' EU–UK relationship whereas the UK's was to seek a number of 'off the peg' solutions. So in 2020 the EU was proposing something which, to the cheers of Brexiters in 2017, Theresa May had said was vital – this was the meaning of her 'red, white and blue Brexit' – whereas the UK was now proposing what she, again to Brexiter cheers, had dismissed as unacceptable.

Second, what was going on was an outgrowth of another Brexiter nostrum, namely that the EU 'always blinks at the last moment'. This had been a claim going right back to David Davis's tenure as Brexit Secretary, much of it based on an erroneous comparison with what often happens at EU summits between member states and the situation of a negotiation between the EU and a departing – or, by now, departed – member. But it took on a new life when Johnson had supposedly renegotiated May's Withdrawal Agreement the previous year, which Brexiters interpreted as the EU having 'blinked'. It was now being given fresh impetus by the new approach of relying on third-country precedents, because the assumption was that since the EU had agreed to them for other countries then, when push came to shove, it would do so for the UK. On this analysis the EU was simply being recalcitrant and when stood up to by a 'sovereign equal' would back down.

One consequence of this belief was that it precluded seeking an extension to the transition period by the end of June, when under the terms of the Withdrawal Agreement it needed to be agreed if it were to happen, because the assumption was that the 'last moment' for the 'blink' would not arrive until the end of December. Extending transition would therefore only defer the necessary crunch moment. But if that analysis were to prove flawed then it would be too late, and the UK would either have to leave with whatever deal it was offered or leave with no deal and accept all the consequences of that.

Of course, part and parcel of this negotiating approach was that the UK was perfectly willing to leave with no deal, or what Johnson, mendaciously, had begun to call 'an Australia-style deal' (mendacious as Australia did not have a free trade agreement with the EU). But if that was a bluff, and if it was called, then there would be no option left but to accept the EU offer.

So this was the situation on the eve of commencing the future terms negotiations in March 2020. But just as they were about to begin, something entirely unexpected and unprecedented was emerging which was to push Brexit from the headlines and to colour the entire negotiating proceedings: the global pandemic of a new and deadly virus.

## THE CORONAVIRUS PANDEMIC AND BREXIT

There is no doubt a book to be written just on the way that the coronavirus – or Covid-19 – pandemic and Brexit intersected. For one thing, it meant that the future terms negotiations often took place by video conference, rather than face to face, which may have inflected them differently. It also meant that, at key times, members of the negotiating teams were in isolation and for a while the British Prime Minister was actually hospitalised. It certainly made the UK refusal to extend the transition period bizarre, and it meant that when that period ended businesses and government were less well-prepared than they might otherwise have been.

Beyond these direct relationships, there was a complex web of interconnections between Brexit and responses to the coronavirus crisis. These included the very clear overlap between those, the self-styled 'lockdown sceptics', who thought that the coronavirus restrictions were overdone, should never have happened or should be lifted quickly, and that the whole thing was essentially a fuss about nothing, and those who supported Brexit, thought it easy and simple to deliver and claimed that it should have already been done. Significantly for the politics of Brexit, that overlap could be seen especially amongst many ERG members, some of whom were to join the new Covid Recovery Group which opposed the restrictions the government imposed to deal with the crisis.

Beyond this political overlap, there was an administrative one shown by reports of how dealing with coronavirus was hampered by political exhaustion from all the Brexit battles of the previous months and that planning for a future pandemic had been entirely sidelined by planning for no-deal Brexit (in the original meaning of 'no Withdrawal Agreement'). In other words, the UK state simply didn't have enough 'bandwidth' to deal with both the pandemic and Brexit. Given that the time frame of the pandemic was beyond governmental control but that of the Brexit process was within it, logically it was the latter that should have been changed.

What both Brexit and coronavirus revealed were some fundamental flaws in the way the UK was being governed and the political discourse around it. Brexit had bequeathed a way of governing which was largely impervious to reason, and incapable of engaging with complexity. Johnson had become Prime Minister because of Brexit and appointed his Cabinet on the criterion of commitment to Brexit. He brought with him many from the Vote Leave campaign as advisers. But all the things which secured the vote for Brexit – the leadership-by-slogan, the boosterism, the appeal to nostalgic sentiment, the disdain for facts and evidence, the valorisation of anger and divisiveness – were, without exception, precisely the opposite of what was needed for effective governance in general, and crisis management in particular.

Because of Brexit, Britain had a Prime Minister who was always in campaign mode, partly because he preferred it and partly because he had no facility for, or even much interest in, governing. The same was true of Cummings and, for that matter, the entire Brexit high command, which had always been characterised by protest and victimhood, not competence and responsibility. That was – literally – fatal in terms of dealing with coronavirus, as was shown during 2020 by the much higher death rate than that of most other countries. But that in turn meant that the coronavirus crisis held up a mirror to the nature and limitations of how Brexiters had approached Brexit and how the Brexit government was pursuing it.

However, if a government configured solely by Brexit was ill-equipped to deal with coronavirus, the pandemic crisis offered the government a convenient cover for how it was dealing with Brexit. For one thing, it meant that Brexit was no longer in the headlines. Had it not been for the crisis, it would have been far more difficult to sustain the pretence that Brexit had been 'done', the central pledge of the 2019 election. The pandemic had the effect of somewhat concealing that pretence.

For another, it offered a shield for the effects of Brexit because the economic impacts of coronavirus were so huge. Economists could warn that the Brexit effects would be far more significant in the longer term than those of coronavirus but, in the political here-and-now, those effects would be dwarfed. That meant that the inevitably adverse consequences of a trade deal (compared with EU membership) could more easily be concealed. On the other hand, it potentially made a no-deal Brexit more politically viable. However, neither was risk-free since both meant a double hit from Brexit and from coronavirus.

At all events, from March onwards the Brexit process and the coronavirus pandemic became inextricably intertwined.

## THE QUESTION OF TRANSITION
## PERIOD EXTENSION

Rationally, the pandemic ought to have caused the government to extend the transition period, which was already considered by most experts to be too short to undertake a negotiation of such complexity. And, after all, its end date was only an artefact of the original Theresa May deal, struck at the time when the leaving date was still set as 29 March 2019. That would have given twenty-two months for the transition and even that was not a generous allowance for the negotiations. As it was, there were only eleven months and in the first of them no negotiations took place anyway. Why not, especially in these dramatically new circumstances, ditch this aspect of May's deal which, in general, the Brexiters affected to despise?

The dogmatic refusal not to seek an extension (which the EU would surely have granted), and government statements that any proposal by the EU to extend would be rebuffed, arose from at least four factors. One was the continuing belief in the 'last-minute blink' theory and the idea that time pressure would force the EU to meet British demands. But the effect was, if anything, to voluntarily recreate precisely the time pressures which the UK had faced in the Article 50 period. The second reason was Johnson's long-standing insistence that there would be no extension, and his determination not to repeat his earlier failure to deliver on a Brexit day at the end of October 2019.

In any case, thirdly, there was no great political pressure to do so. It was true that extension had support in opinion polls, and many commentators and business groups were urging it, as were the devolved assemblies and the Mayor of London. But the Labour opposition did not do so. Labour's stance on this, under its new leader, Sir Keir Starmer, was puzzling because to have called for an extension – even though it certainly wouldn't been heeded – would have set down a marker for the future which could usefully be knitted in with Starmer's wider critique of Johnson's handling of coronavirus as showing his incompetence. That this didn't happen was part of a more general decision by Starmer to barely mention Brexit at all throughout 2020. This was possible primarily because of the overwhelming nature of the pandemic crisis, but it meant that on the crucial issues shaping the UK's entire political and economic future the official opposition simply had nothing to say. It had ironic parallels with Corbyn's approach in the previous parliament.

What underlay Labour's silence was also the fourth factor behind Johnson's refusal to extend the transition. The Brexit Ultras in both the media and Parliament were standing ready to denounce any extension as a betrayal of Brexit, engineered by remainers who did not accept the result of the referendum. That was a trap Labour wanted to avoid and a threat to Johnson, too, because of the overlap, mentioned earlier, between the most hard-line Brexiters in his party and those who opposed the coronavirus restrictions. Despite the size of his majority, there were more than enough MPs in this grouping to defeat him in Parliament and, indeed, he had many times been forced into various U-turns over a range of policies. Within only a few months of his election victory, Johnson was far more vulnerable than would have been expected at that time.

Nevertheless, it cannot be stressed strongly enough that the idea that extending the transition would undermine or betray – let alone reverse – Brexit was pure baloney. Brexit had happened, and that would be totally unaffected by extension. To claim otherwise was untrue and born entirely of the Brexiters' infatuation with the idea of betrayal and their preference for endlessly fighting the Brexit culture war.

Indeed, with Brexit done, the decision on extension was not the last gasp of remainers' rearguard defence but the first big test of whether Brexiters in government and outside could break with campaigning for Brexit and move to governing as Brexiters. It was a test which they all – Johnson included – failed.

Thus the end of June 2020 deadline to apply for an extension came and went with little comment and no drama. The obstacles, both legal and political, to subsequently extending were formidable. So, although some commentators and businesses continued to call for it right up until the end of the year, in practical terms there was never any chance thereafter of it happening.

## PREPARING FOR BREXIT

The refusal to extend the transition period was to cost the UK dearly at the end of the year because what it meant was that, in fact, there was no 'transition' but, rather, an overnight change at the end of December. What the nature of that change was going to be was unknown until the last few days of 2020 because, right up until then, it was not known whether or not there would be a trade deal. However, deal or no deal, some of the changes would be the same, in particular as regards the need for new customs and regulatory checks because they were an inevitable consequence of leaving the single market and customs union. These changes would apply at the borders between Great Britain (i.e. England, Wales and Scotland) and the EU, which also meant, because of the frontstop, the sea border between Great Britain and Northern Ireland, as explained in the previous chapter.

Whilst the EU was moving fairly smoothly to create the necessary new systems, the situation was very different in the

UK. The reason for this had deep roots in the entire Brexit process and had also impacted on planning for the original no-deal scenario of there being no Withdrawal Agreement, as discussed in Chapter Four. The general problem was that the only way of informing people how to prepare for Brexit was for the government to admit the truth of what it would mean, something which, as Brexiters, its leading figures denied and dismissed as Project Fear. This was especially so during the 2017–19 parliament when it was still conceivable that Brexit might be reversed, so admitting publicly what preparations would be needed would be likely to assist the case for such a reversal.

More specifically, for years, despite Theresa May's decision to leave both single market and customs union, the government had promised that there would be frictionless trade or something close to it. That was always impossible, and had been implicitly dropped with Johnson's Withdrawal Agreement. It was also implicit in the behind-the-scenes preparation work the government had begun to do in 2019 after Johnson had become Prime Minister. But it had not been admitted explicitly, presumably because prior to the election there was still the concern that it would feed the campaign against Brexit.

Thus, astonishingly, it was not until February 2020 that any Cabinet minister – namely Michael Gove, who had been a leading figure in the Vote Leave campaign, and was now central to Brexit preparations – publicly and officially admitted[116] that the consequence of the decision taken in January 2017 was border friction, meaning checks and/or formalities such as new paperwork but also new regulatory certifications, and that this would be so regardless of whether there was a future trade deal with the EU. This, evidently, was not until after the 'oven-ready deal' election and just eleven months before the transition period was due to end.

Of course, many businesses had realised long ago what it was going to mean but others – perhaps especially smaller firms – had not unreasonably taken the government at its word. Moreover, many undoubtedly believed the hugely successful Project Fear rebuttal line, and thought that talk of new barriers was the invention of remainers. Additionally, having experienced several postponements of Brexit itself, many assumed that the same would apply to the ending of the transition period. Indeed, right until it ended surveys showed that about a third of businesses expected that the transition would be extended.

As regards the new border between Great Britain and Northern Ireland in particular, preparations were hampered by the fact that, as mentioned earlier, senior government ministers, including the Northern Ireland Secretary and the Prime Minister himself, had repeatedly denied that there was going to be any such border. Johnson had even told Northern Ireland business leaders that any customs forms demanded of them could be thrown 'in the bin'.[117] Understandably. in such circumstances some businesses might conclude that there was nothing to prepare for.

This was a particular aspect of the wider, recurring, issue of having a government that was effectively still acting as if it was a campaign for Brexit and, thus, denying any of its adverse consequences. So, starting in July 2020, successive government information campaigns had limited traction, partly because of all that had gone before in terms of denying the effects of Brexit and partly because they remained coy about what these effects were going to be. Anyone digging into the government websites the campaigns pointed them to would have found two things: numerous areas where the government simply didn't know what was going to happen, and equally numerous areas where it was clear things were going to get worse, more difficult and more cumbersome. Indeed, nowhere in this material was there even a single example of something which was going to get better or easier as a result of Brexit. Yet this was scarcely guessable from the campaign headlines and adverts.

This was because 'everything is about to get harder as a result of our flagship policy' could hardly be the headline of an information campaign from a government led, largely composed of and advised by Vote Leave campaigners. Nor could the government readily explain to a country reeling under the effects of the unchosen disaster of coronavirus why this wholly self-inflicted disaster should be endured. As a result, the initial campaign took on an oddly cheery tone, talking of 'exciting new opportunities', that did nothing to convey the reality of what was to come and which, to the government's apparent bemusement, was little heeded. Unbelievably, towards the end, the government was presenting the new border friction as a business opportunity for growing the 'customs sector', as if this were an economic benefit rather than a cost.

A more realistic, even panicky, note was sounded in the final campaign in the last few weeks of 2020, under the slogan 'time is running out'. But for many firms it already had. Those that were trying to prepare were finding it impossible to recruit the necessary customs staff. Massive lorry parks were starting to be created around the country, and especially in Kent. Kent itself was to be restricted to lorries by new access permits. At the other end of the scale, individuals were beginning to realise that they, too, would be affected, for example by having to use different passport lanes when going on holiday, or having to deal with new restrictions on travelling with their pets.

Inevitably, as each new adverse consequence was reported it was denounced in the Brexiter press as being another example of 'EU punishment' rather than being the inevitable result of hard Brexit.

But even as the government was tentatively admitting that all these negative things were in prospect, it was also implying that everything depended on the negotiations. This in itself hampered preparations because some businesses gained the false impression that, if a deal was struck, there would be nothing to prepare for. That grew directly out of the long-standing confusion between single market membership and a free trade agreement, as discussed in Chapter One, which suggested that a trade deal could allow 'business as usual' to continue.

## NEGOTIATING BREXIT

Despite being hobbled by coronavirus restrictions, the future terms negotiations provided an endless drama right up until the end of 2020. For at least the second half of the year the repetitive report was that a 'zero tariffs, zero quotas' trade deal* was in prospect but that the stumbling blocks were fisheries, LPF and governance. It is of note that each of these issues was to do with managing divergence, demonstrating the point made in Chapter Two that the idea of this being the 'easiest deal in history' because of existing UK–EU convergence was flawed because what was at stake, and what made the deal difficult, was future divergence.

Fisheries was a technically complex issue but, more importantly, one of huge symbolic importance to Brexiters – who

---

\* In principle, a zero-tariffs deal would mean no charges on goods traded between the UK and the EU, assuming they were largely or entirely made within the UK or EU. Zero quotas meant there would be no upper limit on the quantity of goods which could be traded on a zero-tariff basis.

had made it an iconic part of the campaign to leave – and also to some EU member states, especially France and Ireland. In that sense, it had a significance way beyond its economic importance. It was also, arguably, an area where the UK had considerable leverage and the EU had wanted to resolve it prior to other issues, whereas the UK wanted to hold on to it as lever and, also, to resist this 'sequencing' of the future terms talks because of continued resentment at the EU's success in the sequencing of the Article 50 talks (see Chapter Three).

Level Playing Field conditions were, as noted previously, of central concern to the EU in general, but what became especially important as the negotiations proceeded was the particular issue of state subsidies and competition policy. This seems to have been at least in part because Dominic Cummings reportedly had an obsession with the idea of using state funding to support high-tech firms, which EU state aid rules might preclude. Whatever the reason, it was a strange thing for a Conservative government, in particular, to prioritise given its traditional hostility to state intervention. If anything, it was more associated with the 'Lexiters' and with Jeremy Corbyn (though they both generally overstated the restrictiveness of EU state aid rules).

As for governance, any trade agreement was going to need some mechanism to adjudicate on disputes, but there were two particular issues at stake. One was whether, as the EU wanted, there was to be a single agreement with a single governance architecture or, as the UK preferred, multiple separate agreements. That mattered in part because it impacted on whether breaches in one area could be met with penalties in another or not. Secondly, there was a question of trust, and here the UK was paying the price for its behaviour during the Article 50 negotiations, especially for having reneged on the phase one agreement, as well as for the wider shadow over its commitment to the rule of law following prorogation, and, now, the comments of Johnson, Raab and others denying that they had agreed to an Irish Sea border. Thus the EU sought a far more robust governance system than it might otherwise have done, and for reasons explained below that demand hardened towards the end of the negotiations.

Even at the time, there was little point in following each leak and press conference to try to decode what the outcome would be, and there is still less now that we know that outcome. Commentators spent much energy on doing so, however, with many declaring that a deal was certain to be done and others equally sure that there was no possibility of it. Each had some plausibility in that economic rationality dictated that there would be a deal whilst the politics of Brexit, and of the narrow definition of sovereignty the government had adopted, mitigated against it. So, in effect, the two predictions merely encapsulated the ongoing conflict between these two competing rationalities that had characterised the whole Brexit process.

Beyond that, the endless speculation was an artefact of, and in some ways an assistance to, the UK strategy of insisting that no deal was a perfectly possible outcome if it did not get what it wanted. This also explains the recurring pattern of Boris Johnson setting supposedly 'final' deadlines for a deal, or at least substantial progress towards one, which came and went with the talks still continuing. Thus in June, October and December his self-declared deadlines were breached. It's unlikely the EU ever took them very seriously, because the brutal reality remained that, economically, no deal would be far worse for the UK than for the EU and the EU, unlike the UK, did not face any comparable conflict of economic and political rationality because both pointed to protecting the integrity of the single market.

## THE ULTRAS' DEMAND TO SCRAP THE WITHDRAWAL AGREEMENT

However, there was one thing which the EU did care about, and deeply, which was the sanctity of the Withdrawal Agreement, including the Northern Ireland Protocol. As described above, even before the negotiations started there had been indications that the UK government had either not understood or not accepted the provisions of the Protocol, despite having signed up to them. As the negotiations progressed, an increasingly vociferous campaign was mounted by Brexit Ultras, both within and outside the Tory Party, which sought to ditch not just the Protocol but the entire Withdrawal Agreement.

The core propositions of this campaign were set out in a report from the Centre for Brexit Policy – one of an ever-changing array of respectable-sounding bodies through which the Brexit Ultras promulgated their ideas over the years – published in July 2020 and entitled 'Replacing the Withdrawal Agreement'.[118] As its title suggested, it propounded the idea that the government should unilaterally create a new 'Sovereignty Compliant Agreement' to replace the Withdrawal Agreement and present it to the EU. If the EU did not agree, the UK would no longer regard itself as being bound by the existing treaty.

The report listed many ways in which the agreement was supposedly not 'sovereignty compliant', including the Northern Ireland Protocol, and within that the role of the ECJ, as well as the ECJ's position with respect to citizens' rights and other matters, and the size – and by implication even the existence – of the financial settlement. What underlay the latter was the never-ending refusal of the Brexiters to accept or to understand the two-stage process of Brexit i.e. first a Withdrawal Agreement and then a future terms agreement. Thus, even now, well into the second stage, they were still re-fighting David Davis's 'row of the summer' of 2017 over sequencing (and Davis himself tweeted an endorsement of the report).

It's important to be clear – as the report was – that this wasn't about questioning this or that detail within the Withdrawal Agreement, it was that 'the entire WA and [Northern Ireland] Protocol are incompatible with UK sovereignty'. The report received extensive coverage in the pro-Brexit press and an accompanying article[119] by John Longworth, the director general of the Brexit Policy Centre, gave full rein to the sentiments underlying the proposal: the entire agreement was a 'poison pill' deriving from May's lack of belief in Brexit, and the way her government had 'worked hand-in-glove with Remain elements of the British establishment and in cahoots with Brussels and foreign powers'. As a consequence, Britain remained in 'Teutonic chains', paying 'reparations' and facing (in the inevitable Second World War reference) a 'Dunkirk' moment. It was a spectacularly vicious piece of writing, and highly revealing not just of the Brexit Ultras' view of what had been agreed but of their continuing commitment to the culture war against 'treacherous remainers'.

The obvious flaw in the proposal was that the Article 50 negotiations were over, and the EU immediately responded by ruling out any renegotiation. To follow it would entail breaking international law. It also involved an absurd rewriting of history. Johnson had signed the Withdrawal Agreement less than six months before, having put it to the electorate as the 'oven-ready deal' which was the centrepiece of his election campaign. At that election, as noted in the previous chapter, the Brexit Party initially threatened to run a candidate in every seat if Johnson didn't scrap the Withdrawal Agreement but then withdrew that demand and did not field candidates in Tory-held seats. John Longworth, then a Brexit Party MEP (he was later expelled from it), had welcomed this change of strategy and, indeed, had actually voted for the agreement in the European Parliament. Others who supported the proposal, such as Tory MPs Owen Paterson and Iain Duncan Smith, had voted to support the agreement in the British Parliament.

Equally absurd was the proposition that the Withdrawal Agreement was flawed because Johnson had had no time to re-negotiate properly – in fact, the time frames were of his choice and he himself had declared it to be 'a great new deal' – or because Parliament had had insufficient time to scrutinise it. The latter, again, had been of Johnson's choosing but an especially ludicrous twist was when that complaint was made by Iain Duncan Smith, when claiming that there were problems buried in 'the fine print', he was on record as saying that Parliament had had more than enough time to debate it.[120]

Perhaps the apotheosis of this new push by the Ultras came when, towards the end of June, Mark Francois, the Tory MP at that time chairing the ERG, wrote a characteristically crude and bombastic letter to Michel Barnier in which it became clear that he had not understood the key features of the Withdrawal Agreement. Barnier's reply drily pointed out that this was the agreement that he, Francois, had voted for.

At one level, all this might have seemed laughable, but it had a considerable significance. In the long run, it was setting out the grounds for the Brexit Ultras to be able to claim that Brexit had not been done 'properly' and, even, that it had been 'betrayed' (see the concluding chapter). More immediately, it mattered because so often what the Ultras had argued for influenced the policy of Conservative governments. Thus, although these proposals to renege on the entirety of the Withdrawal Agreement did not have any support from the government, at least in public, they had implanted the idea that the government might do so, and with it the idea that it might flout international law.

That possibility came to a head, explosively, in September 2020 when the government unveiled its Internal Market Bill.

## THE INTERNAL MARKET BILL
## AND ITS CONSEQUENCES

The Internal Market Bill (IMB) was, for the most part, a technical piece of legislation about how the UK market would work after leaving the European single market, although it had controversial aspects in terms of the powers of the devolved assemblies. But, crucially, contained within it were clauses that contradicted some of the provisions of the Northern Ireland Protocol by allowing the UK to unilaterally make changes to its terms, rather than doing so by mutual agreement with the EU via the joint committee established to oversee it.

In particular, the proposed legislation meant that the UK government could unilaterally change or do away with customs formalities on goods travelling from Northern Ireland to Great Britain, and unilaterally remove the role of EU law and regulation in state aid policy in Northern Ireland. The latter had a significance beyond Northern Ireland in that it also aimed to prevent the Protocol creating any backdoor role for the EU on state aid policy within Great Britain. In this sense, it was also intimately bound up with the wider ongoing negotiations about the Level Playing Field in the future terms agreement because these included the extent to which the UK as a whole would be tied to EU state aid rules.

These clauses of the IMB were explosive because they would mean the UK breaking the international treaty that was the Withdrawal Agreement and, therefore, breaking international law. What was even more extraordinary was that the Cabinet minister who introduced the legislation, the Northern Ireland Secretary Brandon Lewis, openly and unapologetically *stated* in the House of Commons that it would break international law. It was an unprecedented and astonishing moment. The head of the government's legal department resigned in protest that day, the latest in a growing list of senior civil servants unable to tolerate the excesses of the Brexiter government. Yet Suella Braverman, a former ERG chair who was now the Attorney General, showed none of the principle of her predecessor Geoffrey Cox in a not dissimilar situation (see Chapter Four) and gave the literally incredible opinion that the supremacy of Parliament allowed it to breach international law, to the incredulity of legal experts.[121]

The IMB bombshell brought together, and illustrated, three central aspects of where the Brexit process had now led Britain, which might be called extremism, incompetence and untrustworthiness. First, it was the latest and the most internationally serious example of the 'Jacobinism' with which numerous political, legal and cultural conventions had been thrown aside by the Brexiters – the full-frontal media assault on the judiciary and the illegal prorogation of Parliament being the most egregious previous cases. Second, it showed how Johnson and many other MPs who had voted for the Withdrawal Agreement had not actually understood (or had concealed) the implications of what had been agreed to only a few months previously, and sold to the electorate as an 'oven-ready deal'. This in turn grew out of their long-standing refusal to understand the implications of Brexit for Northern Ireland. Third, even though it didn't in itself amount to the ripping up of the Withdrawal

Agreement that the Ultras were advocating, it showed that the government was quite prepared to renege on parts of it and so might, in principle, go even further in the future.

It was also perhaps another example of the Dominic Cummings 'disruptor' strategy of doing the outrageous and unexpected. If so, like so many of Cummings's ploys, it backfired spectacularly. Even many senior Conservative Brexiters – most notably former party leader Lord Howard – were appalled and opposed it, not least as they recognised the calamitous damage it did to the country's international reputation. Additionally, and unsurprisingly, the EU was horrified and immediately made it clear that there would be no future terms deal if the IMB passed into law. This marked the final evisceration of the already frayed trust the EU had in the UK. It also meant that an unintended consequence of this latest attempt by the UK to 'play hardball' was to make the EU even more determined that if there was a future terms deal it would have to have rigorous governance mechanisms.

The IMB also provoked a strongly negative reaction from Joe Biden, now looking likely to become the next US President. Biden was proud of his Irish heritage, which informed his strong interest in Northern Ireland and the peace process, an interest shared by many other senior US politicians. His intervention also underlined just how geopolitically isolated Brexit was making Britain. That was confirmed when, a few weeks later, Biden defeated Trump. This, in itself, was a symbolically big moment for Brexit, because Trump's victory in 2016 had seemed to validate the Brexiters' project as being not an anomaly but as having caught the tide of history (see Chapter One). With the self-proclaimed 'Mr Brexit' in the White House, and Brexit Britain at his side, the EU would shortly collapse and a new era would begin.

What the Brexiters and Trump shared in their imagination of that new era was a vision of separate nations, unhampered by the constraints of international organisations or multilateral agreements, but making bilateral agreements if and when it was in their interests. A US–UK trade deal was to have been emblematic of how that new world would be, as well as a symbolic affirmation of Brexit itself – symbolic because, as with the idea of an independent trade policy in general, the actual economic benefits would be nugatory, but what mattered was the 'independent' not the 'trade' part of the policy.

With Biden's election, things looked very different. It was already obvious that the fantasy of Brexit heralding a collapse of the EU was nonsense. Now, a trade deal with the US looked less likely (Brexiters had always overestimated what Trump would do in this respect anyway). And there would be a US administration strongly committed to the EU and, more generally, to multilateralism and international cooperation. It was hardly the most propitious of times for the UK to be breaking international law.

This in turn went to the heart of the inadequacy of the Brexiter understanding of what 'independence' and 'sovereignty' mean, as if they permitted untrammelled freedom of action. As had happened so often through the process, Brexit was encountering the hard realities of international realpolitik.

## THE DEAL IS DONE

For all the fevered speculation about whether or not there would be a deal with the EU, it was not until the middle of December that the first tangible sign that it was in prospect emerged. This came with the scrapping of the internationally illegal clauses of the IMB. Whether this was a consequence of Biden's election, Dominic Cummings's resignation in

November (for reasons unrelated to Brexit), the impending economic realities of what no deal would mean, or some combination of these may not be known for a long time, if ever. It did not, in any case, mean there would be a deal; it was just that had the clauses not been removed there would not have been a deal. It was a necessary, but not sufficient, condition for a deal.

At all events, on Christmas Eve 2020, amid a rising death toll and a virtual national lockdown due to coronavirus, which had also caused massive lorry queues to build up at Channel ports (something that may also have concentrated Johnson's mind), it was announced that a deal had been done – the Trade and Cooperation Agreement. It was, inevitably, a hugely complicated document. But in essence it was, equally inevitably, broadly what it was bound to have been ever since Theresa May's Lancaster House speech of January 2017. That had set the path to a hard Brexit that excluded single market and customs union membership, and any role for the ECJ. Johnson's subsequent prioritisation of sovereignty above all else meant that, even within those parameters, the deal was a relatively thin one.

The TCA meant there would be no tariffs and quotas for goods trade but significant new non-tariff barriers to goods trade, and reduced liberalisation of services trade. The idea espoused by Brexiters, most flagrantly in David Davis's claim about 'the exact same benefits', that a free trade agreement could yield anything like the same terms as EU membership had been comprehensively and definitively discredited, as had the promises of frictionless trade and as, most fundamentally, had the proposition that Brexit would be cost-free. They had all been lies or delusions.

Zero tariffs and quotas were hugely important for many

manufacturing industries, and so the deal was much better than having no deal, but it still introduced substantial new barriers, meaning disruptions and costs, between the UK and its largest trading partner. Even the zero-tariffs aspect was not quite what it seemed because of 'rules of origin' clauses whereby goods which had a certain percentage manufactured outside the UK would still attract tariffs. Like other free trade agreements, there was little provision for services, but even by that limited standard the deal was modest.

Overall, some industries and sectors would suffer more than others, but all were set to experience a significant downgrading in terms of trade. Perhaps the biggest irony of the TCA, given the ubiquitous Brexiter claim that 'German car makers' and other EU goods exporters would insist on a good deal for the UK because of the manufacturing trade deficit, was that it was indeed a good deal for such exporters, who had zero-tariff access to the UK market. But in the process, UK services exporters to the EU, who generated a trade surplus, were sacrificed.

As regards what had been the most intractable areas of the negotiation, the fisheries deal did increase the UK share of the catch in its waters, but inevitably created (as for other goods) new barriers with the industry's biggest market, the EU, in the form of complex new checks and paperwork. The EU's initial demands on the Level Playing Field had been somewhat downgraded but what had been agreed was still far more stringent than in most trade agreements and certainly more than those in the EU's deal with Canada.

On governance, the EU had been successful in obtaining a single, over-arching agreement rather than, as the UK government had wanted, a series of separate agreements. With that came an immensely complex governance architecture, consisting of a Partnership Council along with a myriad of over thirty sub-groups. There were also a whole series of mechanisms for reviews, including a five-yearly review of the whole deal.

The deal was not just a trade deal, of course. As its name suggested, it was also about numerous forms of cooperation, including security. Here the picture was similar in that whilst a considerable degree of cooperation would continue, there was nothing that would be improved by the deal and in many respects, including real-time sharing of some EU databases, things would get worse. But, again, it was better than no deal. Also separate from trade was the issue of continued UK participation in some EU programmes, including the Horizon Europe research funding scheme, where these were open to third countries and with the appropriate budget payment. However, the UK had chosen not to continue with the Erasmus+ student exchange scheme.

If all this was much as had been expected since 2017, the big difference was what Johnson had agreed already, namely the frontstop whereby Northern Ireland would effectively remain in the goods single market and the customs union, with a regulatory and customs border across the Irish Sea. These provisions would come into force at the same time as the TCA, on 1 January 2021. Leaving the single market and customs union had been achieved for Great Britain only by *breaking up the single market and customs union of the United Kingdom*. Nothing remotely like this was ever suggested during the referendum campaign, and Theresa May had dismissed it as something no British Prime Minister could ever agree to. Ludicrously, the government tried to spin this as a great deal for Northern Ireland as it gave it the benefit of the European single market and customs union – that wasn't completely absurd in itself, but only served to underscore that leaving those bodies was not good news for Great Britain.

With the transition period about to end, a hurried vote occurred in the House of Commons. The senior researcher at the respected Hansard Society described the proceedings as a 'farce' and a 'constitutional failure'.[122] It was a fitting end to all the other ways in which Parliament and the constitution had been abused over the previous four years. With both Conservative and Labour parties supporting it – Labour once again making itself complicit in hard Brexit, although it could not at this point have prevented it – the vote was easily passed. The deal was done.

It was also a fitting end that, even as the deal was done, the lies continued. Boris Johnson declared that the TCA meant there would be no non-tariff barriers to trade with the EU, which was self-evidently false.[123] He went on to say that he had delivered a 'cakeist' deal and so confounded those who had said that you couldn't have free trade with the EU without conforming with the EU's laws.[124] But this was a lie about his original lie – the critique of cakeism was that you couldn't have the same trade terms as a single market member without being a single market member, which had been proved completely correct.

## A DEFINING, BUT NOT CONCLUDING, MOMENT

The TCA deal obviously marked a decisive moment within the Brexit process, and, for the purposes of this book, the end of my account of it. It finally defined what Brexit meant, the question that had been unasked, and so unanswered, by the 2016 referendum. But it was a moment, not an end point, and what Brexit meant would continue to change.

That was partly simply because, having been cobbled

together in such a rushed process, compounded by the rushed ratification, there were numerous loose ends in the TCA. Also, although export controls on UK goods going to the EU would commence immediately the transition period ended, import controls would be delayed for several months because the UK government was not ready to impose them. Several provisions, especially some relating to Northern Ireland, were subject to phased implementation.

Some crucial questions were still unanswered. One was whether the EU would recognise UK data protection as adequate and, if not, that would have a deeply adverse effect on commercial and security data sharing between the UK and the EU. Another was whether the EU would grant UK financial services regulatory equivalence, with significant consequences for this major industry (some 7 per cent of UK GDP, compared with the 0.1 per cent accounted for by fisheries, which had so dominated the negotiations). These questions lay outside the TCA and were not a matter for negotiation but for unilateral decision by the EU, and even if granted could be taken back at any time. This was where 'taking back control' had led.

Apart from all these 'known unknowns', it was also predictable that many unforeseen issues would in due course arise. Some of the very MPs who had voted for the Withdrawal Agreement the previous year, only to then discover that they didn't like its provisions, had now endorsed the TCA when its ink was barely dry. As had happened before, it was highly likely that some of them would come to say that they had not realised what they had voted for when ratifying it.

The last-minute nature of the deal, along with the other issues of business and governmental preparedness discussed above, also made it inevitable that its implementation just a few days later would be fraught for businesses. There was simply no possibility of firms being ready to deal with all the new export procedures that exiting the single market and customs union would bring. Some degree of disruption to supply chains and trade, at least in the short term, was assured. In the longer term, firms that survived long enough would adjust, and those which adjusted quickly enough would survive, but with new costs and consequent impacts on competitiveness, prices, jobs and taxes.

The situation of Northern Ireland, in particular, was set up in such a way as to make future problems and disputes inevitable. It was clear from the IMB and ministerial statements that the UK government did not really accept what had been agreed, even at the most basic level of the creation of the Irish Sea border, and its complexity meant that no one could fully understand how it was going to work in practice. It was also clear that the Brexit Ultras did not support the Withdrawal Agreement in toto, including the Northern Ireland Protocol, as all the flaws they had previously claimed meant it was not 'sovereignty compliant' still remained in place. This was compounded by the fact that some, at least, still wrongly believed, or pretended to believe, that the TCA in some way superseded what was in the Withdrawal Agreement and Protocol.

Beyond all that, the nature of the governance mechanism ensured that there would be an ongoing institutional arena in which the relationship between the UK and the EU would be negotiated, would be contested, and would evolve. The direction that evolution would take was unpredictable, but that it would happen was, again, inevitable.

That was not just because of the TCA but because of the inescapable fact that, Brexit or no Brexit, the UK is inextricably linked to the rest of the continent by geography, history and economy. Equally inescapably, since the rest of the continent was in a union exerting a massive regulatory pull, the UK would always be shaped by it. The Brexiter truism that 'we are leaving the EU but we are not leaving Europe' was, indeed, true. But what it meant was that, in future, rather than being a large and influential player within its own continent, the UK would be a relatively small outsider, much affected by the EU but with very little power over it.

As the transition period ended, and the UK was fully and finally out of the EU, more than half the country was opposed to what had been done, many bitterly and implacably so. Some were talking of how a closer relationship with the EU could be developed, others were beginning to campaign to re-join. There remained deep divisions between the four nations, between regions, between generations and within families. Businesses, security organisations and all manner of other bodies faced an uncertain future. EU nationals living in the UK and UK nationals in the EU had had their lives permanently unsettled, even when they had settled status. Yet there was little sign of triumph or delight, even from the most committed of Brexiters.

Indeed, already, before the transition period had even ended, before the trade deal had even been ratified, there was the ominous start of the inevitable complaints that Brexit had been betrayed.[125]

It was not an end, but the beginning of a new phase in the unfolding Brexit process.

# CONCLUSION: BREXIT IN RETROSPECT AND PROSPECT

This book has explained how events unfolded following the 2016 referendum, and in this concluding chapter I will try to draw together some key aspects of the account I have given, before discussing what the future may hold.

That the events of the last five years happened as they did was by no means entirely predictable, nor was it inevitable. For example, imagine if the Brexiters had responded to their victory not by jeering at distraught remainers to 'suck it up', but by saying that they recognised that almost half the country had a different view, that many had deep misgivings or were even horrified, but that they, the Brexiters, honestly believed that it would be a change for the better and would work tirelessly to show that was so and to win the support of those who doubted it. Alongside that, imagine if, rather than approaching the EU negotiations in a spirit of suspicion and antagonism, the Brexiters had calmly acknowledged that there was a settlement bill to be paid, that the EU would want the ECJ to have a role with respect to its citizens in the UK given the unusual situation, and that Northern Ireland presented a particularly complex problem that would be addressed carefully and sensitively rather than denying any such problem existed. Such things (they could have said) were as nothing for a great country confidently setting out towards a bright new future.

Whilst it is possible to imagine this, it is hard to do so because it conflicts with almost all of the many strands within the Brexit cause. These included, in some cases, a visceral loathing of the EU, and, in others, the way that Brexit was a means of 'putting one over on' the educated 'liberal metropolitan elite'. In particular, as I have sought to make clear, there was a deep strand within Brexiter political psychology that found comfort in a sense of self-victimhood. Others have noted the same thing, especially the Irish journalist Fintan O'Toole in his analysis of how a certain kind of self-pity, born at once of a sense of grievance and of superiority, was central to both the vote for Brexit and the events that have followed.[126] It is a psychology that precluded any such generous acknowledgement of victory and of responsibility.

The consequence of this was that, paradoxically, Brexiters often seemed as if they would have been happier had they lost the referendum and, conversely, unwilling or unable to take responsibility for what winning meant. At times, they even seemed to act as if Britain was being forced to leave by the EU. To put it more charitably, having not expected to win, they had no real idea of how to deliver on winning and seemed to have given no thought to what would follow. That was compounded by having chosen, as a campaign tactic, not to specify in detail what Brexit meant. It was as if they thought that winning the referendum was the end of the matter when, in fact, it was only the first and easiest step on a very long road.

Of course, Brexiters would give a completely different account, stressing instead that, having won, they expected the whole country to accept the result whereas, conversely, remainers set about trying to delay, dilute or even overturn the decision. Yet this, in itself, shows a lack of preparation for what victory would mean. For the reasons discussed in Chapter Two, it was naïve to expect such a reaction, and thus it was foolish not to be ready to reach out, magnanimously, to allay the concerns that lay behind it. This was especially so because to deliver Brexit would require much effort from those in the civil service and civil society, many of whom undoubtedly had not voted for it. Brexit may, as some of its proponents argued, have been a revolution but, if so, it was an unusual one in requiring those who had not backed it to enact it.

The bigger failure was a refusal to recognise how slender a mandate there was for Brexit. Brexiters constantly invoked 'the 17.4 million' and proclaimed the referendum to have been the biggest democratic exercise in British history (although many general elections had had a higher turnout, and the 1992 election saw a larger absolute number of voters). But that masked the undeniable fact that an almost equal number had voted to remain. That suggested a national ambivalence about Brexit in general, and most certainly didn't provide an endorsement of the particular – hard – form that Brexit took. A more astute and generous response to the referendum victory would have recognised that.

In any case, the Brexiter account of their victory having been subverted by remainers is at odds with the record of what actually happened. For whilst it is quite true that from the day after the referendum there were some who were implacably opposed to it, the government itself pursued Brexit with unflagging energy. Despite what was later said about 'Theresa the Remainer', the reality is that she immediately and unflinchingly embraced the Brexit cause, and for a long time was lauded and applauded by the Brexiters for her approach and, especially, for her championship of the hard Brexit of leaving the single market and customs union.

In fact, one of the principal criticisms of May is how inflexibly she took on not just the project of Brexit, but so many of the flaws that went with it. As outlined earlier in this book, she, quite as much as any who had campaigned for Brexit, poured scorn on remainers, and at least tacitly supported the 'enemies of the people' and 'crush the saboteurs' narrative. Even in her final days as Prime Minister, long after the Brexit Ultras had turned on her, her language was indistinguishable from theirs.

What had made them turn on her was not a failure to deliver their hard Brexit but the fact that, at least from the time of the Chequers proposal in the summer of 2018, she had begun to turn that Brexit into something that was practically deliverable, which became her Withdrawal Agreement. Until the Chequers proposal, the Ultras, including Boris Johnson and David Davis, had supported her. So the issue wasn't that the Brexiters had been thwarted from the outset but that they had been indulged, yet couldn't accept the practical realities of where that led. When faced with them, they retreated into new fantasies about, in particular, how the Irish border could be dealt with.

The same fate would have awaited anyone trying to deliver Brexit. In slightly different form, the same happened to Johnson in that, as discussed in Chapter Six, although the Ultras voted for his Withdrawal Agreement they never truly accepted it, and especially not his version of the solution to the Irish border issue. That was shown when, subsequently, they argued that it should be reneged upon. Then, when Johnson concluded the Trade and Cooperation Agreement, at least some Brexiters almost immediately began to say that it was a betrayal of what Brexit was meant to be, citing, in particular, the new barriers to trade and especially their immediate negative impact on the fishing industry, as well as the Irish Sea border.

## DELIVERING THE UNDELIVERABLE

The heart of the problem, as I have tried to show throughout this book, had two aspects. First, Brexit meant several different things to different kinds of Brexiter and so any actual form of it would split support for it. Second, the core ideas of the Brexit Ultras – about how a free trade agreement could yield similar, if not identical, benefits to the single market and customs union; that the problem of the Irish border was not genuine or was technologically soluble; and, at least arguably, how sovereignty works in an interdependent world – were false. They could not be made true by 'belief in Brexit'.

This meant that no Prime Minister, and no civil service, would ever have been able to deliver them. In short, not only were Brexiters psychologically predisposed to see, and perhaps in some cases even want, betrayal, but they had developed a set of ideas about Brexit that, since they were undeliverable, were necessarily going to be betrayed.

On the other side of the coin, because May had, in fact, so inflexibly and dogmatically embraced hard Brexit, and so signally failed to create any kind of consensual process to deliver it, public opposition grew, and with it the call for another referendum. In the early months of her premiership, many remainers had hoped, and some had actively campaigned, for a soft Brexit of at least single market membership, if not also a customs union. That would have been perfectly compatible with the referendum result and actually in line with what at least some 'liberal' Brexiters has campaigned for prior to the referendum. But the Brexit Ultras were adamantly opposed to this and May endorsed them. It was only later, in April 2018, that the People's Vote campaign started, and not until 2019 that it was in full force.

It is not even true that the parliament of 2017–19 sought to overturn Brexit. The votes on May's Withdrawal Agreement were lost in good part because of the opposition of Brexiters in the ERG and, in the process, this again revealed the recurrent flaw of Brexit. For central to the debate on May's deal were the incompatible positions that voting *for* it could be called betraying Brexit, and that voting *against* it could equally well be called betraying Brexit. To put this another way: suppose that Parliament had voted for May's deal against the wishes of the ERG and, thus, delivered Brexit. The ERG would then have insisted that 'true' Brexit had been thwarted by a 'remainer parliament', just as they do now. As for the votes where Parliament took control of business (leading to the Cooper Act and the Benn Act, as discussed in Chapters Four and Five) these were not attempts to stop Brexit, but to stop a no-deal Brexit – in the sense of no Withdrawal Agreement – something that had never been proposed in the referendum campaign.

So that Brexit unfolded as it did was not inevitable, but it was highly likely because of the flawed nature of the Brexit project, especially as conceived by the Brexit Ultras and enacted, in the first instance, by Theresa May. And even without those flaws, Brexit welded together two broad but incompatible ideas. One was nationalist, or nativist, and was most obvious in seeing Brexit as a way, via ending freedom of movement of people, of reducing immigration. The other was globalist, and was most obvious in seeing Brexit as a way of developing an independent and global free trade policy. These were incompatible not least because ending freedom of movement of people meant leaving the single market which, in turn, meant erecting new barriers to free trade between the UK and its largest market.

Moreover, as noted in Chapter One, the bigger problem was that both nationalism and globalism contained a failure to understand the regionalisation of economics and the multipolar nature of international relations. They also combined to create a strangely nationalist (and highly dated) view of global trade in which removing tariffs between countries was the focus, rather than creating shared regulations across countries so as to remove non-tariff barriers to goods and services trade, and in which the international nature of modern supply chains was all but ignored. It is no coincidence that the TCA ended up being, in essence, a tariff-free deal for domestically produced goods.

## FOLLOW THE MONEY?

The existence of the nativist and globalist strands within Brexit gives the lie to another common, but mistaken, account of how the Brexit process unfolded. But this one is to be found primarily amongst some remainers, rather than Brexiters. It posits that Brexit was devised and guided by global business elites in pursuit of their financial interests, aided by a host of free market and libertarian think tanks. The key, then, to understanding what happened is to 'follow the money'. But this runs into the problem that Brexit is profoundly damaging to many such interests, most obviously those of financial services and the City of London. Indeed, if it were right that global financial interests were so powerful, it would be expected that Brexit would never have occurred. At the very least, it would have been done in a way that protected financial services, whereas, in fact, the eventual trade deal barely covered them at all. That was an artefact of hard Brexit, of course, as no trade deal could replicate what the single market does for financial services liberalisation but, even in those terms, it was at the minimal end of the spectrum.

The way the 'follow the money' account gets round this objection is invariably some version of the argument most eloquently made by the *Guardian* columnist George Monbiot[127] that Brexit is the creature of one kind of capitalism – which he called 'warlord capitalism' but is more often called 'disaster capitalism' – which has captured the Tory Party, and is at war with another kind of capitalism, which he called 'housetrained' and which is horrified by Brexit. That is an important observation and, as Monbiot said, relates to the extraordinary shift in the modern Conservative Party away from its traditional business base, including the City – epitomised by Johnson's reported 'fuck business' comment – which has in turn had a big impact on how Brexit has developed.

But an observation is all it is – it doesn't explain why it was the 'warlord' money rather than the 'housetrained' money which was being followed by the Tory Party. Following the money is sometimes a good dictum, but it doesn't take you very far when it points in quite contradictory directions. To understand why the Tory Party has taken the path it has would require a detailed study of its recent history and its funding, taking in why it incubated such extreme Euroscepticism (as it was then called) long before its funding base shifted, and considering the role of its mainly elderly and nationalist membership.

Beyond that, this type of analysis rests, at least implicitly, on a version of Marxist, or at least materialist, theory whereby the (economic) base is primary and to a greater or lesser extent determining of the (cultural) superstructure. Culture then becomes little more than the dancing puppet of economic paymasters and their interests. When it comes to political explanation, that almost inevitably leads proponents of such analysis to some form of 'false consciousness' argument in order to explain why so many people support and vote for things which are against their economic interests.

And, indeed, this is precisely where Monbiot ended up, in writing that he sees (my emphases added) 'Nigel Farage and similar blowhards as *little more than* smoke bombs, creating a *camouflaging cloud* of xenophobia and culture wars. The persistent *trick* of modern politics – that appears to *fool us* repeatedly – is to *disguise* economic and political interests as cultural movements.'

It's worth bearing in mind that, if correct, this analysis must apply not just to gullible working-class voters but also to 'Lexiter' intellectuals such as Larry Elliott, Monbiot's colleague, the economics editor of *The Guardian*. They too, apparently, were unwittingly doing the disaster capitalists' bidding.

The limitations of such an analysis have long been identified. In particular, it's instructive to recall how in the 1980s writers on the left, especially the sociologist Professor Stuart Hall, started to explain that Thatcher kept winning elections because contrary to the assumption of economic primacy, in Hall's words, 'material interests ... are not escalators which automatically deliver people to their appointed destinations, "in place", within the political ideological spectrum'.[128] It's an important insight that remains true.

Coming to Brexit specifically, viewing leave voters as the unwitting dupes of 'warlord' or 'disaster' capitalism, funded by the likes of US hedge fund mogul Robert Mercer and supported by a network of libertarian think tanks, doesn't take us anywhere. For whilst (some) remainers may believe that to be so, it has a precise mirror-image in the repeated claim made by (some) leavers that remainers are the mouthpieces of the 'global elite', funded by the likes of financier George Soros, one of the donors to the People's Vote campaign, and supported by numerous liberal think tanks. Of course, remain voters would no more accept that to be true of themselves than leave voters would accept the mirror-image accusation aimed at them. Neither claim has any analytical value, nor explains anything. Rather, they are tactics to discredit or demonise opponents.

Ultimately, the injunction to follow the money is not just reductive but is also a circular and unfalsifiable argument. For just as some say that the fact of Brexit is explained by capitalist manipulation of *leave* voters so too, had remain won, some would have said that *that* was explained by the capitalist manipulation of *remain* voters. All you have to do, they'd say then, as they do now, is 'follow the money'. In fact, it would very likely be the same people saying it, since Monbiot virtually does this when pointing to how the remain campaign was funded by global investment banks such as Morgan Stanley and Goldman Sachs. Indeed, it is telling that amongst both leavers and remainers there are many who argue that the opposing side is 'neo-liberal'. Trying to explain Brexit by 'following the money' leads into an analytical cul-de-sac.

It also bears saying that the logic of the analysis that the Brexit process was driven by disaster capitalism was, as most of its proponents confidently predicted, that there would be no Withdrawal Agreement and no trade agreement. That would have created the conditions of maximum dislocation from which disaster capitalists would benefit, but it didn't happen. If it were true that disaster capitalists were pulling all the strings and Brexit had 'followed their plan all along', there would have been no deals.

This is not to deny that disaster capitalists will do all they can to benefit from Brexit, but that is because it is what disaster capitalists do in any situation. Nor is it to deny that a neo-liberal ideology of extreme deregulation was the motivation of one, highly influential, thread within Brexit. The overlap between such ideologues and the Brexit Ultras is plain to see. However, this *was* only one thread, and taking it to be what Brexit was 'really' all about totally fails to understand the alliance of disparate ideas, motivations and interests that Brexit brought together and which shaped the way it has unfolded.

Ironically, when remainers lump together leavers as either advocating or unwittingly endorsing a single plan for Brexit, they replicate the equally flawed Brexiter claim that the 17.4 million were a homogenous group supporting a defined programme. One of the key points about Brexit is that there was never 'a' plan, but multiple plans, or just hopes, from different strands within its coalition and, overall, no plan at all. The Brexiters do not have a secret competence, behind locked doors, whilst presenting an incompetent façade to the public. What you see really is what you get.

## THE POLITICS OF 'AUTHENTICITY'

A far better way of understanding the Brexit coalition, and how durable it has proved to be throughout the culture war that characterised the Brexit process, is through the complex and paradoxical politics of populism. The core proposition of Brexiters was that it was the triumph of 'the people' over 'the elite', and in the years following the referendum they have repeatedly cast all the conflicts it gave rise to in those terms (hence, 'will of the people', 'enemies of the people', and the equation of remainers with 'the Establishment' and the 'liberal metropolitan elite'). As with any form of populism, this entailed treating 'the people' as a unitary whole, which was especially problematic in the case of Brexit given that the country was more or less evenly split – making 'the people' an unconvincingly small proportion and 'the elite' a preposterously large one – and given the self-evidently elite nature of its leaders.

The idea that the largely male, public school and/or Oxbridge-educated Brexit leaders – a category that takes in Boris Johnson, Michael Gove, Nigel Farage, Dominic Cummings, Douglas Carswell, Nigel Lawson, Jacob Rees-Mogg, Daniel Hannan, John Redwood and many other leading Brexiters – were anything other than a privileged elite was plainly ludicrous. That fact was often pointed out, but it had no cut-through with their supporters.

Why? It is not, I think, that those supporters failed to spot the privilege of their leaders. It is that this isn't the kind of privilege to which they object. Such figures – Johnson, most obviously, Farage, certainly, even Rees-Mogg, surprisingly – are seen as being, despite that privilege, still in some way 'ordinary' or, perhaps more important, as 'authentic'. Someone 'you could have a drink with'. There is a parallel with the way that, in the US, the billionaire Donald Trump could appeal to blue-collar voters, but there's perhaps a distinctively British – or more accurately English – twist of class deference.

Political historians have long analysed the phenomenon of 'working class Toryism', and the new populist politics of 'authenticity' is not so very different in its acquiescence to 'the natural order of things'. Indeed, although they would not appreciate or recognise it, Lexiters, with their romanticised imagination of the British working class, are cut from a similar cloth. In this imagination, 'real' working-class people could never aspire to, or benefit from, freedom of movement so as to work abroad or save up for a retirement flat in Spain. Within this universe, too, there is a place for a certain kind of middle-class Brexiter: the well-heeled, Home Counties, golf club member, sick to the teeth of 'political correctness gone mad'.

Crucially, what this populist politics of authenticity means is that whilst its leaders may be highly privileged, in the literal sense of the term, they are not what their supporters mean by 'the elite' which, instead, is associated with the supposedly finger-wagging, 'won't let us say what we really think', prissy, moralistic do-gooders. Graduates with 'Mickey Mouse' degrees. The Human Rights Brigade. The PC Brigade. The Race Relations Brigade. The 'girly swots'. The bleeding-heart liberals.

It's an amorphous group which, together, constitutes a 'them' to which the 'us' – ordinary, common-sense people and their, perhaps not ordinary in the ordinary sense, but still common-sense, authentic leaders – are opposed. For years, this 'we' suffered as the 'silent majority', but with Brexit found its voice. Within this is another, and also crucial, dividing line. As acutely depicted in Jonathan Coe's 'Brexit novel', *Middle England*,[129] the elite in this meaning are 'constantly telling us what to do and say'. They are interfering. They are authoritarian. They make us follow *their* rules. They won't 'let us say what we think', and force us to be other than ourselves, and so to be inauthentic, unlike the flamboyant leaders whom we revere for having kept their authenticity and speaking their minds.

In this cultural universe, the Vote Leave slogan 'taking back control' was doubly potent. It was about freedom from EU control, but also freedom from the control of *them* – who, not coincidentally, were opposed to Brexit – freedom to 'talk about immigration', freedom to celebrate Christmas not 'Winterval', freedom to fly the St George's flag or the Union Jack without being sneered at. In this way it was, of course, partly about nationalism – about 'us' as a nation – but also about internal divisions: about 'us' versus 'them', those who for so long had ruled over us but were now exposed as traitors and saboteurs.

So Brexit provided an umbrella that could link the hardcore

libertarianism of a very small ideological minority with the resentments, victimhood and perceived humiliations of a much larger group. And the spines of that umbrella were 'freedom from the rules'. Almost all the high-profile fights of the post-referendum period were framed by this and, tellingly, it spilled over into objections from many Brexiters to coronavirus lockdown restrictions. Domestically, these ranged from the Miller case on parliamentary approval for triggering Article 50 through to the row (and court cases) over prorogation. They were all battles over whether 'the rules' (laws, conventions) had to be followed or whether the 'will of the people' trumped such niceties.

This umbrella of populist authenticity explains why it has been possible at every stage of the process for Brexiters to depict their cause as being that of the 'left behind', and to adopt a 'prolier than thou' line with their critics, depicting them as metropolitan exploiters of Romanian nannies and Polish plumbers, even in those cases when they, themselves, are well-heeled London-based politicians and journalists. It also serves to gloss over the nationalist-globalist contradiction because it positions Brexit as a project of nationalist pride (so derided by 'the liberal elite') that will lead to global domination, just as when 'we' ruled the world as an imperial power (which the liberal elite tell 'us' we should be ashamed about) and won the war (which the liberal elite insist we didn't do alone).

## CAMPAIGNING VERSUS GOVERNING

The diverse coalition created by this populist politics of authenticity had proved sufficient to win the referendum, and was highly effective in prosecuting the culture war which followed. However, it was totally ill-equipped for delivering Brexit. It certainly couldn't have been expected to yield the open, generous and confident approach imagined at the beginning of this chapter, not least as it was far too angry. For it is striking how, despite winning the referendum and getting Brexit, its supporters have never stopped being consumed by rage, as any social media discussion confirms. More fundamentally, as I have sought to stress throughout this book, Brexiters had developed a successful politics of campaigning but were uninterested in and incapable of governing.

That was particularly serious because delivering Brexit was a complex, technocratic task, requiring deep understanding of international trade and international relations. Very few Brexiters were interested in such things. There had been a plan known as Flexcit (flexible continuous exit), developed by Richard North, a long-standing campaigner to leave the EU and founder of the Leave Alliance, which did engage with these complexities and would have yielded a form of soft Brexit.[130] It had some following amongst soft or 'liberal' Brexiters, but it gained very little political traction and, after the referendum, was entirely swept away by the Brexit Ultras' insistence that only leaving the single market would be 'real Brexit'. That aside, most Brexiters were happy to rely on airy slogans about 'believing in Brexit' or half-understood factoids about how trade and other issues worked.

This failure of serious engagement was part and parcel of the refusal to take responsibility which became evident under May's leadership in two ways. One was that although May completely embraced delivering Brexit, she never took on the Brexiter characteristic of shirking detail and responsibility. It was this which led her to translate hard Brexit into the institutional form which the Brexiters then rejected.

Second, it was illustrated by the conduct of the Brexiters she brought in to her government to deliver Brexit, most obviously David Davis. Here was someone who had been at the heart of what became the Brexit movement for years and had, supposedly, given very serious thought to how it would work. Yet, from the beginning, he showed himself completely incapable of understanding the most basic facts of what Brexit meant, right down to who he would actually be negotiating with, thinking, in common with some other Brexiters, that it would be with Berlin rather than Brussels.[131] As mentioned in Chapter Three, the picture of him at the start of the Article 50 negotiations, sitting without paperwork and grinning inanely opposite the EU team with its bulging files, is one of the defining images of the Brexit process. For much of his tenure he gave the impression of being on the point of resigning, as he eventually did over the Chequers proposal.

In doing so he, as with Steve Baker and subsequently Dominic Raab and others, showed how Brexiters typically preferred to be on the sidelines, where they could indulge their fantasies and criticise the delivery of actual Brexit, rather than in government, where actual Brexit had to be delivered and those fantasies were cruelly exposed. The exception, it's fair to say, was Liam Fox, but his portfolio of international trade involved the one part of the Brexit process which, whilst technically complex, was not fantastical, primarily involving negotiating post-Brexit continuations for the UK of the trade deals the EU already had with other countries and of which Britain had been part of as an EU member.

What under May's government had been evident in the conduct of Brexiter ministers moved centre stage after Boris Johnson came to power and brought with him so much of the Vote Leave campaign team. Yet it also removed the possibility of Brexiter ministers resigning because Brexit wasn't being done properly. They no longer had 'Theresa the Remainer' as a scapegoat since Johnson, if only opportunistically, had fronted the Vote Leave campaign.

That might have led them finally to take serious responsibility for Brexit and to engage with all of its complexities. Arguably, Michael Gove did so as regards border preparations, although what he delivered was inadequate. But the government as a whole, and Johnson in particular, embarked on a much more dangerous path which is set to have long-term effects. Having not understood what Brexit meant when advocating it, he and his government proceeded to enact it by signing agreements with the EU which he did not understand either. In particular, as outlined in Chapter Six, he clearly didn't understand the Northern Ireland Protocol in the Withdrawal Agreement, and didn't understand the limitations of the trade deal within the Trade and Cooperation Agreement. This was not an anomaly or simply a reflection of Johnson's personal limitations, but grew directly out of the entire Brexit process.

There are clearly several linkages between the way that winning the referendum was treated as if that was an end of things, the failure to understand the practicalities of delivering it, and the refusal to take responsibility for it. In addition to these, there is another linkage and it is one of the most puzzling aspects of Brexit.

## BREXIT AS A SYMBOLIC ACT

Throughout the process, there was a strange sense from some of those who argued most vociferously for Brexit as a major and vital change that, somehow, Brexit wouldn't change anything. The most egregious example was Davis's idea (see Chapter Three) that the European Medicines Agency and European Banking Authority could remain in the UK. But it was more widespread and less specific than that. Perhaps the most ubiquitous example, which almost every EU national in the UK will have heard, is when leave voters say to their friends and neighbours from EU countries: 'Oh, but we didn't mean *you* when we said there were too many immigrants'. It was also evident when some Brexiters said that the UK wouldn't erect borders and if the EU did so then that was its business, as if borders were not a consequence of Brexit and, even, as if Brexit was being done *to* and not *by* Britain.

More generally, it was present in the constant implication that, if the EU was 'reasonable', then an agreement could be reached whereby everything (save freedom of movement of people and ECJ jurisdiction) could go on pretty much as before. This reflected, again, the recurring misconception that a free trade deal could create something broadly similar to the single market. That was in evidence in the misleading references during the referendum to retaining market 'access' and to Britain being in a 'free trade zone' from Iceland to the Turkish border, as well as in the endless promises thereafter of 'frictionless trade' and especially in Davis's 'exact same benefits' line. It was still in evidence when, immediately the transition period ended, many Brexiters expressed shock at the fact that new customs and regulatory procedures kicked in, causing significant disruption to trade.

This mindset wasn't necessarily to do with the idea that Britain could 'cherry-pick' some parts of the EU that it liked, or could 'have its cake and eat it', and it was more subtle than simply rejecting warnings as 'Project Fear'. Rather, what underlay such sentiments were two related things. One was a taking for granted of the familiar accoutrements of modern life without realising that they are the product of extensive, albeit largely invisible, institutional arrangements. So 'of course' nowadays planes fly us to wherever we want without restrictions, as if this were not the outcome of complex agreements such as the European Common Aviation Area, and 'of course' nowadays we can travel freely in Europe, as if that were not the outcome of freedom of movement rights. In some ways, Brexiters, who despised EU technocrats and bureaucrats, and railed against extra-national decision making, also treated it as an act of nature that there were Europe-wide regulatory systems from which Britain benefited.

The related underlying issue is that, for many, the vote to 'take back control', with all its emotional resonance, seems not to have been thought about in concrete legal or institutional terms but as a kind of symbolic, feel-good act. That, indeed, was the implication of the first Brexit white paper, discussed in Chapter Two, which affirmed that sovereignty was never lost by EU membership but that 'it has not always felt like that'.

The problem was that, once the Brexit process started, the assumption that familiar systems are an act of nature and the symbolism of taking back control came into collision with the realities of leaving the legal institutions of the EU. That made assumptions and symbolism irrelevant. Or, to put it another way, it made no difference to your EU neighbour that 'you didn't mean her' when she quit her job as, say, a paediatrician to return to Germany, and your child was ill. Just as the vote to leave was not an end but a beginning of the Brexit process, so too did the symbolic act of leaving set in train real, practical and non-symbolic consequences.

Apart from being misleading about what Brexit would mean, there was an even more dangerous consequence of its having been regarded in symbolic not practical terms. As the realities of what Brexit meant began to emerge, the mindset that leaving 'didn't mean that' or 'shouldn't mean that' or 'needn't mean that' easily morphed into the belief that 'the EU is making it mean something that it doesn't, or shouldn't or needn't'. So whereas a rational response would be to say that, by voting to leave, leavers had chosen the consequences, what emerged from it having been treated as a symbolic act was a 'punishment narrative' which Brexiters deployed as another way to avoid taking responsibility. Indeed, in a breathtakingly illogical leap, many even argued that the fact of those consequences and the ascription of them to EU punishment actually proved that it had been right to leave!

## WHY ARE WE WAITING?

The idea that Brexit was primarily a symbolic act and the accompanying claims that it would be quick, easy and have no adverse consequences were perhaps the most dishonest features of the Brexit process. It gave the lie to what emerged as a kind of Brexiter 'political correctness' in which it was deemed offensive and arrogant to suggest that leave voters hadn't known what they were voting for. Manifestly, they could not have done because – apart from the obvious fact that no one had defined or could agree on what Brexit meant – it proved to be neither quick nor easy.

This gave rise to the repeated complaint from some leave voters, egged on by the Brexiter leaders, that it should all have been done 'by now', which no doubt fed the appeal of Johnson's 'get Brexit done' electoral message. They ascribed the slowness, of course, to the EU and to treacherous remainers. Actually, one reason why it did take the time it did was the domestic political dramas which the referendum set in train in the UK. Thus, within the space of five years there were two general elections and two Tory leadership contests, all of which soaked up time. Similarly, when the Article 50 talks reached their second phase, almost nothing happened as regards negotiations with the EU because the UK government entered an internal negotiation as to what it wanted Brexit to be, as well as revisiting what had been agreed about Northern Ireland in phase one because it, apparently, no longer accepted that.

But, even without all that, the reality which had been obscured was that Brexit was bound to take a long time. In fact, it is arguable that it should have taken much longer than it did, and that if more time and care had been taken the outcome might have been better. There was no need to rush to trigger Article 50 with so little preparation and no consensus-building. There was no need to have had such a truncated period for the TCA negotiations. There was no need to create a situation whereby the transition was not, in fact, a transition but ended in an overnight adaptation to the TCA. All of this might have been averted had the Brexiters not pushed for a quick resolution which was quite out of keeping with what, in their own terms, was supposedly the launch of a major new chapter in national history. It became all the more indefensible when, in 2020, the coronavirus crisis emerged.

That impatience was born partly of a paranoid suspicion that Brexit would get reversed, growing out of the wider narrative of betrayal and victimhood. That paranoia would have been present anyway, but was no doubt compounded by the fact that at least some Brexiters must have known that they had fluked a narrow referendum victory on the back of a highly dishonest campaign and that there was no durable majority for Brexit. In short, they knew, even if they did not publicly acknowledge, the point made earlier about the flimsiness of the referendum mandate, especially for hard Brexit. In that sense, though it is not to their credit, they were right to think that if it was not done quickly then it might not be done at all.

## THE CONFLATION OF EXIT TERMS
## AND FUTURE TERMS

Impatience with the time the Brexit process took was also an artefact of one of the recurring motifs of that process. As I have sought to highlight in the preceding chapters, there was a persistent, repeated failure to understand, or to accept, the two-stage nature of that process. From the outset many, initially including Theresa May, seemed to think that the two-year Article 50 period would enfold both the exit talks and the future terms talks. Some, such as Boris Johnson, claimed that both could be completed well within that timescale.

One consequence of this was the early dispute over the sequencing of the Article 50 talks, and the UK idea that there could be parallel talks on exit terms and future terms. That ostensibly finished with the aborted 'row of the summer' of 2017, but it lingered on. Subsequently, this led to endless confusions about what was being agreed or debated at different times.

Examples include the votes on May's Withdrawal Agreement, when Brexiters often complained that it was not the 'Canada-style' deal that they said they wanted, apparently not understanding that any such deal would be the outcome of the future terms negotiations, not of the exit negotiations. It appeared, in a complex way, in Brexiter MPs' rejection of May's deal because of the backstop, which they believed was unnecessary because there were 'technological solutions' to the Irish land border, and yet that deal allowed for the fact that if such solutions could be found they would be incorporated into the future terms agreement and the backstop would not be used. It appeared again during the future terms negotiations, when some Brexiter MPs seemed to believe that, when concluded, these would supersede the Withdrawal Agreement and especially the Northern Ireland Protocol. Indeed, according to Steve Baker, MPs were assured by both Dominic Cummings and Michael Gove that this was so.[32] Or, again, at the same time but in a different way, some thought that if there were no future terms deal then that would justify scrapping the Withdrawal Agreement.

Perhaps the worst example of conflating the two stages of the Brexit process came in the 2019 general election campaign when Boris Johnson campaigned on his 'oven-ready deal' – his Withdrawal Agreement – which he implied was 'the' Brexit deal that would 'get Brexit done', rather than just the exit part of the process. That in turn set up the – to some – bewildering situation that, in fact, the Brexit negotiations didn't go away after he won the election. Equally, it fed the Brexiters' ability to again claim that Project Fear had been discredited when Brexit day came and went without much change – the reason being, of course, that the UK was in the transition period whilst the future terms were negotiated. And that then set up the new surprise, when the transition period ended, that far from being 'done' the country now had to grapple with the concrete effects of Brexit.

## BREXIT IN PROSPECT

At the time of writing, in February 2021, some of these concrete effects were already evident, as both importers and exporters struggled with the new barriers to trade which had been created. This was most visible in images of rotting fish going unsold and empty shelves in some supermarkets, especially in Northern Ireland where the new rules were particularly complicated because of what had been agreed in the 'frontstop' (see Chapter Six for details). It can be expected that such visible impacts will disappear in time, as firms get used to new processes or simply cease to trade, and supply chains are redesigned. But that will only hide the necessary and inevitable fact that significant new costs have been unilaterally added to UK–EU trade by Brexit.

The long-term economic effects will continue to unfold over many years and, like everything else in the Brexit process, will continue to be contested between the advocates and critics of Brexit. Amongst those effects is likely to be the ironic one that whereas control of immigration was such a central theme in the referendum campaign, post-Brexit Britain, with its ageing population, will probably end up using its independent immigration policy to increase the amount of immigration.[133] Yet doing so will now be more complex and bureaucratic without the ease of freedom of movement, whilst the end of that freedom will limit the possibilities for British people to work, study, travel or retire in Europe.

It also seems likely that for some time to come the identities of 'remainer' and 'leaver' will continue to be significant features of the political and cultural landscape, very possibly inflecting traditional voting patterns as, to an extent, happened in the 2019 election. The bigger legacy of that would seem likely to be a moving culture war, taking in new issues apart from Brexit but always reflecting the divisions that Brexit both laid bare and magnified. That could already be seen in the way that, during the coronavirus pandemic, overlaps emerged between 'lockdown sceptics' and Brexiters, as discussed in Chapter Six. Indeed, Nigel Farage pivoted from making Brexit his main preoccupation to criticising the coronavirus restrictions (as well as treading his familiar territory of stoking panic about asylum seekers). As Brexit illustrated, Farage – or, in the future, someone like him – is able to strongly influence politics without necessarily winning seats in Westminster. The populist politics of authenticity will still have plenty of mileage.

In addition, from the day of the referendum result, but compounded by the way that Brexit was undertaken, it has been obvious that the cause of Scottish independence would be boosted. It now seems not inevitable but far more probable than before that this will happen in the coming years. To a lesser extent, the way Brexit was done makes Irish reunification more likely than would otherwise have been the case. Since it has created an economic border between Great Britain and Northern Ireland, that makes a political border between them a logical outcome in due course. Conversely, it will strengthen economic ties between Ireland and Northern Ireland, making a political border between them less logical, although against that, because even Northern Ireland is leaving the single market for services, there will be economic divergence with Ireland as well. The UK single market for goods has already been sacrificed to Brexit. Ultimately, the biggest consequence of leaving the European Union may turn out to be the end of the United Kingdom.

If so, the biggest political losers will be unionists in both the general and the specifically Northern Irish sense. Even if Irish reunification doesn't happen, but especially if it does, much will be written in the future about why the DUP supported Brexit, and the choices they made during the hung parliament of 2017–19 in particular. Part of that history will note how Theresa May's deal sought to maintain the union with Northern Ireland but will also recall how her contemptuous treatment of the devolved administrations, especially Scotland, did so much damage to the wider union. Another part of it will focus on how and why Johnson was so cavalier in agreeing to a Northern Ireland Protocol that, judging by his denial that it created an Irish Sea border, he barely understood and which almost immediately, with the Internal Market Bill, he sought to renege on. At the time of writing, the Protocol is already under stress and facing sustained criticism.

Clearly nationalists in Scotland and Ireland will welcome the opportunities Brexit provides – I make no comment on the desirability of their causes – and from their point of view the end of the United Kingdom, if it comes, will be a positive result of Brexit. But it will be an ironic one for the Conservative and Unionist Party to have set in train and, by definition, will radically change the nature of the remaining rump of the UK.

## Looking backwards to see forwards

Whilst all of this is to a greater or lesser extent speculative, a degree of insight into the future can be gained not by making predictions but by looking back to before Brexit. In particular, as Robert Saunders, professor of politics at Queen Mary University of London, has argued at length, it is instructive to recall the factors that prompted the UK in 1973 to join what was then the EEC in the first place.[134]

This did not come about on a whim, but was the result of years of effort following Britain's initial decision not to be part of the EEC when it was set up. That effort arose from a realisation, from the early 1960s onwards, that this had been a strategic and economic mistake, for which post-colonial, post-great power Britain was paying a huge financial and geopolitical price. That strategic decision was never, as a foundational Brexit myth had it, simply about joining a trade bloc, although trade was a big aspect of it. It was overtly presented at the time, including at the 1975 referendum on whether to continue membership, as being about political and regulatory integration.

The largely Conservative governments which drove this strategy under Harold Macmillan, Ted Heath and Margaret Thatcher were well aware of, but rejected, the idea that it entailed a loss of sovereignty, recognising that by pooling sovereignty it could be enhanced whereas staying outside – or, later, leaving – would give only the illusion of sovereignty in an increasingly interdependent world.

Indeed, one could go further and say that if leaving the EU was possible, as the Brexit process proves it was, then it is abundantly clear that membership was a matter of choice, in which case sovereignty had not been lost. So the very possibility of leaving meant that there was no case for it being necessary on grounds of sovereignty. The question, as those earlier Conservatives had recognised, and many remainers still do, was not one of sovereignty, but of what was the best use to make of sovereignty. So what became the Brexiters' central argument of principle was bogus and, moreover, could not substitute, as they have increasingly tried to claim, for answering questions about the practical and strategic wisdom of using sovereignty to exit the EU.

Through EU membership, the UK did find the strategic role that had eluded it in the immediate post-war period, being able to act as the fulcrum of a wide variety of international bodies and alliances, including being the much-vaunted 'bridge' between the US and Europe. That was an illustration of how, as suggested in Chapter One, having a regional role is the necessary basis for Britain to have a global role rather than, as Johnson and other Brexiters seem to think, being a constraint upon it. The strategic role the UK found through its membership of the EU has now disappeared, but the underlying issues which led to seeking membership in the first place have not gone away, even if the context has changed. Brexit – again because Brexiters treated leaving as an end in itself – put paid to the UK's acquired role without having anything to put in its place.

However, it is not only Brexiters who are responsible for this and, indeed, their success is partly due to the failure of others. For whilst EEC, and then EU, membership created a success-ful national strategy, it was one which was rarely communi-cated or defended publicly. As noted in Chapter One, when Britain joined the EEC in 1973 the Labour Party, which came to power a year after, was deeply split on Europe – the result being the 1975 referendum – and so was hardly likely to engage in such an effort. At the 1983 general election, Labour's policy was actually to leave the EEC. By then, the Tory Party, al-though far more united in favour of membership (how strange, now, to write those words), was in full post-Falklands, Union Jack-waving mode. So no narrative of Britain in Europe was going to be built by the Tories either.

Thus, in those crucial years that followed the 1975 referen-dum, there was a complete failure of leadership from pro-EU politicians to develop any kind of narrative which was positive, let alone enthusiastic, about membership. Instead, and espe-cially after the botched joining of the ERM and the Black Wednesday fiasco in 1992, what developed was an entirely transactional, grudging and often sour approach to the EU. It was dominated by rows over budget contributions and the con-stant search for opt-outs from various EU projects. The British media, so enthusiastic for European membership in 1975, rarely reported on European politics and, when it did, the reporting was almost invariably negative. Headlines such as *The Sun*'s

1990 'Up yours Delors', if not typical, were archetypical and arguably set the course for what became Brexit.[135]

From about that time, the Tory Party began to change in its approach to Europe. That can perhaps be dated from Margaret Thatcher's Bruges speech[136] in 1988 – although, reading that text now, one cannot fail to be struck by how far it is from the Euroscepticism of those who became Brexiters (e.g. 'Our destiny is in Europe, as part of the Community'). At all events, the Maastricht Treaty turmoil of the early 1990s began the long civil war within the party that ultimately led to Brexit.

The Labour Party also changed, but in the opposite direction, partly because British social democrats began to see that the EU offered protection from the excesses of Thatcherism. Yet although Tony Blair was undoubtedly the most pro-European Prime Minister since Heath, he did not really use the 1997 moment to recast the British narrative about the EU. And whilst the Blair governments did successfully promote eastwards expansion of the EU, they never trumpeted what a triumph that was for both Europe and for British strategic interests. Moreover, largely because of Gordon Brown's opposition, Britain failed to join the Euro. Had it done so, Brexit would surely have become all but impossible.

Perhaps the most damaging effect of the failure to build and communicate a positive narrative about EU membership was in relation to freedom of movement of people. The reasons for that are complex, relating to the wider issue of immigration, which in turn relates to that of Britain's changed place in the world and its confusion about its post-Empire role. It's a topic that is well beyond the scope of this book. At all events, immigration was invariably configured in, at best, economic terms, and freedom of movement of people was subsumed within immigration in ways quite different to how it is understood within the rest of the EU.

So in all of these ways, political leaders since 1973 failed to undertake perhaps the key task of leadership: the provision of a coherent and compelling story of what was being done and why, right down to the basic, strategic reasons that had informed applying to join. Overall, there was no attempt to develop an account of Britain's changing place in the world and how EU membership facilitated and allowed it. Within that, there was no narrative about how Britain was, through the EU, facilitating a post-communist Europe, a pan-European regulatory space, and a new set of freedoms and rights for British people along with all other Europeans.

Nor was there a narrative explaining how, both in shaping the EU and securing its numerous exemptions, Britain was getting exactly the kind of European Union and exactly the kind of membership that it wanted. Instead, a wholly negative view of Britain as 'put upon' by the EU, and a wholly transactional view of its membership, was able to take root almost unchallenged. More than anything else, it was firmly established in the public mind that the EU was in some way an external, antagonistic constraint upon Britain.

All this is very far from being an account of the referendum result – that is not the purpose of this book – although it does help to explain both that and the suspicious, paranoid and often hostile way that politicians and the pro-Brexit media approached the Brexit negotiations. In other words, it goes some way to explaining why the scenario of 'Brexiter generosity' with which I began this chapter did not come about. More generally, it is a reminder that what I have called the Brexit process, the process since the vote to leave, grew out of what had preceded that vote. However, my point in providing this background is a different one, relating to the future, not the past.

## A new debate?

The questions which Brexit now poses are actually a re-posing of the ones faced in the 1960s and 1970s: how is the UK, or what survives of it, to relate to the EU and, with that, to the wider world? One of the sillier Brexiter slogans was 'we are leaving the EU, not leaving Europe' – silly because it is either a geographical truism or ignores the political reality that the bulk of European countries belong to the EU. But, even if inadvertently, it points to an important truth. The EU isn't going away, and the UK sits adjacent to it, and is going to have an evolving relationship with it.

So without even considering the question of re-joining (which I think is highly unlikely to happen, at least for many years, perhaps decades, if at all), the issue is how that relationship is to be conducted. The terms of the TCA mean that both closer and more distant relationships may develop, and that in large part depends upon whether UK policy continues to be entirely defined by Brexit and by the Brexiters' frame of reference.

On the face of it, there is no reason at all why it should be. Brexit, in the precise sense of Britain having left the EU, has happened. Indeed, it happened in January 2020. So the question of whether to leave or not is no longer one of any relevance or meaning. Yet there is every possibility that it, or at least the beliefs that surround it, will continue to hold sway. Thus it is easy to envisage the UK continuing to treat the EU as a punitive antagonist, and for Brexiters to endlessly denounce any cooperation – and, indeed, the agreed terms of withdrawal and of future relations – as being a 'betrayal of the 17.4 million'. In particular, it is easy to envisage Brexiters arguing that the TCA should not be renewed when it is reviewed in five years' time.

That would mean a 'Groundhog Day' for UK–EU relations, endlessly reliving that one day in 2016 as their sole, defining moment. Such a scenario would be consistent with the Brexiter psychology I have sketched in this book: one of perpetual campaigning, perpetual grievance, perpetual self-victimhood, and perpetual hostility not just to the EU but to the supposed 'Establishment' or 'liberal elite' which might seek to have less antagonistic, and closer, relations with the EU.

Somewhat related to this is the question of what the UK does with Brexit. Some Brexiters, as suggested previously, treated the vote to leave as an end in itself, and have been bemused by the process that has followed. But others, many of them very influential, envisaged it as a means to extensive deregulation and the pursuit of a more neo-liberal agenda than would otherwise have been possible. That would entail not just a looser relationship with the EU but, almost certainly, ending the TCA altogether because of the Level Playing Field commitments on labour and other standards that it contains. It seems highly likely that those with this agenda will continue to claim that it was mandated by the 17.4 million (though that is clearly untrue for many, if not most, of those voters) and if so then, again, we will remain stuck forever in the same debates as the last five years about the 'will of the people'.

Against this, changing political demographics may enable the UK–EU relationship to be framed differently. The age profile of the vote to leave means that, in due course, those younger voters who were predominantly pro-remain will become influential and, indeed, some will assume positions of political leadership. However, it shouldn't be assumed that those who were in their late teens and early twenties in 2016, however ardently pro-EU they may have been then, will still see it as a burning cause once they reach their thirties, forties and fifties. It may be that, by then, being out of the EU is the new normal, and they will see other issues as far more important or pressing, most obviously the climate crisis. It's not even inconceivable that the global nature of that crisis and the responses needed to solve it will make global, rather than regional, political institutions the focus of the next generation of political leaders.

On the other hand, it is perfectly possible that what develops is a politics in which even the bitter divisions of the Brexit process are mild by comparison. If the economic consequences of Brexit (along with coronavirus) turn out to be as severe as many expect then there will be a fertile ground for the 'punishment narrative' to develop into a more extreme hostility to the EU. It would also be likely to see even more anti-immigrant sentiment, and an even greater search for 'enemies within' developing out of the 'Brexit McCarthyism' identified at various points in this book. It is a scenario which becomes even more plausible if, at the same time, the United Kingdom has dissolved, leaving an English, or England-dominated, rump.

In this scenario, an obvious arena for a new and worse 'Brexit 2.0' would be a campaign to leave the European Convention on Human Rights (ECHR), which would in turn violate key parts of the TCA, assuming it was still in force. Even during the referendum, when leavers spoke of the things they disliked about the EU, they often pointed to judgments made not by the ECJ but by the European Court of Human Rights, which adjudicates on the ECHR. Typically, these related to things like the deportation of foreign terrorists or prisoners' voting rights. Very often this was based on misunderstandings or myths but, as Brexit has shown, that need make no difference.

As it becomes clear that being a signatory to the ECHR predated and wasn't due to Britain's EU membership (though would be a requirement of re-joining), and hasn't been affected by Brexit, this could well be a new cause for the 'politics of populist authenticity' described above. It would also be very much in line with the numerous ways that Johnson, in particular, has shown disdain for political and legal conventions. For that matter, it's worth recalling that before the referendum, Theresa May, whilst at that time arguing to remain in the EU, advocated leaving the ECHR regardless of the outcome of the vote.[137]

## A different kind of debate?

These and other conceivable scenarios are not inevitable – that must be true if only because it is possible to envisage a variety of scenarios – any more than the Brexit vote and the events which have unfolded since were inevitable. They will be a matter of the choices made, the debates had, and the decisions taken in the future. This book sheds no direct light on them, but it does have an indirect message to those who will be involved in such choices, debates and decisions. It is that whilst beliefs, opinions and emotions are a legitimate and inevitable part of any politics, they can ever be enough to make workable policy. Evidence, honesty and rationality are vital to that.

Brexit is obviously something which bitterly divides people to the point that, as I said in the introduction to this book, it has been as if there was 'remainer truth' and 'leaver truth', and sometimes there has even been the 'post-truth' suggestion that the truth doesn't matter. But it is important to draw distinctions between different kinds of issues at stake in Brexit. Some of those are perhaps endlessly contestable. The debate about sovereignty is at least arguably an example because its conceptual meaning is fuzzy and the kinds of evidence that can be adduced in debating it are highly diverse and, themselves, contestable. Some issues are less contestable in principle, but do not have clear-cut evidence to decide on them. That might, for instance, apply to the implications of different economic growth rates as between the EU and other parts of the world.

However, again and again during the Brexit process claims were made which were incontestably false, or at the very least deeply misleading, whether as a result of misunderstandings or, on occasion, lies. For example, it was false to claim that there could be frictionless trade between the UK and the EU if the UK left the institutions of the single market and customs union (which had created frictionless trade). It was false to say that leaving those institutions had no implication for the Irish border or the Good Friday Agreement. It was false to say that the UK would not have any financial obligations to settle on leaving. It was false to say that the UK could negotiate its leaving terms before starting the legal process to leave. It was false to claim that the judges in the various legal cases were seeking to prevent Brexit rather than giving a purely legal judgment. It was false to claim that Level Playing Field conditions were only sought by the EU after trade negotiations had begun. It was false to claim that lengthy prorogations are normal when there is a new Prime Minister. It was false to claim that the UK had not agreed to an Irish Sea border in the 2020 Withdrawal Agreement. It was false to say the TCA meant there would be no non-tariff barriers, and it was false to say that it showed it was possible for Britain to 'have its cake and eat it'.

All these, and numerous other falsehoods, many of them mentioned in this book, were not just occasional features of the Brexit process; they permeated it. If the response to that is to say that remainers also promoted falsehoods then, even if it were true, it is irrelevant. The fact is that Vote Leave won the vote and Brexit was the policy. So it is that and what followed from it that requires analysis. No doubt in an alternative universe where the remain campaign had won someone would be writing a book about what followed from that.

Not only was the Brexit process characterised by falsehoods, it also saw the deliberate, concerted discrediting of any attempt to warn about the consequences through the ubiquitous dismissal of these as 'Project Fear' so as to falsely present Brexit as entirely cost-free. That often involved the construction of ludicrous false representations, so that warnings of a reduction to trade, for example, were referred to as if they were claiming all trade would end; or reminders of the EU's role in promoting peace were referred to as if they were claiming that Brexit would lead to World War Three. Seldom has so short a phrase been so effective and so damaging. It rendered rational debate all but impossible, and when combined with accusations that Project Fear was the work of saboteurs, traitors and enemies of the people, Brexiters created a horrifically toxic political culture which is one of the worst legacies of the last five years.

Again, the response to that can't adequately be that remainers were often extremely rude to and dismissive of leave voters. That's not a justification and, anyway, it was on nothing like the same scale; for example, there was no attack on Brexiters comparable to the 'enemies of the people' headline. Moreover, many of those most aggressively attacked – such as judges and civil servants – became targets simply for giving apolitical, technical opinions, such as when the then head of the HMRC received death threats simply for identifying, as requested of him, the costs of new customs procedures.[138] There is an urgent need to cleanse our political culture of such things and to affirm rationality in political discourse. The dangers of not doing so are profound, as many horrific historical parallels attest.

## FINAL WORDS

Not only is there the need for a fresh debate about the UK's new and evolving relationship with the EU which leaves behind the now dead question of Brexit in its literal sense, there is also the need for a debate conducted on new and better terms. The Brexit process has shown what happens when false claims and promises are used as the basis for policy, and the result is a grimly ironic one. For what it has brought about is a situation which pleases almost no one.

Of course, there are many for whom Brexit was never of much interest, however they may have voted, if they voted at all. That is still the case. So some may be perfectly content with Brexit because they never cared much either way. But those who most wanted to remain in the EU are for the most part still unhappy, and in some cases devastated, bitterly resentful of what has been done to them and their country by Brexit and Brexiters. Yet those who most wanted to leave are for the most part equally unhappy, because the Brexit they have got is nothing like what they were told, or believed, that they would get. As a result, they, too, are bitterly resentful of what they see as the betrayal of Brexit by remainers or by the Establishment.

That resentment is misplaced, though, because Brexit could never have lived up to the promises they made or that were made to them. It is not an accident that this has been the outcome. Although the way the Brexit process has unfolded was not inevitable, and with better political leadership it need not have been so divisive and toxic, it was always going to fail to deliver what was promised to those who voted leave in June 2016.

The central flaw of that promise was that Brexit could be done without any cost, not just in an economic sense, but in political and cultural senses. It was a false promise, and that can be seen by the fact that it has been very far from cost-free, in any of those senses.

Even those who deny that the promise of Brexit being cost-free was made cannot in good faith deny that the Brexit of 2021 is nothing like that promised in 2016, if only because nothing like the Irish Sea border was even mentioned. And if that is to be ascribed to remainer sabotage – despite the fact that remainers clearly haven't got what they wanted, and despite the fact that it was agreed by the Prime Minister who led the Vote Leave campaign – then the point still holds, because those 2016 promises failed to consider what imposing Brexit on a country with only marginal and shallow support for it would mean. That failure was compounded when, after the marginal result, Brexiters insisted on the hardest of Brexits and bludgeoned their compatriots with the wholly unjustified claim that this was the 'will of the people'.

Irrespective of the explanation given, neither Brexiters nor remainers have got what they want. The future is not going to change that, even if the Brexiters now push to overturn what has been agreed with the EU in pursuit of the same false promises about what Brexit could or should be if done differently. Equally, the process of having tried to turn these false promises into policy means that there will never, as some committed remainers still hope, be a way of the UK going back to 23 June 2016, before the vote that started that process. The future is not going to change that, even were the UK to eventually re-join. That country, that world, of 23 June 2016 has gone for ever, as, strictly speaking, have leavers and remainers.

Whatever the future of the UK and its relationship with the EU, it will be a different one to what Brexiters promised and a different one to that which remainers tried to hold on to. How it unfolds from now on will depend not least upon what lessons are learned from the events that unfolded over the last five years, which in turn will require understanding how and why they happened. This book is hopefully a useful aid to doing so.

# ABOUT THE AUTHOR

Chris Grey studied Economics and Politics at Manchester University, where he then completed a PhD on the regulation of financial services, which began a career researching and teaching, broadly, the interface of politics and business. After working as a lecturer at Leeds University, he moved to Cambridge University where he became Professor of Organisation Studies at the Judge Business School and was a fellow of Wolfson College.

He then moved to Warwick University and subsequently to Royal Holloway, University of London where he is now Emeritus Professor of Organisation Studies in the School of Business and Management. He has held visiting professorships at Copenhagen Business School, Denmark, at Université Paris-Dauphine, France, and been a visiting fellow at the Stockholm Centre for Organizational Research, Sweden. In 2015 he was made a fellow of the Academy of Social Sciences (FAcSS) in recognition of outstanding contribution to social science.

Since 2016 he has written a popular and influential blog on Brexit (now entitled 'Brexit & Beyond') which has led to him being described as 'the best writer on Brexit' by the Europe editor of *The Economist*, 'the best guy to follow on Brexit for intelligent analysis' by the London Bureau Chief of ARD German TV and 'a must-read for anyone following Brexit' by the law and policy contributing editor of the *Financial Times*.

His writing on Brexit appears on House of Commons reading lists and the Northern Ireland Assembly website, and has been quoted by Reuters, the *Financial Times*, CNN, *Prospect*, *The Observer*, *The Times*, the *Irish Times*, *The Scotsman*, *The Guardian*, *Liberation*, *The Week*, the *New European* and many others. Apart from his blog, his commentary on Brexit has been published by *New Statesman*, *Prospect*, the *i*, *PMP Magazine*, *Byline Times*, the *New European* and *The National*, amongst others, and he has appeared on the BBC, the Australian Broadcasting Corporation and Germany's ARD, as well as giving invited expert evidence to the Scottish Parliament. In 2020, he was described in the *Irish Times* as 'the doyen of Brexit commentators'.

# ENDNOTES

1 Lord Ashcroft, 'How the United Kingdom voted on Thursday… and why' Lord Ashcroft Polls 24 June 2016 https://lordashcroftpolls.com/2016/06/how-the-united-kingdom-voted-and-why/

2 Christopher Grey, 'What actually happens if Britain leaves the EU?' The Conversation 7 October 2015 https://theconversation.com/what-actually-happens-if-britain-leaves-the-eu-48619

3 Official Journal of the European Union C326/1 EUR-Lex https://eur-lex.europa.eu/legal-content/EN/TXT/?uri=CELEX%3A12012M050

4 For example, see Dominic Raab, 'If we play clever, we can keep our EU trade' The Times 25 July 2016 https://www.thetimes.co.uk/article/if-we-play-clever-we-can-keep-our-eu-trade-szrk9wc05

5 E.g. Kevin O'Rourke, *A Short History of Brexit: From Brentry to Backstop* (London: Pelican, 2019); Harold D. Clarke, Matthew Goodwin and Paul Whiteley, *Brexit: Why Britain Voted to Leave the European Union* (Cambridge: Cambridge University Press, 2017); Tim Shipman, *All Out War: The Full Story of Brexit* (London: William Collins, 2016)

6 At the start of 2021, the pound was about 15 per cent weaker relative to the euro than on the day before the 2016 referendum. See 'How has Brexit affected the value of sterling' Economics Observatory 22 February 2021 https://www.economicsobservatory.com/how-has-brexit-affected-the-value-of-sterling

7 John Springford, 'The Cost of Brexit to June 2019' Centre for European Reform 16 October 2019 https://www.cer.eu/insights/cost-brexit-june-2019

8 E.g. Tim Shipman, *All Out War: The Full Story of Brexit* (London: William Collins, 2016)

9 See Rosa Prince, *Theresa May: The Enigmatic Prime Minister* (London: Biteback, 2017)

10 'Brexit: key quotes from non-UK figures' BBC News 12 October 2016 https://www.bbc.co.uk/news/world-europe-37632305

11 'Reality Check: Has Corbyn changed his mind on Article 50?' BBC News 22 July 2016 https://www.bbc.co.uk/news/uk-politics-uk-leaves-the-eu-36866170

12 Daniel Korski, 'Why we lost the Brexit vote' *Politico* 20 October 2016 https://www.politico.eu/article/why-we-lost-the-brexit-vote-former-uk-prime-minister-david-cameron/

13 Michael Gove, 'The facts of life say leave' Vote Leave 19 April 2016 http://www.voteleavetakecontrol.org/michael_gove_the_facts_of_life_say_leave.html

14 'Statistics on UK-EU trade' HC Library Briefing Paper 7851 10 November 2020, p. 18 https://commonslibrary.parliament.uk/research-briefings/cbp-7851/

15  John Springford and Sam Lowe, 'Britain's services firms can't defy gravity, alas' Centre for European Reform 5 February 2018 https://www.cer.eu/insights/britains-services-firms-cant-defy-gravity-alas

16  Rowena Mason, 'Brexit talks may be the most complicated negotiation ever, says Davis' *The Guardian* 12 September 2016 https://www.theguardian.com/politics/2016/sep/12/brexit-talks-may-be-most-complicated-negotiation-ever-says-minister

17  Jill Rutter and Hannah White, 'Planning Brexit: Silence is not a strategy' Institute for Government September 2016 https://www.instituteforgovernment.org.uk/sites/default/files/publications/IfG_Organising_Brexit_briefing_final.pdf

18  Jon Craig, 'Brexit "have our cake and eat it" note caught on camera' Sky News 29 November 2016 https://news.sky.com/story/tory-brexit-plan-photographed-in-downing-street-10676337

19  Guy Faulconbridge, 'Disputed memo says Britain has no Brexit plan' Reuters 15 November 2016 https://www.reuters.com/article/uk-britain-eu-idUKKBN13A0OC?edition-redirect=uk

20  Kate McCann, 'Theresa May rebukes David Davis over warning that UK could leave single market' *The Telegraph* 6 September 2016 https://www.telegraph.co.uk/news/2016/09/06/theresa-may-rebukes-david-davis-over-warning-that-uk-could-leave/

21  Dan Sabbagh and Jasper Jolly, 'Nissan was offered secret state aid to cope with Brexit, minister concedes' *The Guardian* 4 February 2019 https://www.theguardian.com/politics/2019/feb/04/government-letter-to-nissan-reveals-brexit-promise-to-carmarkers

22  Dave Burke, 'Senior Tories including Michael Gove pen a letter to Theresa May demanding "hard Brexit" and a clean break from the EU' *Daily Mail* 19 November 2016 https://www.dailymail.co.uk/news/article-3952270/Senior-Tories-including-Michael-Gove-pen-letter-Theresa-demanding-hard-Brexit-clean-break-EU.html

23  Liam Fox, 'Liam Fox's free trade speech' Manchester Town Hall, Manchester 29 September 2016 https://www.gov.uk/government/speeches/liam-foxs-free-trade-speech

24  Theresa May, 'The government's negotiating objectives for exiting the EU' Lancaster House, London 17 January 2017 https://www.gov.uk/government/speeches/the-governments-negotiating-objectives-for-exiting-the-eu-pm-speech

25  Tim Shipman, *Fall Out: A Year of Political Mayhem* (London: William Collins, 2017), p. 12

26  Interview with Philip Hammond, Witness Archive, UK in a Changing Europe November 2020 https://ukandeu.ac.uk/brexit-witness-archive/philip-hammond/. Hammond suggests that hard Brexit was definitively set by May's conference speech but, as I suggest above, this is not compatible with the fact that a month *later* hard Brexiters were still lobbying her for hard Brexit.

27  James Slack, 'Enemies of the people' *Daily Mail* 4 November 2016 https://www.dailymail.co.uk/news/article-3903436/Enemies-people-Fury-touch-judges-defied-17-4m-Brexit-voters-trigger-constitutional-crisis.html

28  'Nigel Farage calls for more resignations after Sir Ivan Rogers quits' *The Guardian* 3 January 2017 https://www.theguardian.com/politics/video/2017/jan/03/nigel-farage-calls-for-more-resignations-after-sir-ivan-rogers-quits-video

29  Jim Gallagher, 'Advice in a time of belief: Brexit and the civil service' UK in a Changing Europe 10 July 2019 https://ukandeu.ac.uk/advice-in-a-time-of-belief-brexit-and-the-civil-service/

30  Ben Riley-Smith, 'Businesses that speak out for Britain's EU membership will be punished, vows John Redwood' *The Telegraph* 28 September 2014 https://www.telegraph.co.uk/news/politics/conservative/11127836/Businesses-that-speak-out-for-Britains-EU-membership-will-be-punished-vows-John-Redwood.html

31  Heather Stewart, 'Firms bidding for government contracts asked if they back Brexit' *The Guardian* 1 March 2017 https://www.theguardian.com/politics/2017/mar/01/firms-bidding-for-government-contracts-asked-if-they-back-brexit

32  Anna Fazackerley, 'Universities deplore "McCarthyism" as MP demands list of tutors lecturing on Brexit' *The Guardian* 24 October 2017 https://www.theguardian.com/education/2017/oct/24/universities-mccarthyism-mp-demands-list-brexit-chris-heaton-harris

33  Anna Soubry, 'Why I will defy Mrs May to vote for a Brexit safety net' *Mail on Sunday* 5 March 2017 https://www.dailymail.co.uk/debate/article-4282586/Why-defy-Mrs-vote-Brexit-safety-net.html

34  John Major, 'Sir John Major's Chatham House Speech' 27 February 2017 http://www.johnmajorarchive.org.uk/2015-2/sir-john-majors-chatham-house-speech-27-february-2017/

35  Alain Tolhurst, '"Bitter and angry" John Major savaged by Tory Eurosceptics' *The Sun* 28 February 2017 https://www.thesun.co.uk/news/2972095/john-major-savaged-by-tory-eurosceptics-after-former-pms-craven-speech-attacking-theresa-mays-brexit-strategy/

36  For an extensive and influential discussion of this, see Fintan O'Toole, *Heroic Failure: Brexit and the Politics of Pain* (London: Head of Zeus, 2019)

37  Kevin Maguire, 'Nigel Farage wants second referendum if Remain campaign scrapes narrow win' *The Mirror* 16 May 2016 https://www.mirror.co.uk/news/uk-news/nigel-farage-wants-second-referendum-7985017

38  Tim Hume, 'Brexit: Petition calling for second EU vote was created by Leave backer' CNN 27 June 2016 https://edition.cnn.com/2016/06/26/europe/uk-second-referendum-petition/index.html

39  Aubrey Allegretti, '"Extreme EU loyalty" amounts to treason, says Tory MEP David Bannerman' Sky News 25 July 2018 https://news.sky.com/story/extreme-eu-loyalty-amounts-to-treason-says-tory-mep-david-bannerman-11448380

40  Ross Logan, 'Cameron ordered to guarantee Gibraltar sovereignty after "unacceptable" Project Fear claim' *Sunday Express* 29 May 2016 https://www.express.co.uk/news/uk/674869/David-Cameron-guarantee-Gibraltar-sovereignty-unacceptable-Project-Fear

41  HMG Cm 9417 'The United Kingdom's exit from and new partnership with the European Union' February 2017, p. 5 https://assets.publishing.service.gov.uk/government/uploads/system/uploads/attachment_data/file/589191/The_United_Kingdoms_exit_from_and_partnership_with_the_EU_Web.pdf

42  HMG Cm 9417 para 2.1, p. 13

43  For a full account of the issues posed for Ireland by Brexit see Tony Connelly, *Brexit and Ireland* (London: Penguin, 2018)

44  Lisa O'Carroll and Stephen Collins, 'Irish leaders fear Brexit will bring economic disaster' *The Guardian* 16 October 2016 https://www.theguardian.com/world/2016/oct/16/irish-pm-calls-brexit-summit-to-confront-looming-crisis

45  'Reality Check: Would Brexit mean border controls for NI?' BBC News 7 June 2016 https://www.bbc.co.uk/news/uk-politics-eu-referendum-36462023

46  'Media Mole', 'The Brexit Minister David Davis thinks the Republic of Ireland is part of the UK' *New Statesman* 18 July 2016 https://www.newstatesman.com/politics/uk/2016/07/brexit-minister-david-davis-thinks-republic-ireland-part-uk

47  Nicholas Watt, 'Brexit: Tory resentment of Irish power within EU' BBC News 11 December 2018 https://www.bbc.co.uk/news/uk-politics-46528952

48  Greg Heffer, 'Boris tells Brussels: 18 months is MORE than enough time to get "great" Brexit deal' *Express* 6 December 2016 https://www.express.co.uk/news/politics/740453/Brexit-News-Boris-Johnson-EU-chief-negotiator-Michel-Barnier-18-months-deal

49  Official Journal of the European Union C326/1 https://eur-lex.europa.eu/legal-content/EN/TXT/?uri=CELEX%3A12012M050

50  HMG, 'Prime Minister's letter to Donald Tusk triggering Article 50' 29 March 2017 https://www.gov.uk/government/publications/prime-ministers-letter-to-donald-tusk-triggering-article-50/prime-ministers-letter-to-donald-tusk-triggering-article-50

51  Henry Mance, 'David Davis warns Brexit timetable will be "row of the summer"' *Financial Times* 14 May 2017 https://www.ft.com/content/01396086-38ae-11e7-821a-6027b8a20f23

52  Ibid.

53  Hansard HC Deb, 24 January 2017, vol. 620, col. 169

54  Thomas Colson, 'Boris Johnson promised frictionless trade after Brexit but now his government admits new border checks are "inevitable"' *Business Insider* 11 February 2020 https://www.businessinsider.com/boris-johnson-michael-gove-admits-brexit-border-checks-are-inevitable-2020-2?r=US&IR=T

55  The 'thought experiment' in this sub-section up to this point is adapted from my article 'The ultimate Brexit counterfactual' *Prospect* 1 August 2018 https://www.prospectmagazine.co.uk/politics/the-ultimate-brexit-counterfactual

56  Daniel Boffey, 'How Juncker's Downing Street dinner turned sour' *The Guardian* 1 May 2017 https://www.theguardian.com/world/2017/may/01/how-junckers-downing-street-dinner-turned-sour

57  Faisal Islam, 'No signed "future" trade deal within two years, says Theresa May' Sky News 5 April 2017 https://news.sky.com/story/no-signed-future-brexit-deal-within-two-years-says-theresa-may-10824347

58  See, for example, Tim Shipman, *Fall Out: A Year of Political Mayhem* (London: William Collins, 2017), Tim Ross and Tom McTague, *Betting the House: The Inside Story of the 2017 Election* (London: Biteback, 2017)

59  'Theresa May's general election statement in full' BBC News 18 April 2017 https://www.bbc.co.uk/news/uk-politics-39630009

60  I am only going to talk about the broad features of the national campaign, but I'd argue the same was true in Scotland and Wales though perhaps slightly less true in Northern Ireland. This can be seen by reading the parties' manifestos, all of which, including those I refer to, are accessible via the DeHavilland manifesto library https://www1.dehavilland.co.uk/manifesto-library-%E2%80%93-general-election-2017

61  Alex Morales, 'May should fire Hammond for Brexit "sabotage", Nigel Lawson says' Bloomberg 12 October 2017 https://www.bloomberg.com/news/articles/2017-10-12/may-should-fire-hammond-for-brexit-sabotage-nigel-lawson-says

62  Julia Hartley-Brewer, Tweet 12 October 2017 https://twitter.com/JuliaHB1/status/918603594567471104

63  Nigel Farage, Tweet 29 June 2017 https://twitter.com/Nigel_Farage/status/880477525306216448

64  Laura Kuenssberg, 'Three key concerns about Brexit talks' BBC News 19 July 2017 https://www.bbc.co.uk/news/uk-politics-40655843

65  Robert Peston, 'The Angela Merkel and Theresa May comedy double act' ITV News 19 January 2018 https://www.itv.com/news/2018-01-29/the-angela-merkel-and-theresa-may-comedy-double-act

66  'Slide presented by Michel Barnier, European Commission Chief Negotiator, to the Heads of State and Government at the European Council (Article 50)' European Commission 15 December 2017 https://ec.europa.eu/commission/publications/slide-presented-michel-barnier-european-commission-chief-negotiator-heads-state-and-government-european-council-article-50-15-december-2017_en

67  Maïa de la Baume and Judith Mischke, 'Barnier dashes Britain's trade hopes' *Politico* 16 November 2017 https://www.politico.eu/article/brexit-trade-barnier-dashes-britains-hopes-of-something-better-than-canada-deal/

68  Dan Roberts, 'EU chiefs acting like gang leaders over Brexit threats, says Liam Fox' *The Guardian* 8 March 2018 https://www.theguardian.com/politics/2018/mar/08/european-chiefs-issuing-threats-to-secure-brexit-deal

69  'EU trade deal "easiest in human history"' BBC News 20 July 2017 https://www.bbc.co.uk/news/av/uk-40667879

70  George Parker and Duncan Robinson, 'London battles to keep hold of two main EU agencies' *Financial Times* 16 April 2017 https://www.ft.com/content/72ead180-229a-11e7-8691-d5f7eocd0a16

71  Agnes Chambre, 'UK will not be allowed to host European Capital of Culture after Brexit vote' PoliticsHome 23 November 2017 https://www.politicshome.com/news/article/uk-will-not-be-allowed-to-host--european-capital-of-culture-after-brexit-vote

72  'Brexit: Kate Hoey says Ireland would have to pay for physical border' BBC News 27 November 2017 https://www.bbc.co.uk/news/uk-northern-ireland-42137597

73  Richard Vaughan, 'EU to insist Brexit deal be legally binding after David Davis gaffe' *i* 12 December 2017 https://inews.co.uk/news/politics/eu-insist-brexit-deal-legally-binding-david-davis-gaffe-110115

74  Hansard HC Engagements (PMQs), 28 February 2018, vol. 636, col. 824

75  GATT is the General Agreement on Tariffs and Trade which was subsumed within the WTO when that was formed in 1995. In the interests of concision I am simplifying, and ignoring many aspects of, what was wrong with Rees-Mogg's claim. For detail, see Ian Dunt, 'What one piece of Jacob Rees-Mogg nonsense tells us about Brexit tactics' Politics.co.uk 21 May 2018 https://www.politics.co.uk/blogs/2018/05/21/what-one-piece-of-jacob-rees-mogg-nonsense-tells-us-about-brexit-tactics/

76  Peter Ungphakorn, 'One last go. The Article 24 red herring in less than 400 words. Think "highway code"' 16 February 2019 Trade β Blog https://tradebetablog.wordpress.com/2019/02/16/one-last-go-article-24/

77  Lars Karlsson, 'Smart Border 2.0: Avoiding a hard border on the island of Ireland for Customs control and the free movement of persons' November 2017 Publications Office of the European Union http://publications.europa.eu/resource/cellar/a9c80272-fcca-11e7-b8f5-01aa75ed71a1.0001.03/DOC_1

78  Something subsequently suggested by ex-Chancellor Philip Hammond, see Interview with Philip Hammond, Witness Archive, UK in a Changing Europe November 2020 https://ukandeu.ac.uk/brexit-witness-archive/philip-hammond/

79  Tony Connelly, 'Brexit: How a week in politics has made a backstop deal more remote' RTÉ 17 June 2018 https://www.rte.ie/news/brexit/2018/0615/970823-tony-connelly-brexit/ (web version updated, but quote as at date cited)

80  Statement from HM Government 6 July 2018 https://assets.publishing.service. gov.uk/government/uploads/system/uploads/attachment_data/file/723460/ CHEQUERS_STATEMENT_-_FINAL.PDF

81  Quoted in Andrew Sparrow, 'Barnier rejects customs plan set out in May's Brexit white paper – as it happened' *The Guardian* 26 July 2018 https://www.theguardian. com/politics/blog/live/2018/jul/26/brexit-not-too-late-for-uk-to-change-its-mind-and-stay-in-eu-on-same-terms-says-french-minister-politics-live

82  Rob Merrick, 'Brexit secretary admits the government must ensure "there is adequate food supply" if UK leave the EU with no deal' *The Independent* 24 July 2018 https:// www.independent.co.uk/news/uk/politics/brexit-secretary-food-supply-dominic-raab-uk-leave-eu-no-deal-a8461771.html

83  For a more extensive discussion of this important issue, see Fintan O'Toole, *Heroic Failure: Brexit and the Politics of Pain* (London: Head of Zeus, 2019), and on 'Dunkirk spirit' see pp. 86–91 in particular

84  Andrew MacAskill and Anjuli Davies, '"Insecurity is fantastic," says billionaire funder of Brexit campaign' Reuters 11 May 2016 https://uk.reuters.com/article/uk-britain-eu-donations-hargreaves/insecurity-is-fantastic-says-billionaire-funder-of-brexit-campaign-idUKKCN0Y22ID

85  Patrick Wintour, 'German ambassador: second world war image of Britain has fed Euroscepticism' *The Guardian* 29 January 2018 https://www.theguardian. com/politics/2018/jan/29/german-ambassador-peter-ammon-second-world-war-image-of-britain-has-fed-euroscepticism

86  Full Brexit statement from Theresa May, 21 September 2018 *Politico* https://www. politico.eu/article/full-brexit-negotiations-statement-from-theresa-may/

87  David Davis, 'There has long been an alternative to this discredited deal. It's the Canada-style plan that Tusk and Barnier offered us' ConservativeHome 19 November 2018 https://www.conservativehome.com/platform/2018/11/david-davis-there-has-long-been-an-alternative-to-this-discredited-draft-deal-its-the-canada-style-plan-that-tusk-and-barnier-offered-us.html

88  Chris Mason (BBC political correspondent), Tweet 13 December 2018 https:// twitter.com/ChrisMasonBBC/status/1073356135116218368

89  'Rare speech by EU's Deputy Brexit negotiator on UK talks' *Channel 4 News* 29 January 2019 https://www.youtube.com/watch?v=kNe8qK_-wUI&ab_channel= Channel4News

90  'The Malthouse Compromise – an official explainer in full' ConservativeHome 3 February 2019 https://www.conservativehome.com/parliament/2019/02/the-malthouse-compromise-offical-explainer-in-full.html

91  'Donald Tusk: Special place in hell for Brexiteers without a plan' BBC News 6 February 2019 https://www.bbc.co.uk/news/uk-politics-47143135

92  More accurately, this was the date if the UK participated in European Parliamentary elections, as, in the event, it did. Otherwise, it would have been 1 June.

93  Jon Stone and Andrew Woodcock, 'David Davis is "thick as mince" and "lazy as a toad", says Vote Leave chief' *The Independent* 18 July 2017 https://www. independent.co.uk/news/uk/politics/david-davis-thick-mince-lazy-toad-dominic-cummings-a7845911.html

94  Martin Kettle, 'This is no normal transition of power. It's a hard Brexit coup' *The Guardian* 25 July 2019 https://www.theguardian.com/commentisfree/2019/jul/25/power-brexit-boris-johnson-radical-conservative-party

95  Tom McTague, 'British Jacobins on the march in Brexit revolution' *Politico* 16 September 2018 https://www.politico.eu/article/boris-johnson-brexit-fantasy-explained-britain-perpetual-revolution/

96  'Dominic Cummings: Anger at MPs "not surprising", PM's adviser says' BBC News 27 September 2019 https://www.bbc.co.uk/news/uk-politics-49847304

97  'Kwasi Kwarteng criticised for "biased judges" comment' BBC News 12 September 2019 https://www.bbc.co.uk/news/uk-politics-49670901

98  Helene von Bismarck, 'Shutting down parliament is worse than a coup. It's a mistake.' *Foreign Policy* 29 August 2019 https://foreignpolicy.com/2019/08/29/shutting-down-parliament-is-worse-than-a-coup-its-a-mistake/

99  Chris Patten, 'Is Britain becoming a failed state?' Project Syndicate 20 August 2019 https://www.project-syndicate.org/commentary/britain-brexit-failed-state-by-chris-patten-2019-08?barrier=accesspaylog

100 Peter Foster and James Crisp, '"Despairing" EU officials braced for showdown with Boris Johnson after combative Commons performance' *The Telegraph* 26 September 2019 https://www.telegraph.co.uk/politics/2019/09/26/despairing-eu-officials-braced-showdown-boris-johnson-combative/

101 Andrew Woodcock, 'Brexit: Boris Johnson accused of being "out of his depth" after rebuff in talks with EU's Juncker' *The Independent* 18 September 2019 https://www.independent.co.uk/news/uk/politics/brexit-boris-johnson-jean-claude-juncker-eu-meeting-negotiations-northern-ireland-a9110411.html

102 Alan McGuinness, 'Tory MP Daniel Kawczynski defends bid to get Poland to veto Brexit delay' Sky News 21 October 2019 https://news.sky.com/story/tory-mp-daniel-kawczynski-defends-bid-to-get-poland-to-veto-brexit-delay-11841185

103 Sam Fleming, George Parker and Arthur Beesley, 'Boris Johnson warns of return to Irish customs checks' *Financial Times* 1 October 2019 https://www.ft.com/content/488cd226-e467-11e9-9743-db5a370481bc

104 David Allen Green, 'Boris Johnson subverts the rule of law' *Financial Times* 11 September 2020 https://www.ft.com/content/5f57d498-d3e0-11e9-8367-807ebd53ab77

105 For which, see Jonathan Tonge, Stuart Wilks-Heeg and Louise Thompson (eds), *Britain Votes: The 2019 General Election* (Oxford: Oxford University Press, 2020)

106 Dominic Wring and Stephen Ward, 'From Bad to Worse? The Media and the 2019 Election Campaign' *Parliamentary Affairs* Vol. 73, issue (supplement) 1, September 2020 https://academic.oup.com/pa/article/73/Supplement_1/272/5910280

107 Sir John Curtice, 'Brexit: Do Britons now agree about leaving the EU?' BBC News 31 January 2020 https://www.bbc.co.uk/news/uk-politics-51268688

108 Fergal O'Brien, '$170 billion and counting: the cost of Brexit for the UK' Bloomberg News 10 January 2020 https://www.bloomberg.com/news/articles/2020-01-10/-170-billion-and-counting-the-cost-of-brexit-for-the-u-k?utm

109 See Iain Anderson, *F\*\*k Business: The Business of Brexit* (London: Biteback, 2019)

110 'The Irish Times view on Brexit day: Britain's great leap backwards' *Irish Times* 30 January 2020 https://www.irishtimes.com/opinion/editorial/the-irish-times-view-on-brexit-day-britain-s-great-leap-backwards-1.4156666#.XjMl8OF_a2U

111 Matt Honeycombe-Foster, 'Dominic Raab slaps down Michel Barnier as he insists there will not be customs checks in the Irish sea' PoliticsHome 2 February 2020 https://www.politicshome.com/news/article/dominic-raab-slaps-down-michel-barnier-as-he-insists-there-will-not-be-customs-checks-in-the-irish-sea

112 Gail Conway, 'UK Govt will not have a border in the Irish Sea – Lewis' RTE News 14 February 2020 https://www.rte.ie/news/2020/0214/1115361-brandon-lewis/

113 Tim Shipman, 'Brexit team seeks to evade Irish sea checks on goods' *Sunday Times* 23 February 2020 https://www.thetimes.co.uk/article/brexit-team-seeks-to-evade-irish-sea-checks-on-goods-mv3pqjkcm

114 HMG CP211, 'The Future Relationship with the EU: The UK's approach to negotiations' February 2020 https://assets.publishing.service.gov.uk/government/uploads/system/uploads/attachment_data/file/868874/The_Future_Relationship_with_the_EU.pdf

115 Daniel Boffey, 'We won't budge on escaping EU's rules, says UK Brexit negotiator' *The Guardian* 17 February 2020 https://www.theguardian.com/politics/2020/feb/17/britain-wont-follow-eu-trade-rules-after-brexit-says-uks-chief-negotiator

116 Lisa O'Carroll, 'Michael Gove confirms post-Brexit trade barriers will be imposed' *The Guardian* 10 February 2020 https://www.theguardian.com/politics/2020/feb/10/checks-on-eu-bound-goods-inevitable-gove-tells-business-leaders

117 Patrick Daly and Megan Baynes, 'Johnson tells Northern Ireland businesses to "bin" customs forms' *Belfast Telegraph* 8 November 2019 https://www.belfasttelegraph.co.uk/news/northern-ireland/johnson-tells-northern-ireland-businesses-to-bin-customs-forms-38674258.html

118 'Replacing the Withdrawal Agreement: How to ensure the UK takes back control on exiting the transition period' Centre for Brexit Policy July 2020 https://centreforbrexitpolicy.org.uk/wp-content/uploads/2020/07/REPLACING-THE-WITHDRAWAL-AGREEMENT-How-to-ensure-the-UK-takes-back-control-on-exiting-the-transition-period-12-July-20.pdf

119 John Longworth, 'Why Britain must ditch the Brexit deal' *Politico* 13 July 2020 https://www.politico.eu/article/why-uk-britain-boris-johnson-must-ditch-the-brexit-withdrawal-agreement-deal/?fbclid=IwAR0RsJm881CRltt9vkOGIzlLmhmayHH_aY6lW_6YBJUK2q3WDFaGbMJkU1c

120 Adrian Zorzut, 'Video resurfaces of Iain Duncan Smith trying to stop MPs scrutinising Brexit agreement he now wants rewritten' *New European* 5 August 2020 https://www.theneweuropean.co.uk/brexit-news/video-of-ids-commons-speech-against-wa-scrutiny-found-on-85954

121 Michael Savage and Toby Helm, 'Top lawyers slam Suella Braverman for wrecking UK's reputation' *The Observer* 12 September 2020 https://www.theguardian.com/politics/2020/sep/12/top-lawyers-slam-suella-braverman-for-wrecking-uks-reputation

122 Dr Brigid Fowler, 'Parliament's role in scrutinising the UK-EU Trade and Cooperation Agreement is a farce' Hansard Society Blog 29 December 2020 https://www.hansardsociety.org.uk/blog/parliaments-role-in-scrutinising-the-uk-eu-trade-and-cooperation-agreement

123 Faisal Islam, 'What Boris Johnson's mistake tells us about our future' BBC News 24 December 2020 https://www.bbc.co.uk/news/business-55442982

124 'Post-Brexit trade: UK having its cake and eating it, says Boris Johnson' BBC News 30 December 2020 https://www.bbc.co.uk/news/uk-politics-55486081

125  Martina Bet, 'Brexit deal betrayal as Johnson's non-tariff barrier claims torn apart by experts' *Daily Express* 26 December 2020 https://www.express.co.uk/news/uk/1376851/brexit-news-deal-eu-uk-trade-talks-boris-johnson-non-tariff-barriers-single-market-spt

126  Fintan O'Toole, *Heroic Failure: Brexit and the Politics of Pain* (London: Head of Zeus, 2019)

127  George Monbiot, 'Brexit stems from a civil war in capitalism – we are all just collateral damage' *The Guardian* 24 November 2020 https://www.theguardian.com/commentisfree/2020/nov/24/brexit-capitalism

128  Stuart Hall, *The Hard Road to Renewal: Thatcherism and the Crisis of the Left* (London: Verso, 1988)

129  Jonathan Coe, *Middle England* (London: Penguin Random House, 2018)

130  *Flexcit: A plan for leaving the European Union* The Leave Alliance 2018 (updated edition) http://www.eureferendum.com/documents/flexcit.pdf

131  David Davis, Tweet 26 May 2016 https://twitter.com/DavidDavisMP/status/735770073822961664

132  Steve Baker, 'Boris: take back control' *The Critic* 24 May 2020 https://thecritic.co.uk/boris-must-take-back-control/

133  Jonathan Portes, 'After Brexit, Britain's hard line on immigration won't hold' *The Guardian* 29 January 2020 https://www.theguardian.com/commentisfree/2020/jan/29/brexit-britain-hard-line-immigration-openness

134  Robert Saunders, 'Brexit in Historical Perspective. The Age of Britain in Europe' 31 January 2020 The Gladstone Diaries (blog) http://gladstonediaries.blogspot.com/2020/01/brexit-in-historical-perspective-age-of.html

135  Stefan Stern, 'The great Brexit "up yours": How three decades of Euroscepticism made the UK go full tabloid' Politics.co.uk 21 August 2019 https://www.politics.co.uk/comment-analysis/2019/08/21/the-great-brexit-up-yours-how-three-decades-of-euroscepticism-made-the-uk-go-full-tabloid/

136  Margaret Thatcher, 'Speech to the College of Europe ("The Bruges speech")' Margaret Thatcher Foundation 20 September 1988 https://www.margaretthatcher.org/document/107332

137  Anushka Asthana and Rowena Mason, 'UK must leave European convention on human rights, says Theresa May' *The Guardian* 25 April 2016 https://www.theguardian.com/politics/2016/apr/25/uk-must-leave-european-convention-on-human-rights-theresa-may-eu-referendum

138  James Blitz, 'UK's Brexit officials targeted with death threats and personal slurs' *Financial Times* 20 October 2018 https://www.ft.com/content/a1defo3a-d2fb-11e8-a9f2-7574db66bcd5

# INDEX

air travel 105
Article 50
    ECJ ruling 139
    extensions to leaving process 159–60,
        164, 165, 172, 176, 191–2, 195
    formally triggered 75
    legal challenge 55, 65–6
    not immediately triggered 24
    parliamentary vote 55, 67–8
    terms 10
    time pressures 90–91, 120, 186
authenticity 255–8
automobile industry 50, 51–2, 53, 105

Baker, Steve 99, 128, 260
Barnier, Michel 14–15, 103, 110, 133, 139, 232
    Barnier staircase 104, 209
Barwell, Gavin 99
Basu, Neil 154
BBC, *Daily Politics* 123
Benn Act ('Surrender Act') 176, 178, 181,
    189–90
Benn, Hilary 151, 176, 202
Benn, Tony 33
Bercow, John 151, 160–61, 192
Bettel, Xavier 28
Biden, Joe 235–6
Blair, Tony 81, 273
Brady, Graham 154–5
Braverman, Suella 234
Brexit
    incompatibility of nationalist vs
        globalist ideas 11–12, 250–51
    minimal scrutiny (2017 election
        campaign) 92–9
    multiple models 7–8, 113, 123, 126, 142–7,
        259
    shifting terminology 9

symbolic act 261–4
    *see also* outcome of Brexit; preparations
        for Brexit; process of Brexit;
        transition period
'Brexit means Brexit' 30–31
Brexit in name only (BRINO) 9, 143
Brexit Party 29, 165, 179–80, 188, 197–8, 200,
    232
Brexit Ultras
    dissatisfaction with outcome 9, 11,
        29–30, 111, 248–9
    and the Irish border 118
    repudiation of Withdrawal Agreement
        230–33
    Withdrawal Agreement Bill debate
        193–4
    *see also* European Research Group
        (ERG); UKIP; Brexit Party
Brexiters
    definition 2n
    ill-equipped for delivering Brexit
        258–61
    misconceptions 266–7
    motivations 251–2
    privileged elite 256
    promises 41–2, 52, 57–8, 129, 188
    psychology of betrayal and victimhood
        13–14, 72–3, 246, 276
Brown, Gordon 34, 273
budget contributions *see* financial
    settlement

Cable, Sir Vince 100
Cameron, David 2, 23, 27, 32, 39–40
Canada, CETA (Comprehensive Economic
    and Trade Agreement) 209–210
Canada option *see* hard Brexit (Canada
    option)

297